Praise for *As Time Goes By*

"I have a GPS for my car to help me find my way. If I wanted a 'GPS for my life' I'd go to Abigail Trafford. She's the best guide to help me find my way in the second half of life."

—Harry R. Moody, Ph.D., director of
Academic Affairs, AARP

"Abigail Trafford proves she is a great storyteller and an original thinker as she maps out the new territory of intimate relationships in the second half of life. Whether you are married or single, alone or in a relationship, this wonderful book is for you."

—Mary Pipher, Ph.D., author of *Letters to a Young Therapist* and *Seeking Peace*

"Everything I have ever wanted to know about sex and the second journey but didn't dare ask, Abigail Trafford has answered in her revealing book, *As Time Goes By*. Her own experience as well as those of others makes for an honest, forthright, and compelling read."

—Joan Anderson, author of
A Year by the Sea and *The Second Journey*

As Time Goes By

As Time Goes By

Boomerang Marriages,
Serial Spouses, Throwback Couples,
and Other Romantic Adventures
in an Age of Longevity

ABIGAIL TRAFFORD

Basic Books
New York

Published by Basic Books,
A Member of the Perseus Books Group

Throughout the book, asterisks indicate that names, identifying
details, and some events relating to the individual have been
changed. No case study, other than those in which real names are
used, is or is intended to be descriptive of any living individual.

Books published by Basic Books are available at special discounts for
bulk purchases in the United States by corporations, institutions, and
other organizations. For more information, please contact the Special
Markets Department at the Perseus Books Group, 2300 Chestnut
Street, Suite 200, Philadelphia, PA 19103, or call (800) 810-4145,
ext. 5000, or e-mail special.markets@perseusbooks.com.

Library of Congress Cataloging-in-Publication Data
Trafford, Abigail.
As time goes by : boomerang marriages, serial spouses, throwback couples, and other
romantic adventures in an age of longevity / Abigail Trafford.
p. cm.
Includes bibliographical references and index.
ISBN 978-0-465-00280-1 (alk. paper)
1. Middle-aged persons—Psychology. 2. Middle-aged persons—
Sexual behavior. 3. Middle-aged persons—Attitudes. I. Title.
HQ1059.4.T69 2009
306.81084'40973—dc22
2008037930
10 9 8 7 6 5 4 3 2 1

For the grandchildren
Brooks · Sophia · Lila

Contents

Acknowledgments

First I want to thank all the men and women whose stories appear in this book. They invited me into their hearts and their lives to tell the tale of love in an age of longevity. They spoke of pain as well as joy, laying bare secrets and sharing the wisdom they had gained from experience. I am grateful for their courage and candor, their warmth and friendship. Their insights will help the next generation as it moves into this unprecedented period of vitality in later life.

I also want to thank my editors at the *Washington Post* for their support. Frances Sellers and Mary Hadar have nurtured ideas as well as copy for my column, "My Time," about life after 50. Some of the people in *As Time Goes By* have appeared on the pages of the *Post.* I also appreciate all those who have responded to the column with their personal stories and observations. They, too, are part of this book.

Much of my research took place at the Stanford Center on Longevity, where I was a visiting scholar in 2007. I am grateful to the Center's director, Laura L. Carstensen, for her support and guidance. So many people at Stanford and in the Bay Area gave me their expertise and hospitality. My thanks go to Jill Chinen, Lauren Smith, Randy Bean, Jane Hickie, Tom Rando, Adele Hayutin, Steve Goldband, Marc Freedman, Richard Adler, Janet Rutherford, Gordon and Sharon Bower, and Carolyn and Philip Cowan.

Throughout the months of interviewing and writing, I was supported by my web of kinship—friends and family members who provided encouragement, meals, lodging, and laughter as well as editorial guidance: Henry and Deborah Allen, Merribel Ayres, Triny Barnes, Norman Birnbaum, Candace Boyden, Edith and Lincoln Boyden, Perry and Annie Boyden, Chris and Bunny Clark, Susanna and Moose Colloredo, Beth Colt and Peter Simonds, Buffy and Jim Colt, Ann Crittenden and John Henry, Josh and Amy Eden, Tom and Mary Edsall, Toby and Sandra Fairbank, Caroline Herron, Art and Eloise Hodges, Pat Jackson, Emma Jordan, Becky Lescaze and Mark Borthwick, Noel and Terry Miller, Jack and Angie Olson, Garril Goss Page, Max Reid, Trip and Heddy Reid, Geoff Schaefer, Harvey Sloane, June Spencer, Sophia Stone, Arthur and Agnes Terry, Beth Terry, Jim and Maude Terry, Bonnie Trafford, Stella Trafford, Nicholas von Hoffman, Eric Wentworth, Clare Whitfield, Sherley Young. My two book clubs—one of couples, the other of women—provided regular insights. So did the Cosmos Group, organized by my friend Florence Haseltine, a monthly meeting of women in science and medicine.

The book has two stalwarts—my agent, Gail Ross, who prods me, and my editor at Basic Books, Jo Ann Miller, who emboldens and sustains me. With clarity and compassion, Jo Ann helped shape the book. Both Gail and Jo Ann share my belief in the revolutionary power of love in later life. I am grateful to them for their support and friendship.

Finally, I want to thank my home team of editors: my daughters, Abigail Miller and Victoria Brett, and my friends: Mary Edsall, who edited successive drafts; Heddy Reid, who read early versions and reviewed the manuscript; and Susan Dooley Carey, Mary Hadar, Harvey Rich, and Jim Terry, who reviewed the final copy.

Thank you all very much.

Prologue: Arc of Love

It's a small thing, an intimate gesture. I am visiting a man I knew in childhood. On the kitchen counter is a French press coffeemaker—glass with red trim. He makes the coffee—very strong, he knows I like it very strong, half regular and half decaf—and he brings me a cup in bed. So I can lie there with my thoughts, while he works at his desk. We know each other's habits. We know the way we once were as children, and how far we have gone in our lives. We are Sixties People—we came of age in the 1960s; we're in our 60s now.

Sipping my coffee, I think about the arc of love and intimacy over a lifetime. How do people invigorate relationships at this unprecedented stage of life? How do they find love if they become single? Longevity, like a rogue wave, has washed out traditional patterns of mating. Yet, it is also creating a new landscape for meaningful relationships.

My friend and I are not married. Ours is a long friendship. Each of us has been divorced. Our intimate narratives are very different. Our needs and fears overlap and diverge. We have the spark, we share a history. We laugh. I help him pick out a Medicare prescription drug plan. We talk about global warming.

Lying there in the cool of the morning, I realize how much the past reemerges now. My résumé includes two marriages, two children, and three grandchildren. But my intimate narrative is so much more. How to capture in that storyline: the thrill of young marriage, the deep joy experienced with my second husband, the anguish of breaking apart, the richness of singlehood, the glory of children, the reward of work, and the generativity of friendship? Mine is a complex story of affection and sorrow, of ecstasy and heartbreak, of momentary and eternal bonds. Each relationship has been transformative. So much of who I am is shaped by whom I've loved and who has loved me.

The same is true for the core of eight women who have been my lifelong friends. Among them they have a total of five long marriages, three divorces, three remarriages, one re-divorce, and two widowhoods. They are mothers and grandmothers; two have suffered the death of a child. But for all their different trajectories, they have much in common in their rhythm of attachment and loss and renewal: separate plots in the quest for love, but similar struggles for intimacy and individual growth. In a long life, you have a lot of opportunities for finding love—and for enduring loss. Both are life-changing. Each loss forces you to a new chapter. Every encounter with love is an awakening. An intimate narrative is like an epic: it sweeps high and low; it starts early, long before marriage; and it runs 'til death. I wonder: What is the new credo for love when a life may span 100 years?

My friend and I sit down for breakfast. He picks up the sports section. I'm preoccupied. He knows I've been ruminating on the nature of relationships in our generation. I'm searching in my head for a thesis—and an explanation. He puts down the paper.

"You know the cliché: there's no 'I' in 'T-E-A-M.'" He waits for me to absorb this sports talk . . . and to adapt it. In generations past, marriage was restricted to the sports-team concept of "we": life was short and the game was swift, and the goal of marriage was to form a union to enhance wealth and power of the family and "score" with a next generation of children. Self-expression, mutual satisfaction, and the pursuit of happiness were not in the contract. But today, life is long. Marriage, like all intimate relationships, has a new script.

"There is an 'I' in 'M-A-R-R-*I*-A-G-E'!" I reply. My friend smiles and I continue:

"Marriage is also a relationship. And there are two 'I's' in 'R-E-L-A-T-*I*-O-N-S-H-*I*-P.'"

It's a beginning: I have a structural image of the arc of love in an age of longevity. One "I" is the lifelong trajectory of the individual; two "I's" mark the story of coupling. Both stories entwine to create the larger narrative of a long life shaped by relationships and personal development. Sometimes the stories overlap; sometime they diverge. There are many chapters in this narrative. How do you end up with a coherent tale?

Something huge is happening in the realm of marriage and relationships as people live longer, healthier lives. Now at least I have a conceptual map to chart these new realities.

All around me I see a rush of problems—and possibilities—as people try to navigate long-standing relationships and embark on new ones. I am surprised by the amount of upheaval in marriage from breakups and bitter estrangements, too often leading to emotional paralysis and the slow wait for death. At the same time, I am awed by the regenerative power of affection and attachment, by the novel configurations of "coupledom." How do people reinforce this power far past the age when in previous generations they would rarely have been alive?

We finish breakfast. I am restless. I want to know more.

✦

A few years ago I wrote *My Time: Making the Most of the Bonus Decades After Fifty,* in which I chronicled the new stage of vitality that comes after midlife but before traditional old age. I named the period "my time" because, at this point, you have largely completed the tasks of adulthood—raising a family, finding your niche in the workplace, establishing yourself in the community. "My time" is a chance to do what you really want to do—to dream, to reach out, to give back, to go to school, to create relationships and nurture old ones, to crown a meaningful career or begin a new one, to make a difference.

Since *My Time* was published in 2004, I have given talks on the promise—and pitfalls—of longevity, addressing the 2005 White House Conference on Aging and participating in the annual meetings of the American Society on Aging and the National Council on Aging. I carry the "New

Stage—Not Old Age!" message to libraries and community centers, to campuses and conferences, to bookstores, churches, and family rooms. Again and again, one set of questions keeps coming up: Why do relationships change so much in these decades? What keeps the spark alive? How do you overcome the loss of a partner—to death, divorce, or disease?

At a meeting at the library in Maryland's Prince George's County, a woman sums it up: "What is happening to marriage? All around me I see people getting into trouble. After the children leave home, when one of them retires, couples announce they are splitting up. . . . I'm afraid." Others nod. A man stands up and talks about the stress of retirement. The term is "retired spouse syndrome," a constellation of symptoms from depression and drinking too much to irritability and health ailments. Is it a problem of too much togetherness? Not enough in common now that it's down to the two of you? The lack of purpose—of something meaningful to do? The discussion shifts back to the impact of illness on marriage, the fear of running out of money. Then a woman asks: "I want to take a job in another city and leave my husband behind. The assignment is for a year. Is this normal? Am I crazy?" After some uneasy laughter, people give her support. In good and not-so-good relationships, there seems to be a longing to carve out more separateness: to seek adventure or a retreat—alone—to expand the borders of an inner world, of private space.

Yet, there's also a longing for closeness. A man says that he's recently widowed. More hands go up from those who have become single through the death of a spouse or a divorce. Are they really "unmarried" when they have been married for so many years? Now they have more time to focus on relationships—but who is there to focus on? The risks of loneliness and social isolation increase in these years. All the research shows that loving relationships are associated with better health and well-being.

The children are gone. The job may be gone. You may be very alone—married or unmarried. Yet you need the glue of human connection to make the most of the time left. How do you find these connections to see you through a period that could last twenty, thirty, or more years?

✦

I set out to find answers to these questions. In 2007, I go to Stanford University as a visiting scholar at the Stanford Center on Longevity. The center's director, psychologist Laura L. Carstensen, shows me how the growing importance of relationships fits into later-life development. I learn that the brain changes from being mainly cognitive and intent on acquiring information (to get ahead) to being more emotional and focused on relationships (to get "whole"). This shift puts a priority on loving connections. I also learn that with maturity comes another plus for relationships: the art of settling, a greater ability to accept and accommodate a partner.

I'm impressed by the consensus building among many experts around the richness of relationships in this period. I talk to Robert W. Levenson as well as Carolyn and Philip Cowan at the University of California, Berkeley; John M. Gottman at the University of Washington, Seattle; Betsey Stevenson at the University of Pennsylvania; Stephanie Coontz at The Evergreen State College, Washington; and Andrew Cherlin at Johns Hopkins University.

There are not a lot of studies on long-term marriage and later-life relationships because the phenomenon of longer, healthier lives is so recent. But research hints at the impact of maturity on seasoned love: how wisdom can soften rough edges and sharpen emotional aptitude—to enhance a committed relationship or soothe a troubled one.

As I travel the country collecting stories, I am inspired by the innovative ways people are confronting problems and creating new models of connection. In Connecticut, I visit a couple who keep separate households—a living apart, loving together relationship. In California I stay with a boomerang couple: they married young, split up, and remarried each other years later. While this is rare, the boomerang is an apt metaphor for many long-lasting marriages: you start out in love, drift apart into separate spheres, and then reunite once the children are grown.

I also get to know several throwback couples. In a throwback romance, you rediscover someone from long ago. "Remember when" becomes an aphrodisiac. One throwback couple in South Carolina carry the torch for each other for more than twenty-five years before they finally marry.

Then, too, I'm moved by the stories of long-married couples who go through a renaissance in this stage. I talk to a couple in California who tell me this is the best period in their marriage. I hear the same thing from a husband and wife in Georgia. And again in Massachusetts. I'm also impressed with how readily men and women start over. In Washington, I go to the wedding of a couple in their 60s; he is a widower, she a divorcee. They join the expanding ranks of serial spouses—men and women who have more than one marriage in a lifetime.

Still, I can't escape heartbreak: the twenty-seven-year itch and gray divorce. A woman in Virginia tells me: "After thirty years, my marriage just burned out." I start to wonder: Is velvet stagnation what snuffs out older relationships the way conflict breaks up younger marriages? I also see how people get trapped in fatal engagements. You fall for a cad; you're seduced by a gold-digger; you stay with an abuser. I learn that as you get older, you become more trusting and optimistic. That makes it easier to be generous in love—and to be taken advantage of.

Meanwhile, the past comes to a head. As a friend says: "Secrets don't get buried anymore." People live too long to live out a lie. At the same time, they live long enough to hold out for a Last Hurrah of love—in marriage, in friendship, in family relationships.

The dynamic variety of relationships in this stage is stunning. I find a much more complex portrait of love than expected. Far from conforming to a somnolent and sexless stereotype, men and women of a certain age are literally kicking up their heels and rewriting the script of love.

✦

Some of the storytellers in these pages are in their early 50s and struggling to renegotiate their relationships; others are in their 80s and can put their intimate narrative in perspective as they add new chapters. Many have been married to only one person, deepening the bonds of attachment and enjoying the payoff of shared memories—but also raising the risk of marriage fatigue. Many others have had more than one partner, clearly delineating different chapters—but also raising the risk of shallow compartmentalization, and thus complicating the story line. As a woman in a second marriage quips at a cocktail party in Washington: "I came in in the middle of his movie."

His movie; *her* movie. *Their* movie. Longevity has turned mating into a trilogy. Whether you are a spouse in one long relationship or the veteran of several marriages, you are starring in three movies at once. Can the institution of marriage expand to include *his* and *her* scripts, which are lifelong and only sometimes simultaneous? Can it open out beyond the narrow focus just on *their* movie, the legal union, which is the traditional definition of marriage?

The more I look for answers, the clearer it becomes that what I am seeing is the restructuring of the institution of marriage itself. Longevity is imposing a new construct for intimate relationships, a revised concept of family and generational ties that expands the social structure of marriage.

The restructuring of marriage is happening very rapidly. By 2010 more than 80 million Americans will be between the ages of 50 and 80. Every day, 8,000 Americans turn 60. By 2030 one in five will be over the age of 65.

It's a perfect storm: Where the evolution of marriage intersects with the forces of longevity, you may find yourself in the midst of a sometimes crushing, disruptive passage. But out of havoc, a fresh terrain for relationships is being created. Several features stand out in this uncharted territory:

- *Be prepared for predictable jolts.* Just as young couples confront such predictable stresses as bearing children and striving for success in a job, older men and women face predictable stresses around health and retirement. The jolts come fast: The ominous PSA test. Breast biopsy. Coronary bypass surgery. The death of a high school classmate. The divorce of an adult child. The retirement party. Stopping a career, starting another. Moving out of a community and into a new one. But these jolts, which signal the end of traditional adulthood, are also beginnings. For a surprising number of people, loss turns out to be liberating. It can free you up in relationships. You embrace a new boldness, an attitude of "If not now, when?" and "What have I got to lose?"

- *Being single is an integral part of your narrative.* Most people will spend significant chapters of their lives as single persons even though they marry. If you are young, you can expect to have a period of singlehood before getting married and having a family. You are also likely to be single after marriage, especially if you are female, since two-thirds of married women outlive their husbands. And this period can last many years. Lady Bird Johnson, who died in 2007, was single for more than three decades after the 1974 death of President Johnson—a whole lifetime in generations past. You may also be single between marriages—or "single" during marriage if you spend time apart or are on different emotional pages. For many men and women, these periods are creative and rewarding. You need private space to grow. Intervals of individuation are an opportunity to widen your circle of friends and family and to adjust your compass for partnership.

- *Relationships tend to get better with age.* Experience counts. You're more skilled in relationships, better able to handle disappointment and negotiate conflict, more willing to be open about yourself and more tolerant of others. Good marriages tend to get better, and even bad marriages may get easier. "Often these couples rediscover each other when they have time to be partners again. There is a reblooming of lives and partnerships," explains Berkeley psychologist Levenson. "A lot of couples have this renaissance." Older people are generally happier than younger people—what researchers call a *positivity* factor. The age advantage can also bode well for new partnerships.

- *Marriage is not enough.* You need an intimate circle—a network of people you cannot imagine your life without. Call it your marital team. A spouse may take up the largest space in your circle, but you need to make room for others: your closest friends, certain relatives, most likely your children, perhaps a former partner. This is your family of choice. Whether you are married or single, you need about ten people in your intimate circle, according to Stanford's Carstensen. If the number falls below three, you can get into trouble. You're at greater risk of poor health, emotional isolation, and despair. Research shows that intimate circles are crucially important, emotionally rich, and remarkably stable.

✦

As Time Goes By illuminates the many new facets of love in an age of longevity. I conducted most interviews in person with follow-up discussions on the phone. Sometimes I talked to couples and individuals in a group. As a condition of the interviews, I showed the men and women who are named in the book their stories before publication. If people requested anonymity, I changed their names and identifying details. But the story lines and quotes are their own. Some examples are composites crafted from multiple interviews and personal stories sent to me at the *Washington Post,* where I have written a column called "My Time" since 2004. Asterisks indicate that names, identifying details, and some events have been changed. In my travels, I find that people are very eager to talk about their relationships, past and present. They invite me into their living rooms and refer me to their friends. They are teachers and salesclerks and doctors and government workers. Most would be described as middle and upper-middle class. They are generally in good health.

They are reassured when I tell them the problems they are encountering, which seem strange or unique to them—retirement anxiety, financial worries, health concerns, sexual issues—are actually common conditions. I point out that there are universal patterns in how people bond in these later-life decades. The more we talk, the more excited they become about starting a national conversation on what it is to love as time goes by.

PART ONE

Turmoil

1

The Big Churn

Y ou start hearing stories: About the man who retires and his wife keeps working and they begin to fight. (He says: Where are you going? She says: Can't you find something to do?) About the divorced grandma who falls in love, and her adult children think the man is vile. About the couple who sell the family home because he's sick of mowing the lawn and the toilets drip and they need the equity in the house to live on, but they don't know where to move. After a while, she asks the doctor for a prescription for Prozac. About the husband who decides to become a minister and goes to seminary in another state, leaving his wife behind—a sabbatical, they explain. About the wife who walks away from a thirty-year marriage, the man with two ex-wives who starts to speed-date, the widowed grandfather who finds his college girlfriend on the Internet.

Just when you think life is supposed to be calming down, longevity has changed the rules on you. By age 50, around 90 percent of men and women are or have been married. But marriage is only part of the larger story of coupling in this stage.

The generation of the Big Chill is now the generation of the Big Churn. *"Will you still need me/Will you still feed me/When I'm 64?"* People are scrambling to find out—in marriage and other committed arrangements. The generation of the Big Churn is also the generation of the Big Choice.

Never have there been so many different possibilities for intimate relationships in this stage of life. You don't need social approval anymore. You can cohabit as an unmarried couple. You can live separately and be a married or unmarried couple. You can be travel companions. You can be friends.

And all this churning is not just about you. It's also about the churn in the institution of marriage. The old wedding mystique of the past no longer fits the new reality of relationships.

'Til death? That was easy to promise when life expectancy was relatively short. "Marriage was designed for men who went to sea at 25 and women who died in childbirth," quips Thomas Detre, professor of psychiatry at the University of Pittsburgh School of Medicine.

Today, death usually comes at an advanced age. Meanwhile, there are other kinds of "partings." Divorce ends a significant percentage of unions. And most divorces are followed by remarriages, some of which lead to re-divorces. In time, death catches up with divorce as a marriage breaker. Chances are the surviving spouse will get involved in new relationships—creating a swelling population of serial spouses and seasoned partners.

One relationship until death? Even in a long marriage, there are internal partings caused by conflicting demands of work, children, ambitions, and responsibilities. You may be married for more than thirty years, but you can probably point to several distinct phases in your marriage—distinct relationships, even—all with the same person.

Staying together for the sake of the children? What children?! The children are grown and have their own families. Only a minority of married couples—about 41 percent—have children at home. In 1880, 75 percent of married couples in the United States had children at home.[1] To be sure, the hands-on rearing of children remains a main focus of mar-

---

1. These data on marriage patterns come from Betsey Stevenson, an assistant professor at the Wharton School at the University of Pennsylvania. She is the author, with colleague Justin Wolfers, of the 2007 study "Marriage and Divorce: Changes and Their Driving Forces," *Journal of Economic Perspectives* 21, no. 2 (Spring), pp. 27–52. (Hereafter, I refer to this research as the "Pennsylvania marriage and divorce study.")

riage—but that covers only the early chapters of a relationship. What is the mission of marriage once you get past the child-rearing phase?

"This is a massive experiment. People have to try to sustain marriages long past the time people were expected to live, long past the time of child bearing and rearing," says historian Stephanie Coontz, author of *Marriage, a History: From Obedience to Intimacy, or How Love Conquered Marriage.*

How do you master the arts of love in this unprecedented stage of life?

The Big Churn is a series of paradoxes.

✦

Paradox: New road. No road map.

What to expect when you're expecting to live a long time . . . is *terra incognita.* There are handbooks for young couples raising children, but not for older lovers starting down a new road of togetherness.

Most couples go through a transition period. Fissures that could be plastered over during adulthood get exposed as people spend more time together. New cracks appear when relationships are tested by health problems and job changes. It can take five or more years to make the transition and learn how to accommodate each other in this new stage.

Sally Crandel*[2] is speeding down a country road in a 300-horsepower Ford Expedition SUV, careening around the curves, turning up the volume on the Classic Rock radio station ". . . Can't Get . . . No Satisfaction," pushing down the gas pedal as she comes up over a hill, and then, damn, a Stop Sign! The road is about to dead-end into the main street into town. She brakes hard, but can't stop in time; so she guns the Ford hard to make a left turn, misses the pavement, and ends up in a ditch. She's lucky. No one coming either way. A soft landing. She unfastens the seat belt and crawls out. Right light broken, fender bashed in a bit, mirror smashed. A

---

2. Throughout the chapter, asterisks indicate that names, identifying details, and some events have been changed.

teenager comes along in a pickup truck and pulls her out. *"Don't tell your husband,"* the kid jokes. And Sally laughs.

And then she gets back in the Ford, puts her head down on the steering wheel, and weeps. She retired three years ago from being an assistant principal at an elementary school in Seattle. Her husband, Donald*, worked for the city police department. His dream was to buy a place in the country and go fishing in the river with his grandsons. The way he used to do with his grandfather. And so that's what they did. They moved away from traffic jams and bought an old farmhouse in Sequim on Washington's Olympic Peninsula.

But Sally knows that Don is not happy. He misses the old neighborhood, his buddies. The house is demanding. The chimney smokes. Don is good with his hands; he rebuilt the front porch. Last week, he asked her to paint the trim. But she's been too busy. She's joined a book club and volunteers at the local library two days a week, reading stories to children. He nags her: *"When are you going to paint the porch?"* Don putters around the house, waiting for her. *"Sally, you're always out. Can't you sit still?"* Her book group is reading *1491*, about the continent before Columbus, and she is amazed to learn that right here where they are living, smallpox so ravaged the native populations of the Northwest that the first European explorer to Puget Sound found deserted villages, abandoned boats, and human remains scattered on the beach. But all Don cares about are sports and local politics. He watches TV. For reading, he'll pick up *People* magazine when he goes to the supermarket. *"Honey, did you know that Julia Roberts went to Morocco?"*

Sally opens the glove compartment and finds the two speeding tickets from last month. This is not like her—Straight Arrow School Marm, showing young people how to grow up and be responsible adults. She loves her husband: his cop jaw, street wit, and straight talk about people. He helped her all those years to navigate in the shark tank of a large urban school. But she can't please him anymore.

She drives home . . . slowly . . . and doesn't say anything about the accident. She gets a beer from the fridge. Don has put the chicken in the oven. He's watching the news. She sets the table, the chicken is ready. She is suddenly hungry and helps herself to more potatoes, gets another beer. He watches her gulp down her food. She starts talking too fast—about the library, about plans to add space for digital research . . . a room with computers and hey, what about serving cappuccinos for people to meet and talk?

He thinks to himself: She eats like a pig. The beer makes her talk too loudly. She's gonna get fat. He picks at his food.

Sally and Don are caught up in the Big Churn. Theirs is a good marriage. For more than forty years, they've pulled together with clearly defined roles: they went to work; they raised their two children. They led satisfying parallel lives, each one proud of the other. But the old roles are gone. Now that they are suddenly alone together, they realize how far apart they are. Sally is frustrated that Don isn't *doing* more—he just putters around the house. She's shocked that he doesn't read real books now that he's got the time. Has he always been like this? The move has been stressful. Sally feels betrayed. She's supported him in his career and put his work first. She supported his decision to retire at 55—although she wanted to keep working, to stay on at the school. She supported him in taking on a house in the country. It was his dream, not hers.

Don also feels betrayed. He supported her in her career. All those years, when she complained about not having enough hours in the day? He worked out the finances; they both have pensions. They had the means to retire. Now she has the hours, and still she fills them up and is never home. The children are scattered across the country. It's down to the two of them—and she's always in a rush. Always a project, always a phone call about the library. And now, the beer. He stocks up on Pyramid Hefe Weizen and Heineken Premium Light when he does the marketing. Where is his wife?

The phone rings. It's their son in Kansas City. He and his wife have two sons, 11 and 8. Hey, Dad, could we visit next month? The kids want to see the black bears in the Olympic Game Farm. Maybe go fishing like

Don did with his grandfather. Don smiles at the prospect. So does his Sally. They both get a lift from the phone call.

Unexpected upheaval is a normal part of adjusting to this new stage of life. You have to get to know each other again. Perhaps you're surprised and even upset by what you discover in your mate, in yourself. If you've been married for many years, you may be stuck in old habits and rituals. You arrive at this transition period on separate tracks. You have to get out on the same platform and create a new agenda for the relationship. Don and Sally have a lot going for them: shared history and mutual enjoyment of grandchildren. But they are reaching a break point that is forcing them to redefine themselves and their roles in the marriage.

✦

Paradox: You have lots of time. You have little time.

Statistics tell you that you can look forward to many more years of vitality. You have also entered the mortality zone with rising death rates. Instead of counting years from your birth, you start to count back from that fixed point in the future.

In a time study, men and women were asked: "Who would you like to see—a family member or someone new?" Older people replied "family"; younger people, "someone new." When the beginning of the question was changed to "You are diagnosed with X disease and have only a short time to live," younger people responded like older people and preferred a family member. And when the question was changed again to "You are likely to live another twenty years, what would be your preference?" both older people and younger people replied "someone new." "It is not age, but perception of a future that determines choice," says Laura Carstensen of the Stanford Center on Longevity, who led the time study.[3]

How you perceive the time left influences your behavior and decisions. Do you want to stick with the status quo, or are you open to something

---

3. Laura L. Carstensen, Derek M. Isaacowitz, and Susan T. Charles, "Taking Time Seriously: A Theory of Socioemotional Selectivity," *American Psychologist* 54, no. 3 (March 1999) (hereafter referred to as the "Stanford socioemotional selectivity study").

new? A friend is married to a man whose cancer is in remission, but with a cloudy prognosis. The immediate moment is precious to them. "I'm spending money," she tells me. If they want to go out to dinner, they go to a good restaurant. "It's the cancer talking," she explains. Another friend who jogs every day and has no medical complaints celebrates his 50th birthday; he realizes he can expect to live another thirty years—too long to stay in an unsatisfactory marriage, long enough to bond with someone else. He leaves his wife of twenty-five years and starts over. Perception of time shapes relationships in this stage.

"When the future is expansive, novel experiences with others are at a premium," report Carstensen and her colleagues. "When time is limited, familiar social partners are valued."

✦

Paradox: More people are single. More people are coupled.

Many men and women become single in this period through the loss of a spouse. A close friend from childhood calls to tell me the news. Her husband has pancreatic cancer. It is very quick. Within three months, he is dead. We were all in each other's weddings. A lifetime of friendship, and all of us reeling: saying good-bye to the one who is gone, embracing the widow as she rebuilds her life. Death is uneven in marriage, leaving more widows than widowers.

Then, too, middle- and later-life divorces make news. You go to a fiftieth wedding anniversary. A big celebration with dancing and singing, all the grandchildren flying in for the occasion, a sense of accomplishment in the room, husband and wife a symbol of the old-fashioned marriage: go forth and multiply . . . live (happily) together ever after. She is smiling. He stands up to give his toast. In retrospect, a clue. He thanks them all for being here; he thanks his wife for all she has done for him, for the family. Now it is his turn to do what he's always wanted to do. Everybody claps and cheers and drinks champagne. More toasts; more dancing. The next morning the man announces at breakfast that he is leaving the house and getting a divorce. The family is undone. It turns out that he had gotten involved with someone else.

"Twenty years ago, we rarely saw a divorce among older adults. Now we do," says marriage researcher Andrew J. Cherlin of Johns Hopkins University. "Older adults are using the same set of values as younger men and women are using. They are saying to themselves—if younger adults aren't staying with unhappy marriages, why should we?"

At the same time, more and more older people are married than in previous generations. For starters, longer life spans allow more couples to survive into old age. But the demographic blockbuster is the increase in remarriage in this age group. Public attitudes now encourage re-mating among those once thought past the age of romance. Older men and women have greater opportunities to find a partner after the death of a spouse or a divorce—what researchers call a "thicker remarriage market." In fact, those over 65 are as likely to be married as younger men and women.

All this churn creates a dynamic dating world for recently unmarried men and women—and some unhappily married people. Online matchmaking sites and personal ads in magazines have become a boon to older men and women. You don't have to hang out at a bar or hassle friends to fix you up. You can shop online for a mate the way you pick out a refrigerator. At Match.com, men and women over 50 account for about 20 percent of the seekers and are the fastest-growing segment on the site. E-harmony has also seen a steady increase in older participants—a 66 percent jump from 2006 to 2007. Success rates are elusive, but the anonymous safety of technology legitimizes the search.

"Passion is a desire to live fully," says Jane Juska, a former schoolteacher in Berkeley, California. Several years ago, she placed a personal ad in a magazine: "Before I turn 67, I would like to have a lot of sex with a man I like." That ad drew hundreds of responses, and Juska set out on her journey to find the perfect lover. She found several and described her exploits in A Round-Heeled Woman.[4] Passion is a decision not to sit on the sidelines. "You give up passion and you give up life," she says.

---

4. Jane Juska, A Round-Heeled Woman (Villard, 2003).

✦

Paradox: Older people are sexy. Few believe that.

Older men and women are as responsive to—and as capable of being brought to life by—sexual pleasure as younger lovers. A recent study by researchers at the University of Chicago found that desire and a range of sexual activities persist into the 80s and beyond.[5]

But ageism continues to warp public perceptions of love and romance among older people. I visit my 95-year-old stepmother in her assisted-living facility. She is a Southern Belle and she puts on a coral shade of lipstick to go with her coral and green paisley shawl when we go down to the dining room for dinner. "See that man over there?" I look across the room at a man with white hair, hunched over his walker as he inches toward a table. "He's attractive, don't you think?"

I smile. I am also a little embarrassed. This is the privacy barrier between generations. Children—no matter how grown up—don't like to think of their parents *that way!* They don't want to see anybody in a parental role being attracted to others and (maybe) having sex. But longevity is breaking down those barriers between generations.

Look at who is coming for Thanksgiving dinner! A woman, 48, calls me in distress about her mother-in-law, 70. Hers is not the usual mother-in-law story about messing up the old family recipe for cranberry jelly. This is the new mother-in-law story about the merry widow with a new boyfriend who is a decade younger. "Here's this other guy. . . . Is he going to carve the turkey?" It's not only the young who are defying social conventions; it's the old folks, too, who are behaving like young people. "It's weird being around the two of them," she continues. "They are making goo-goo eyes at each other. They're like teenagers in the throes of passion. It's all kind of overwhelming. We don't expect this with someone who's that age. It's freaky."

---

5. Stacy Tessler Lindau, L. Philip Schumm, Edward O. Laumann, Wendy Levinson, Colm A. O'Muircheartaigh, and Linda J. Waite, "Study of Sexuality and Health Among Older Adults in the United States," *New England Journal of Medicine* 357, no. 8 (2007) (hereafter referred to as the "Chicago sexuality study").

The Responsible Generation—parents between the ages of 35 and 50—now faces the Rebellious Generation of people over 60. How does the adult child respond when Grandpa and his girlfriend (or Granny and her lover) are coming to visit—where do they sleep, in the pullout double sofa-bed, or on separate cots in the unheated space over the garage? And what do you tell young children about sex and morals and commitment when the Medicare set is out for romantic adventure?

✦

Paradox: Love in these years is wonderful. Love in these years is dangerous.

You look around at those golden long-lasting marriages that continue to thrive. Jimmy and Roselyn Carter: how closely they work together on their projects, on their books, on stewarding their family. Actors Paul Newman and Joanne Woodward: how they contradicted the Hollywood image of in-and-out relationships. You hear the refrain from friends and family members; you say it about your own marriage: *We are happier now than ever before.*

You smile at new marriages. Former Vermont governor Madeleine Kunin, at 72, married an 80-year-old man. "Without expecting it, without looking for it, we fell in love," she told the *New York Times.* She had been divorced; he was a widower. Now these serial spouses are blending their pasts as they create a joint chapter in their marital narratives.

But the dark side of romance does not disappear. Passions can run just as high at 80 as at 18—with the same disastrous results. Great-grandmother Lena Driskell of Atlanta was convicted at age 79 of shooting and killing her 85-year-old boyfriend because he took up with another woman. "I found out he was cheating on me," said Driskell at her trial. To be sure, such an event is rare. But it is a reminder that relationships can be just as tumultuous and jealousy just as raw in later decades as they are in youth. The simple fact that you are older doesn't mean your heart can't be broken. You have to watch out for the predator, the manipulator, the user. In short, you can love smart—and love stupid. The point is, you continue to love.

✦

Paradox: You yearn for closeness. You seek freedom.

At last, it's "my time," a period of liberation when you are freed from the earlier tasks of adulthood. You want to do things you've always wanted to do, but haven't had the time until now. You need space to spread your wings, to do some reckoning about life. You also need close, loving relationships. The push for independence comes up against the pull of connection. This push-pull can create friction in your marriage, among your friends, and in your family.

If you're single, you generally get support to take flight. A woman, 62, remembers that when she took a fellowship in Rome to study Italian and religion for six months, her grown son said to her: "Now, Mom. If it doesn't work out, you can always come home."

But if you are married, carving out independence vis-à-vis your spouse is more complicated. And it's risky.

Arnold Kessler* doesn't understand what happened to his ordered world. At 60, he is on top: a successful real-estate developer in Houston with a dynamic wife, three healthy, intelligent children, a nice house on Memorial Drive.

But he doesn't know his wife anymore.

Mary Amalfi* is an Army brat. Her father, a forward artillery observer in the infantry, survived World War II and married a soft, sad German woman. Mary has her father's black hair, her mother's pale skin. She has also inherited their talent for languages. In her high school years, she is sent to live with her aunt and uncle in Washington to attend a Catholic girls' school. History grabs her with the assassination of President Kennedy. The school shuts down in mourning. The headmistress takes all the girls to Pennsylvania Avenue to witness the funeral procession. In the rain, they slosh through the mud in their school uniforms and hats. She can still feel the rainwater around her ankles.

Mary is part of the Fault Line Generation, a cohort of men and women born in the 1940s, with one foot rooted in the more traditional 1950s, the other foot thrust into the turbulence of the 1960s. Her social imprinting begins with Sputnik in 1957, a symbol of the technological revolution that cracked the complacency of the postwar years. It ends with President Kennedy's death in 1963. In that period, Mary absorbs the Camelot messages of hope, opportunity, and faith that the world could be made a better place. After all, the president challenged her to ask what she could do for her country.

She joins the Peace Corps. She can speak Spanish and Portuguese and she travels throughout Latin America. Finally she settles in Houston to work in a nonprofit community outreach program. The women's movement is in full swing and she jumps onboard. She doesn't get married until age 30. That's when she meets Arnold, a Texas Aggie, who loves a good party and makes her laugh, who pursues her across Mexico one summer—who goes on to make a killing in Houston's building boom. Right down the yellow brick road to happily-forever-after. Three children in six years. Four houses in fifteen years. Mary adjusts to his schedule. She cuts down on her hours, shifts to volunteer status. But when the last child leaves for college, she goes to work full-time at a social service organization.

And then, while at church, she sees the announcement of a program in Rio de Janeiro to work in the *favelas*, the slums tucked into the cliffs above the city. Weird, thinks Arnold, but he says to her: *"Sounds interesting."* He knows the script. After all, they are both committed to gender equality. *"I think I'd like to apply,"* she says. *"Sure, go for it,"* says Mr. Success, summoning up his politically correct *anima*—all the while thinking she'd never get it.

She gets it.

The marriage turns upside down. Arnold is astounded. Mary tries to explain: it's only for a year, she'll be working with an international team, it's a great opportunity, something she's always wanted to do; she'll get time off, they can take romantic trips together—explore the Amazon rain forest, visit Machu Picchu. For God's sake, there are direct flights from Houston to Rio. The children are away. Lots of couples have commuter marriages. "He hasn't been able to see the positive aspects of this," she says. "Throughout our marriage his career came first. It seemed to me it was time to have some reciprocity."

Arnold gets angry. Go away and leave him? Beneath his blustery salesman persona is the insecurity of a boy who grew up in Texas City, whose father ran a gas station and left the family when Arnold was 8; his mother went to work in the school cafeteria. Mary's "great opportunity" feels like abandonment to him. Why can't she be happy in Houston? He doesn't have to work on weekends anymore. She says she will suffocate if she has to stay in Houston full-time. They need a change. Why doesn't he come with her? For God's sake, he's a partner in the firm. He likes it in Houston. What is she thinking? What is wrong with her? Let's try couples therapy, she says. What? Who needs therapy—we've been married almost thirty years!

She goes to Rio. Every six weeks, she flies back to Houston. They have a traditional Thanksgiving with the kids—she cooks the turkey and makes the broccoli casserole because it's a family favorite. Their son brings home a girlfriend. The children are impressed with Mom's stories—the ninety-eight-foot statue of Christ as Redeemer, the swirling black-and-white tile sidewalks, the goat farm in Teresopolis.

Arnold sits with his arms folded. What is going on with his wife? Off saving the world? He has his work. There are plenty of women asking him how he's doing, shaking their heads, poor Arnold, offering to cook him a meal. Dammit, he knows how to cook. Hey, he's been Ken the Enabler to Gloria Steinem's Barbie! A liberated woman's dream! He's supported and encouraged his wife. And he made good money to get a fancy address and put three kids in college. And now he's alone in an empty house. He goes to the gym. He plays some golf. His PSA is slightly elevated but he's not going to tell her.

They haven't had sex since she decided to leave. Even on these visits, when she comes to him in bed—he won't let her touch him. He pushes her hand away.

Mary and Arnold are free-falling in their marriage. Their final landing place is uncertain. For some couples, time apart is a healing sabbatical. For others, it is a prelude to divorce. You may not know which at first.

Ask yourself: How much space do you need? Or consider whether something else is going on in your relationship. There is a difference between a time-out and a breakup. In a time-out, you stay in touch with each other. At some level, you both buy into the novel arrangement. Each spouse derives some benefit from the time apart, and the relationship changes in positive ways. Therapists point out that if there is a strong bond to begin with, couples can usually reignite the spark when they come back together and refigure the balance between connectedness and selfhood.

For most people, the urge for more independence does not translate into a year's separation or travel thousands of miles away. It may take the more conventional form of a consultancy in another city that lasts several months, a semester at a university, separate vacations; the husband who walks the Appalachian Trail with a grandson, the wife who joins her college classmate in New Zealand to build houses for Habitat for Humanity.

Or it's a more subtle pathway. The need for separateness is fulfilled by finding a new purpose: acting in community theater and never being home for dinner because of rehearsals and performances. Doing *pro bono* legal work on mortgage foreclosures and never being home for dinner because that's when the clients are available to meet.

There is no standard formula for finding a balance. Some people need a lot of space; others need a lot of closeness. Everyone needs a combination of the two. In the past, the balance was determined by the separate spheres of working and raising a family. But that structure no longer exists. It's up to you to build a new structure.

It takes time to figure out the new balance. A man who has been traveling in his job may want to tip the scales toward closeness—enjoying home and the amenities he has worked so hard for. A woman, freed of the main responsibility of children, may want to throw herself into work and take a new assignment that pulls her away from the home front. The awkward phone calls: Where are you? What are you doing? Why aren't you _____ (at home, doing your own thing)? Why can't you _____ (understand, get a grip)? The mixture of guilt, anxiety, and frustration boiling up until it overflows the bowl of marriage.

Preferences for closeness and independence go deep inside. Insecurities may come to the surface in this unscripted period. To many family therapists, what older couples need to sustain a relationship through this transition are the pillars of confidence and trust. The more confident you are in yourself, the more secure you are in the relationship, the easier it is to carve out separate space—for yourself and your spouse. Ultimately, you want to bring your individual pursuits back into the marriage as a way to enrich the relationship.

✦

Paradox: You dream. You settle.

It is a time when you loosen up and imagine great visions for the future. It is also a time when you compromise: you settle for what you can realistically expect in a relationship.

Nora Sweet* of Memphis aims her sights high. If she stands up straight, she measures five feet one inch. Always a skinny kid, but she was born with dreams—one in particular: tall, dark, and handsome. She finds her prince during her senior year at the University of Tennessee in Knoxville, a pasty-faced, brown-haired English major whose parents have old money. They look down on her because she is scrappy and her family is poor. Nora and her prince marry after graduation and have two children. But after that, the fairy-tale marriage quickly crumbles. She is 28 when they have sex for the last time. Five years later, he leaves her for someone else.

Nora becomes a familiar woman's story. She raises the kids alone. She trains as a paralegal, gets a job in a prestigious local law firm, rises up to become an expert in estates and wills. A good salary, Armani suits, children who do well in school. But there is something she keeps hidden in her skinny body: lust. She is consumed by sexual longing. She deals with it privately and waits for another prince to come her way.

Decades go by. No one comes her way. At 51, she decides to be proactive. She goes online; she becomes a member of a dating service. The longing for sex burns in her. One summer she joins her cousin and his wife on a camping trip to Wyoming. They get in the camper and take off. With them is their friend Mike*: six foot four, dark eyebrows and gray hair, close to 300 pounds. He used to be a bus driver in Lexington, Kentucky, but diabetes forced him to retire on disability. Nora quickly seduces him, the first sex with a partner that she's had in a quarter of a century, but she knows her body well and this is what she wants. They tour the Grand Teton mountains in each other's arms.

Mike is cautious. He has never married. He takes up two places on the sofa. His face is flushed—but he's always smiling. They start seeing each other regularly. Nora has found an outlet for her lust and he's sexually inventive—like her. About five years into the relationship, they decide to buy a condo together. Nora has the job and the money. Doesn't matter, she tells him, that she's supporting him. She wants him; she wants a life together. He adores her, adores her bony body. A week before they move in, he is rushed to the hospital with a suspected stroke. It turns out to be a very mild one—a TIA, or trans-ischemic attack; he completely recovers. But he is 58 with diabetes and high blood pressure, and he's facing an uncertain future. She realizes she would rather have him sick than not at all. They both feel the pressure of mortality. On impulse, they take a weekend trip to Las Vegas and get married.

Her children wonder what has happened to their career mom who wears dressed-for-success suits—marrying an overweight bus driver? Nora and Mike return from their blackjack honeymoon, husband and wife. They buy a fifty-two-inch plasma TV for their condo. They join the local church and listen to Garth Brooks—*she will be in your dreams/that's when she's/more than a memory.* In the morning, she whips up a yolkless omelet for him for breakfast and he waits for her at the end of the day. She glows.

Nora spent years waiting for fantasy man. With Mike she is finding happiness with a real man; he is not the prince of old dreams but a loving partner in the shared minutia of daily life.

"Settle" is not a dirty word. Not when it opens the door to real intimacy. The same settling takes place in long-term relationships. At a certain point you accept your mate and accommodate those things that are bothersome. She's always late; he factors that into plans and prompts her early to get ready, instead of berating her. He doesn't get a promotion and plateaus out at work; she keeps her job and tightens the family budget, instead of taking out her disappointment on him. He doesn't look like George Clooney, she doesn't resemble Diane Keaton; instead of regrets over wrinkles, they appreciate each other—his crooked grin, her sweet hands.

"Young people say: *I don't want to settle*. . . . Settling is exactly what we need to do," says Stanford's Laura Carstensen. You get to the settling point when you calibrate your needs and dreams to the reality of your partner. *Just my Bill, an ordinary man.* You settle in an old marriage. You settle in a new relationship. You settle in a circle of close relationships. You settle.

✦

Paradox: Marriage is a façade. Attachment is real.

All marriages and prime relationships have a façade, a public persona that greets outsiders and keeps them at bay. Children, included. *Pas devant les infants*, the French say. Not in front of the children. Each relationship is a private story with different layers of complexity. When life was relatively short, the façade might have endured to the grave. But longevity has strained the marriage façade. If a relationship is too distant or conflicted, it is hard to maintain the public persona for so many decades. And why should you?

At your graveside, you don't want your children to say: *they should have gotten a divorce!* But what constitutes a good marriage? Sometimes the truth comes out after one of the partners dies.

Filmmaker Doug Block films the kiss that rocks his world, a kiss that lasts twelve seconds, the deep, slurpy wedding kiss of his dad starting a new life in a new state with a new wife, shortly after the death of Doug's mother. Doug and his siblings are in shock. They don't remember Dad kissing Mom like that. And yet, their parents were married for fifty-four years. They raised three children, went on family vacations, had picnics in the backyard. Typical American Family: there are photos and videos to prove it.

Doug is a husband and father himself when his mother dies unexpectedly of a virulent pneumonia at age 77. A few months later, his father announces that he is moving with his secretary of forty years to Florida. The family house at 51 Birch Street[6] in Port Washington on Long Island, New York, is put up for sale. "I guess I was stunned," says Doug. He is dealing with the shock of his mother's sudden death, his father's sudden remarriage, and "the fact that my father seemed so much happier, so much more emotive, around this new woman."

During the two weeks of clearing out the house for sale, Doug gathers up old photos and family films. He gets to know his mother anew when he stumbles upon her diaries: boxes of handwritten and typed pages that reveal the passionate intelligence of a suburban housewife frustrated with herself and her marriage, a woman filled with desires that were played out in therapy and in fantasy. As she wrote about her husband: *"I've been too much for him all along."*

Meanwhile, Doug gets to know his father anew. Do you miss Mom? No, replies the father. What was the marriage like? A functioning association, not a loving association, explains the father. "It's surprising how little we knew," says Doug.

Today, says Doug, his parents probably would have gotten divorced. Or they wouldn't have gotten married in the first place. "They were mismatched," he says. Maybe she would have lived with his father for a while and moved on, found fulfillment in a career, found a more like-minded partner. And his father might have had a happy marriage earlier in life.

But his parents lived at a time when women were under pressure to marry young, and men were under pressure to marry them. Their role as parents was to provide for children. Do whatever it took: stay in a marriage

---

6. *51 Birch Street* is a documentary film, now available on DVD. For further information, go to http://www.51birchstreet.com.

that made them miserable, move to the suburbs when they missed the city, get a job that allowed three kids to go to college. Because that's what parents were supposed to do. And they did a great job! In a family video of his parents celebrating their fiftieth anniversary in the backyard with balloons flying and guests laughing, his mother, white-haired with a grand smile, turns to her son and says into the camera: *"Aren't you glad we got married?"*

Well, yes! It was a long marriage! A statistical triumph! At the heart of this story is ambivalence. There is nothing pure about love. There is pride, anger, jealousy, hope, disappointment. As time goes by, there is the glue of shared memories and the creation of a family. In a "functioning association," estrangement may be combined with loyalty. Boredom mixed with kindness. But it's still a marriage with bonds of interdependency and attachment.

Ask yourself: *Aren't you glad you got married?*

For most people, the answer is yes. And it should be. As you look back, you have to respect the past. Even if a relationship was empty or turned ugly, it may have given you children and a network of friends. You probably had some good experiences. Previous marriages and relationships make up your legacy. They are part of who you are.

✦

Paradox: Old rules. New rules.

A lot of couples get trapped in the changing rules of marriage. The differences between Doug and his parents reflect the transformation of marriage in one generation. Unlike his parents, Doug and his wife both have careers. They married later—in their 30s, rather than in their 20s. They lived together before marriage.

Yet the basic struggles in a relationship transcend generational differences. "I've always thought marriage was great but hard work. We're all mismatched. You're always wrestling with an imperfect partner . . . always acknowledging that you're imperfect. It's a constant struggle. Whose marriage is easy I'd like to know," says Doug. "I think I have a pretty good marriage."

It's the structure of marriage as an intimate partnership that has shifted. And so have expectations and responsibilities. Economists look at it this way: marriage used to be cast as a *production unit*. How does a couple produce happiness and well-being for themselves and their family? In marriages formed a generation ago, spouses, like members of a small firm, tended to specialize in different areas. One spouse would specialize in the marketplace (usually the man); the other would specialize in the home (usually the woman). Specialization was the most efficient way to raise children, advance in a job, and participate in the community.

Today, the trend is away from specialization toward the *complementarity* of shared roles, interests, talents. Both partners are likely to hold jobs. Both partners participate in the running of the household and the raising of the children. Instead of a *production unit*, marriage has become a *consumption unit*. You pool your assets to generate the resources you then use to *consume* what you need for the well-being of your family. "Essentially we've moved into a world where you can buy almost anything you want—any service, any goods," says University of Pennsylvania social economist Betsey Stevenson, who, as co-author of the Pennsylvania marriage and divorce study, has analyzed changing patterns of marriage and divorce. In the past, she explains, if you liked pies, "you wanted a pie maker for a spouse. Now you can buy a pie."

What you need in a spouse is someone who can help you pay for the pie. And then the question becomes: Do you both like pies? Maybe one of you would rather spend money on bowling. Common interests and values are critical to the consumption model of marriage. Do you both like to hike, watch Western movies? If you disagree, how do you resolve your differences? In the production model, spouses have clear and separate functions. The consumption model requires a lot more negotiation and involves more overlapping responsibilities.

The consumption model also changes how you choose a spouse. These days, there is more "like" marrying "like": you tend to match up with someone who is like you—same age, same education, same background, even same earning power (what researchers call "assortive mating"). Men and women tend to bring the same kinds of resources to the union.

This is a huge shift in mating rules and expectations. In earlier generations, you would have looked for a mate to provide what you didn't have or couldn't attain. In the early 1970s, when women were asked about the most important characteristic in a spouse, they answered: *a man who was a good earner.* Today, the answer is more likely to be: *a guy who understands me, who is a good friend.*

The trend toward the consumption model of marriage can catch older couples off guard. If you grew up in the era of specialization, you now find yourself in a changed marketplace of relationships. Longevity reinforces the newer model. "As you get older, if you don't have things to do in common, it's more problematic," continues Stevenson. "When you go into retirement, this is a real issue. If you don't like doing the same stuff, what are you going to do together? With kids, it was easy. Now it's just the two of you. How can a marriage survive another twemty years?"

That is the question older men and women are answering with their lives. Over the past 300 years, marriage has evolved from a relatively short, social-business partnership for producing the next generation into a romantic partnership—what scholars call "companionate" marriage— based on love, choice, and mutual benefit. In the process, the bar for marital satisfaction was raised. Now longevity is raising the bar even higher.

Retired Spouse Syndrome

As the Caterpillar asked in *Alice in Wonderland*: *"Who are YOU?"* And Alice replied: *"I—I hardly know. . . . I know who I WAS . . . but I think I must have been changed several times since then."*

Who are you? You know who you were once upon a time: teacher, engineer, social worker, office manager, police sergeant, lawyer, nurse . . . soccer mom, single mom, Mr. Mom, Little League coach, school volunteer. . . . And now? *You must have changed several times since then.*

In a workaholic culture, people define themselves by their job. When you retire, you lose an identity, a built-in network of colleagues, and a structured schedule. You look across the bed. Maybe your spouse has already left for work and you're alone. Or you're single and wonder: Who are you going to see today? In traditional adulthood, you follow a rigid to-do list; now you are cut loose. You swing between drift and chaos. And you may even drive those around you a little crazy.

There are many guises of retired spouse syndrome. The retiring spouse becomes a drag; the nonretiring spouse seems unavailable and unsympathetic. Or vice versa. Perhaps you are suddenly locked together at home for the first time. Research by sociologist Phyllis Moen of the University of Minnesota shows that the first two years after leaving a job are a common time of marital strife for both men and women.

Besides, you're not really retiring. Retirement is an obsolete word. Chances are you're going to find new work, new purpose. But no one tells you that after leaving the big job, you enter a transition phase that could last a decade. Thanks to longevity, you're in a novel period in the life span. Like adolescence, this "adult-escence" or "middle-escence" is a sometimes stormy period that marks the end of one life segment and the beginning of another. Just as teenagers are breaking away from childhood and moving on to starter adulthood, men and women in their 50s, 60s, and 70s are breaking away from traditional adulthood and moving to . . . *what next?*

Perhaps you haven't a clue what to do next. Maybe you should get that knee replacement. You've got time now. You think about visiting the grandchildren. Go on a trip. The Human Resource folks at the office held seminars on financial planning, but did anyone mention marriage? Or depression?

The key to managing this transition after the big job ends is the quality of your relationships. How connected and engaged you are with others— your friends, your adult children, your partner. Even with preparation, official retirement can put your life and your relationships on the line.

No, not you, you say. You have a good marriage. You are looking forward to this time together. How bad can retirement be?

Ask Reese and Cheree Cleghorn of Washington, D.C.

Reese has it all: energy, ambition, brains. For nearly twenty years, he has been dean of the University of Maryland School of Journalism. He and his wife of twenty-five years live in the fast lane with other successful couples who are drawn to the nation's capital to make their mark. Reese plans his retirement. His wife, Cheree, is happy that he is happy to step down and teach; now he can write and she can build up her Internet health counseling service. They can do some traveling.

At his retirement party, all his friends, colleagues, and students come to pay tribute. He is a star. He has a wonderful wife. He's made a difference. "Aren't we two of the luckiest people in the world?" says Reese.

"Three months later, we were in free fall," says Cheree.

Born in 1930 in Lyerly, Georgia, population 293, Reese has a Mark Twain boyhood running along the railroad tracks and going to the drugstore for hot ice. He smiles at the memories: his Scots ancestry; the Methodist church; his great-great uncle, the Confederate general. His folks are solid citizens. With a handsome craggy face and a twinkle in his eye, he has all the graceful charm, irreverent wit, and friendly warmth of the Southern Gentleman Journalist.

But hidden behind the Mark Twain boyhood, a successful career, and a good marriage is the shadow of loss—partly historic coming from the Old South and the legacy of the Civil War, but mostly personal: the loss of his older brother, a "blue baby" born with purplish lips; he couldn't play baseball but he diagramed out the 1937 World Series game for Reese. Three years later, when Reese was 10, his 17-year-old brother died. "I loved my brother," Reese says.

And the loss of his father, who'd once been prosperous and was ruined in the Depression, never regaining his economic foothold in life. He wore a three-piece gray suit to Reese's graduation—Reese had jumped a grade and graduated cum laude—and after that, his father took to his bed, incapacitated by a thrombosis; he died when Reese was 16. "He gave up everything. . . . The sparks had gone out."

That would not happen to Reese. His way out of the shadow of loss is to excel. By the time he goes to Emory University in the footsteps of his father, the shy boy, who was not an athlete and hadn't been particularly popular at school, starts to blossom. He joins a fraternity, becomes president of the student government and editor of *The Wheel*, the college newspaper. "I became outgoing," he says. "I came into my own." He finds his wit, his talent for writing. He finds friends.

Reese belongs to the "Southern Mafia" of writers who bonded in their coverage of the civil rights movement; mostly they were boys from small towns in the South, who understood the struggles in a way Yankees never could, who were called "liberal" when that was a dirty word in the South, who helped change the country with their news stories.

In the journalistic chase for the big story, Reese finds challenge, fulfillment, and friendship. Whenever the shadow of loss darkens—as it would with the breakup of his first marriage—he turns to his work . . . and thrives. "Survival was something I learned early," he says. "My profession was my salvation. I drew great satisfaction from it."

In midlife he finds another source of salvation: Cheree, his second wife. They meet at the newspaper in Charlotte; he is the editor of the opinion page—and she is fifteen years younger, smart, feisty, and just starting her career. "She was stunningly beautiful," he says. They ride the roller coaster of success for the next several decades.

And then he steps down from the deanship. Another loss; different from earlier losses because "retirement" is supposed to be a normal, welcome milestone. But he experiences the shift to teaching as a real blow and the shadow falls.

For the first time, his days have no beginning. He feels a huge physical weight bearing down on him, an unbearable heaviness of being. He sleeps twelve hours a day. At first his wife is not too concerned. He'd been hard at it for nearly twenty years. "Then it became clear to me: this was darker. He was more remote," says Cheree. "I could not reach him. It was a distinct kind of loneliness."

Sluggish . . . miserable . . . confused. Reese would forget a phone number, forget his computer password, forget a street address. He becomes a stranger in the house: the Southern Gentleman is gone. He is irritable and snaps at the woman he loves. He looks haggard, ancient. One evening when they are out to dinner, the waiter turns to Reese and asks: "And what would your daughter like?" Reese is furious. Deeper into darkness he goes.

It is a severe depression. He has never had a clinical depression before. But with the end of the big job, he loses the salvation of work. No more onward and upward in a career to pull him out from the shadow. His lifelong solution to loss has now become another loss. All he has left is the shadow . . . and his wife. "I was absolutely terrified. I knew enough to be terrified," says Cheree, who had made a career in health care.

The crisis of retirement switches to the crisis of illness. Cheree knows that depression can be treated. But knowing this does not take away the pain when he lashes out at her, or ease her fear that he might not come back, even with treatment.

A dual dance begins. She gets him to a doctor. All the while she is struggling with her own retirement from a suburban Washington hospital and confronting a far bigger loss: the prospect that the love they have shared might be gone. As she says to the doctor: "There is no law that says he has to keep loving me just because I'm good at taking him to the doctor." And what about his stabbing words? "I need help. When he lashes out, I don't know what to do here. I'm not a blank board myself. I'm trying to figure out what I'm going to do."

The doctor reassures her that the reason Reese lashes out at her is because she is a safe target. With the depression, the doctor says, Reese is not himself. Who is he? Who is she? Are they still a "we"?

They draw on the past. They had a strong marriage going into this crisis. "Very few people are lucky enough to find soul mates. That's important. We are both Southerners so we have a common understanding of history. We have common values. We share intellectual interests. I'm one of his biggest fans. He's one of mine," she says. Reese agrees: "We had a very robust relationship from the start. We're very candid, we don't flirt around, we don't do anything we shouldn't do."

What they have is a large dose of *positivity*—positive feelings and experiences in their marriage that buffer them in times of crisis. Reese gets into the care of a neuro-psycho-pharmacologist and is treated with medication. It's hard work and takes a couple of years. Slowly his humor comes back and so does his life. Today he is teaching again and is pursuing two book ideas. Cheree is getting her life back, too, updating her website for consumers to get health information.

To be vulnerable like that and survive . . . together. To come so close to losing it and then get another chance. "Now, in a lot of ways, he's younger. He has a wonderful sense of play," she says. He loves being with his grandchildren. "He's so mischievous. He can make me laugh." And he credits her with saving his life. "When I got so depressed, I couldn't have made it without Cheree. I don't think I would be alive. She's had to put up with enormous difficulty," he says.

Also crucial is the support of his circle of friends, the Southern Boys who have borne witness to his long life. Once again they all sit in the garden on a warm spring evening and tell stories and laugh together. As one of his friends says to Cheree: "Reese collects people the way others collect antiques. He's such a good friend, and he keeps them until they *are* antiques."

Reese feels that he has climbed a mountain to keep all that he holds dear. The crisis deepens their marriage. Amazing, he says, to love more completely, to attach more firmly, to become more grateful. And they are both wiser about what can happen in this phase of life.

As Reese says: "Watch out when the big job ends."

Retirement usually leads to a new and rewarding chapter. But getting there can be a rough passage. Like childbirth, leaving the big job is a life-changing event that alters the dynamics of a couple and reorients the bond with friends and family. In the glossy brochures about Caribbean cruises and retirement communities in Arizona, there is no mention of the need to mourn the official end of a working life. No bulletins about the heartbreak that can occur in a marriage when you turn in your badge. No instruction manuals for you and your family on how to cope with unanticipated consequences of retirement.

It's important to be alert to the magnitude of changes ahead so you aren't taken by surprise when you encounter signs of retired spouse syndrome. This is a time to inventory your relationship assets. Reese and Cheree are successful because they have three good fairies on their side: a committed marriage before retirement; access to appropriate medical treatment—and the good fortune that treatment worked in his case; support of a community of lifelong friends and colleagues.

◆

Another critical factor in surviving retired spouse syndrome is the role of the individual. Reese takes responsibility for his depression, for his behavior, and for getting treatment. There is an "I" in marriage and it's up to him to regenerate his health, his work, and his life in the wake of stepping down from the big job. The two "I's" in a relationship can't move on to a new chapter if one "I" balks or shuts down.

Some people don't make it. The end of a job throws you into a pit of despair. Your spouse can't reach you. Friends fall away. The future darkens. You lash out. You retreat. There are many ways to snuff out life. Some people do it slowly. They start drinking too much. Cocktail hour moves up to 4 P.M. Lunchtime, too. Every night is TGIF. Meanwhile, you look for safe targets. With no boss to complain about, you pick on your spouse— on whomever comes your way. You flounder around the house. You don't do much of anything. Your health starts to deteriorate. You withdraw and become increasingly isolated. You wait for death.

Other people come to the end more quickly.

Hal and Mimi Seidel*[1] grow up in Wisconsin. She falls in love with his brain: he is smart, confident. They have been married nearly thirty years. She manages the office of a law firm. He has a good job at a machine tool plant. Their children are away—one in college, the other working in Chicago. About ten years ago they move into their dream house, farther out in the country. And then out of the blue, the company offers Hal an early retirement package. A year's salary. The whole operation is moving out of state. Who can refuse the velvet handshake? "He decided rather suddenly to take this package," says Mimi. "He was under a lot of stress."

Six weeks later, Hal is home, a *retiree*, age 58, unemployed, looking for work, sort of. "He said he wanted to try different things," she says. He gets a job doing maintenance at a high school, has a fight with the boss and quits. At the plant, he was a supervisor; he's used to telling others what to do. "He wanted a supervisor job. He never had to do a résumé

---

1. Throughout the chapter, asterisks indicate that names, identifying details, and some events have been changed.

before—he'd worked at the plant all his life. He was really lost trying to look for a job. It's not a hotbed of jobs here, especially for people pushing 60. He did not ever finish the résumé. He didn't go for any job interviews. All along he became more unpleasant," she says.

He never hurts her. But he scares her. She'd come home from work and he'd be a bear. "He was losing control of his life. He was trying to control mine. As he was feeling more desperate, his behavior got worse," she says. "He got more depressed. I knew he was more depressed." She tries to talk to him about it. "He would not entertain any help or counseling or medication." He pushes her aside. He grows angry. One day he throws the plastic computer stand against the wall, leaving a dent.

A week later, they have a huge fight. A shelf in the closet had fallen down and they argue about how to fix it. Put the shelf in this way. No, that way. Shut the (blank) up! Why are you so angry? He ignores her. She fights back: What about the dent in the wall? What do you mean you're not angry? He throws her words back at her. "He said I was turning into some horrible person. I tried to stay calm. He stomped off to bed," she says.

The next morning, Mimi gets dressed and goes to the gym before work. Hal is still asleep. "I said good-bye. He stirred. I went off."

After work, she stops at the grocery store. By the time she comes home, it has started to snow. She goes into the house but he isn't there. She puts the groceries on the counter. She looks upstairs. She looks in the basement. Even the dog isn't there—the red-haired mutt retriever the children left behind. She sees a light in the barn and walks across the field. There are no tracks in the snow.

"I opened the door. The whole barn was full of gray smoke of exhaust. The car was still running. I saw him in the back seat. I tried to open the door. The dog was in the car with him. I screamed his name. I touched him. He was warm." She turns off the engine. She calls 911. She opens up the back of the barn and smashes windows.

He is dead. He leaves no note.

"I didn't know how really desperate his depression was. He never talked about taking his life. He just boom did it," says Mimi. "Retirement—that was the thing that triggered this. He was a man who was extremely centered. He always seemed to know what to do; he always knew who he was. He lost that comfort with himself. He lost that confidence. He lost his identity. He wasn't a supervisor—he wasn't a person anymore. He felt that way.

"It's a warning. It's a warning to people to be prepared for the changes in your life. Be humble about needing help. Here we were. We were going to retire together and do all these things. Wow. Yes, I loved him. Yes, I certainly did. I assume he loved me too. He said he did. It was not easy all the time."

This kind of loss is devastating. It is a reminder that the transition of "middle-escence" is a vulnerable period. Most people do not succumb to a severe depression after retirement—just as most women do not suffer from a postpartum depression after giving birth. But like a parent with a newborn, you may find yourself dealing with the swing of some strong emotions: relief and joy mixed in with unease and unexpected sadness. The future seems overwhelming; the present, uncertain.

It's a time to take special care of yourself; to give yourself some slack—to spoil yourself. You've put in many long decades of pleasing the employment gods. If the talons of depression clamp down on you, it's an emergency for you and your family and it requires medical attention. As Mimi says, *Be humble about needing help.*

✦

Several years ago in Japan, doctors began noticing a new "contagious" illness—a stress disorder that graying husbands were giving to their long-suffering wives. Exiled from the workplace and a rigid corporate culture of command and control, these homebound martinets turned on their wives, barking orders, nitpicking every detail of dinner, demanding service. Retired husbands were making their wives sick with stomach ulcers, rashes, throat polyps, and slurred speech. So many wives of retired men were showing up with stress-related problems that physicians in Japan started calling it "retired husband syndrome." The problem has prompted a rise in divorce among older Japanese couples. The number of divorces among those married for twenty years or more has doubled since 1985.

American wives can relate to the plight of their Japanese sisters. We have our cocktail napkins with retirement jokes: *For better or worse, but not for lunch.* And *Retirement is twice as much husband and half as much money.* But postretirement marital malaise is much more complex in the United States.

For starters, both spouses are likely to be in the workforce. In Japan, the at-home wife is the one who shows signs of retired husband syndrome. In the United States it is the retiring spouse who may be at greater risk of stress-related symptoms. But both partners go through an adjustment phase when one or both retires, which affects the marriage. The daily routine as well as the power balance in the relationship is in flux.

Wives in the workplace confront many of the same issues of identity, structure, and community as husbands when they leave a prime job. So there is *his* retirement and *her* retirement and *their* new life to figure out. It all adds up to retired spouse syndrome.

Timing is important. Spouses are often out of sync. A husband, after thirty years on the job, is eligible to retire, while his wife, who may have postponed her career to raise children, is offered a promotion to a more demanding job. He wants out; she wants in. His career is ending, hers is taking off. He wants to move to South Carolina and play golf. She doesn't want to leave where they live, where she has friends, a job, room for grandchildren—and a life. Most problematic, says Minnesota's Phyllis Moen, are situations in which the husband retires and the wife continues to work.

The out-of-sync sinkhole is another variation of retired spouse syndrome. At issue is not just timing but the fact that couples often have very different visions of the future. The challenge is to merge your dreams of what the next chapter will be. You may be surprised when you learn what your partner is envisioning.

"I come from a very authoritative household," begins Belinda McHugh.* Old man McHugh is a fixture in South Boston; he knows everyone in the neighborhood. When he walks into Connolly's drugstore, he is greeted as a king. The year Belinda graduates from Boston College, she gets married. Four children before she is 30. "I was heavily into the wife and mother role. I was not swamped by it—I was developed by it. That was a huge part of my development," she says.

Her husband is ten years older and manages a tow-trucking company. He makes good money, getting illegally parked cars in Boston towed off to nearby Charleston. Never a slow period in a city where a parking space is more precious than a house in the suburbs. But it is grueling physical work—calls at all hours, hoisting vehicles onto the truck. He's sick of it. When a new boss takes over, he starts thinking about retiring. Maybe getting a place down on the Cape. He is 60.

The year before is full of change: Belinda earns a certificate in health care management. Two daughters get married. Her first grandchild is born. "A heck of a year," she says with a smile.

And then her husband comes home and tells her his dream: a cabin far, far away. No traffic. A fishing rod for company. And her. But she is not ready. She's been offered a job at Harvard Pilgrim Health Care. Their timing is out of sync. So are their visions of the future. Belinda likes being with people. The idea of spending the next thirty years alone with her husband and a fishing pole appalls her.

They sit down and talk, perhaps for the first time in a long busy marriage. She says: *I want a soul mate.* He says: *I just want to be left alone.* "There were huge differences in how we were going to live out the rest of our life," she explains. The age gap between them becomes more acute. He is slowing down. She is revving up into a new job. He is done with the full-time treadmill; he wants a quiet life. She's eager to soar.

They talk and struggle for two years to overcome their differences. Belinda thinks about the old adage from Margaret Mead: a woman needs three husbands—one for youthful sex, one for raising children, one to be a joyful companion of old age. "I was not going to get the joyful companion of old age," she says.

They try to adjust their clashing visions of a future life. "We had better talks than we ever had," she says. They become closer in their relationship even as they draw farther apart in their destinies. "He just wanted to have a smaller world. My life was going to get bigger. He wanted me to be less than I was. I wanted him to be more than he was," she says.

They let each other go. They solve their dilemma by parting and getting a gray divorce. He remarries within a year. She takes back her maiden name. They create separate lives but remain close. They continue family rituals. So much binds them.

Belinda thinks about the social revolution of longevity and wonders how people are going to work out relationships in an era of expanded life spans. It seems an unconventional accommodation in this period of life, she says, to reestablish an occasion of grace with your spouse of thirty years—as you live apart for another thirty years!

But in the new construct of marriage, there are many variations on the theme of a long married life. Adult children—those in their 20s and 30s—need to prepare for the imperatives of longevity, she says. "This is our generation's life work—to help people figure this out and get involved much earlier in life. To say to them—*you've got the long haul here!*"

As Belinda and her "wasband" carve out a different pathway in these later years, they—like many older couples—are showing the young how to manage the long haul. "What a gift to the next generation," she says. "I'm excited."

✦

Women seem to have an easier time with retirement. One factor has to do with the identity issue. Early on in marriage, women tend to have multiple identities—the manager who is primarily responsible for the house, the mom who takes the lead in raising the children, the consumer who shops for groceries and calls the plumber to fix the washing machine, the planner who arranges the social calendar for the family and organizes vacations, the family spokesperson who writes the holiday cards. Their selfhood is more fluid (another kind of problem), not so fixed on being a police officer or an insurance salesman. Men tend to see their social value as mainly linked to their job. That makes the loss of a job title a bigger blow to identity. These are crude generalizations, of course. Many women derive their main identity from the workplace, and many men are involved in multiple roles at home and at work. But in general, men root more of their identity in the job.

The other factor revolves around relationships. Women seem to have more intimate friends—a more available structure of emotional support outside the marriage. This network is crucial as you get older. Part of it is practical: retirement wipes out the built-in social structure of a job—the bonding among colleagues that takes place on assignment, around the water cooler, in the cafeteria. You are thrown into your personal circle outside of work. The challenge for many men is to build up a team of friends and family. The marriage may be central, but you need more than one person in your life.

Research shows that you shift priorities in personal development toward emotions and relationships as you age. When you are younger and are climbing up the life ladder, you tend to concentrate on acquiring knowledge and gaining experience. You want to be a success. As you get older—after age 50 or 60—you become more attuned to emotions and relationships. This is true of both men and women. Instead of getting ahead, these years are about getting whole and being connected. It's not what you know but how you feel.

Over the life span, explains Laura Carstensen, director of the Stanford Center on Longevity, a person goes from being mainly cognitive and rational to being more sensitive and emotional. The psyche's compass moves from acquiring information (necessary to get ahead and survive in youth and adulthood) to showing emotions (necessary to connect and survive in the later years). "How you feel becomes more important over time. We change our priorities. The early years are about information gain: what you know. The later years are about emotional regulation: how you feel," says Carstensen.

This is not to say that younger people aren't emotional and older people aren't rational. It's that your preferences have shifted with age.

Getting older puts a premium on relationships. If you've not paid much attention to friendship beyond work and family, you have some catching up to do. What's more, as you get older, another change is taking place in your social environment: you tend to have smaller but closer networks than younger people. This is natural selection at work. Quality of relationships becomes more important that quantity. When you're young, you're eager to make a good impression and meet people. You are more concerned about what others think of you. But in later years, you don't so much care what most other people think of you; more important are the love and goodwill of the ones you hold dear.

You settle on your intimate team: those people you can't imagine your life without. You go deep into these lasting relationships—you recover the friend from childhood, you create new bonds with adult children and grandchildren, you cherish the cousin from family Thanksgivings past, you gather up a friend from work, from child-rearing years; and, of course, if you are part of a couple, you hold your partner closer.

"People get more selective as they age. They prune their social networks," continues Carstensen. This is the *socio-emotional selectivity theory* of aging. It is one of the reasons you are happier than a younger person. Your network, though smaller, is more meaningful. It is also more stable. "The inner core hardly changes across adulthood," says Carstensen. "Love is about the core." And the core is about love.

You need about ten people in your core, she says. If you get down to three, you may become too isolated emotionally. Like a baby who is not held enough, you are at risk of "failure to thrive."

Jolts like retirement or an illness push the emotional regulation button and test the resilience of your circle. Some couples, alone together, week after week, get too locked into each other, draining the energy and surprise out of the relationships. There is too much togetherness. The balance between intimacy and independence is out of whack. Unless you make an effort, you can lose touch with your circle.

People who are single tend to hone their friendship skills. Without a partner, you may pay more attention to your intimate circle—this core is your "marriage." You are more likely to nurture your circle all through the different chapters in your life. You come to retirement with a strong social network already in place.

Mona Kreaden of New York City is no stranger to transition. She worked in the trucking industry. She lived in Israel. She was married for six years in her 20s. She went to graduate school when she was 50. Recently, she retired from an administrative post at New York University. She is now active in The Transition Network, a nonprofit association for women who are undergoing transitions in their work (job loss, job search), their personal life (marriage, divorce, widowhood), or their health.

Mona has an intimate circle of about eight people: childhood friends from Montreal and Toronto where she grew up, university friends, New York friends, and family members (her niece lives nearby)—men and women from different parts of her life from near and far, who respond to different parts of who she is, who are there for her and vice versa.

She has two pieces of advice for those who are coupled: "As a single woman, you are not going to get one person to be all things. It's very important to develop a coterie of friends—so you get the nourishment you need," she says. "I worked hard to get my friendships. I won't let them go."

And second: "You need to know how to listen," she says. In the first phase of a relationship, there is the click of connection. New friends make you laugh. They confer social status and acceptance. They tap into a special interest—in music, in sports. "They fill a need in you," says Mona. Then if the connection is to evolve into real friendship, "you have to come to that place where it's not about you," she says. "You have to be willing to put yourself aside and learn about the other person. If your judgment is good, it becomes an equal exchange."

This framework applies to couples, too, especially now that you are spending more time together. You can't expect your partner to fulfill all your needs. And to have a friend in your spouse, you have to put yourself aside and listen. "I know how to listen," says Mona. "To get a good friend, you have to be a good friend."

✦

You want to know what's normal—but there is no normal. The average age of retirement is about 62. But some people work into their 80s. Others opt out or are booted out in their 50s.

Making the transition to a new chapter is a long process. Sometimes the seeds of retired spouse syndrome are planted long before you step down from the big job. Issues can simmer because you are simply too busy at work to deal with them. Your spouse understands the pressure you're under and accommodates . . . for a while.

You look forward to retirement. But there's deferred maintenance that needs to be done on your marriage.

In 2001, John Patterson gets a much-needed and demanding job: head of information technology at Children's Hospital in Los Angeles. "A high-stress period," he says. The position involves installing state-of-the-art equipment and integrating systems and databases for doctors and nurses to improve patient safety and medical outcomes. His wife, Nina, stays in their house in Northern California. He has an apartment in LA. They alternate going down, coming up on most weekends.

The job is taxing—because he is the one between doctors and nurses and administrators and patients and vendors and consultants. "I was Jabba the Hutt." He'd call Nina every night. How are you doing? Nina is busy. She is a Jungian analyst. They moved from Massachusetts a few years earlier and she has to get licensed to practice in the state of California. The burden of making money weighs heavily. At that point, the last two of five kids are in college. They are stretched out; both working, both burdened. At first, the pattern of commuting is hard.

"When I work, I work. When I'm engaged, I'm engaged," says John. "At night, I'd go down to a watering hole and eat and drink. My blood sugar was out of whack. I was moody, irritable. I was on this roller coaster down there. I'd come home and think: If this doesn't stop or change, I don't think I can take it."

After about five years, circumstances change. The kids are through college. John's father has died, leaving them an inheritance, which helps to ease the burden of making money. And a new leadership team takes over at the hospital.

John is happy to retire and come home. He is 63.

But three months later, he and Nina are at a break point. "I said to myself: *I can't live with him if he's going to be like this,*" she says. "I felt besieged and unable to live up to his expectations or even understand what they really were."

John and Nina aren't used to being together all the time. To a certain extent, they have lived on separate tracks throughout much of their marriage. Nina is five years older than John and has two daughters from a previous marriage. She and John go on to have a son and twin daughters. For more than thirty years, they struggle to keep the family afloat emotionally and financially.

Suddenly with John's retirement, they are thrust together every day with much less to do in a small place. "This is the first time we are living together on a day-to-day basis and there are no children as a distraction—or something else for us to focus on," says Nina. "We found out in a new way that we are two very different personalities; our rhythms are different, our emotional configurations are different. Also when John started to retire, he was stressed out from the job. He was exhausted. It was such a huge change from constantly working hard. He was extremely moody."

John has all the signs of retired spouse syndrome. He isn't eating properly, his blood sugar is up, his days have no structure. He flies off the handle about little things—if someone telephoned during dinner. "John had to learn to take care of himself and not be all things to all people," says Nina.

John and Nina reframe their marriage. They have three things going for them:

1. *Deep commitment.* John and Nina have been tested over more than three decades together. They've moved about every ten years: Los Angeles to Boston to Philadelphia to Northern California. They've raised five children and sent them to college. They faced the stepfamily challenge of blending Nina's daughters with their own three children. How hard it is to be a stepparent; how hard it is to be the one in the middle between steps. They both have worked—he in information technology and hospital management, she rebuilding her practice every time they move. To survive they have bonded on a deep level.

"I've never considered divorce," says John. In the midst of an argument, both occasionally bring it up but neither wants to go past posing it as a threat to get attention. Nina had gone through the divorce of her parents as a child and her own divorce. She knows the trauma involved in breaking up. "Things would have to be unbearable for me to do that. We just know the grass isn't greener," she says. If a spouse were alcoholic, or physically abusive, and staying together would be dangerous, then she believes divorce would be a healthy option. But she knows John, she knows what they have achieved together, she does not want to lose him. And he does not want to lose her.

2. *Time apart.* The first step was to get a break from each other. John goes off on a meditation retreat. It's only for ten days but he meditates and remains silent the whole time. It gives him a chance to examine his life and put his retirement in perspective. After he comes back home, he sleeps long hours. He eats specially prepared food: broccoli stir-fried in olive oil, steamed shrimp, sprouted wheat bread. He takes long walks. He detaches and reckons with the changes he is undergoing. He starts to think about what lies ahead. He listens to the stories of other men in transition. Some are getting divorced and they talk about their marriages. He notices that one or both spouses persist in erroneous beliefs about each other. They don't see each other as they really are. They have this fantasy—of what they want and don't have. They feel unknown by the other. "Who else is going to see you as you really are? That's really being very unconscious," says John. And he thinks of Nina. They really know each other.

He then gives himself permission to do nothing for six months. "I had the predictable anxiety," he says. He uses the metaphor of the lobster. The hard shell of the exoskeleton provides security but allows no growth. When the lobster "sheds" its outer shell, it grows. But it is also vulnerable. "It's *terra incognita*," says John. "I didn't know what it means to have the exoskeleton melt away." Retirement sheds his outer shell. Finally he is able to focus on the *terra incognita* and separate the changes within himself from the changing dynamic of the marriage.

3. Safe zone. Over the years, Nina and John learn that they have to create a safe zone where they can come together and iron out problems. Creating that safe place is a conscious decision. They each set up protective boundaries so that discussions don't escalate beyond their respective limits. They choose a place. Now it is on the hiking trails near where they live. They go there and walk and talk. They have always loved to take walks together. "The way we could talk," says John. About everything. About men and women, about love, about books, about a news event— any way to get to the bedrock of their relationship, to bring up the hard stuff and face it. "The other day, we took a long walk on the beach. We knew we were in a safe zone," he says.

Before they married, they each had been in relationships that did not turn out to be safe. "We both knew what that was like," says Nina. So they have worked at preserving their safe zone. When the anxiety meter rises, "I tend to use self-deprecating, though sometimes too pointed, humor—irrespective of who has hurt whom. I can't stand the tension," says John. "I don't do well with a lack of harmony." When John was 13, his mother was institutionalized, and he went to the nursery to get thirty flowering bushes, so that when she returned, "things would be nice for her." But his mother didn't notice the beautiful bushes—didn't notice the boy who was trying to please her, heal her; she was just angry and disappointed that life hadn't treated her better. As husband and father, John can't stand the feeling of not being able to make a woman happy.

Nina's response to that kind of anxiety is to get quiet. "She does knitting or retreats into a book," says John. In her silence, he feels his mother's disappointment. "More often than not, I can pull myself back from" the legacy of his mother's unhappiness.

They keep going back to the safe zone. It doesn't help to gloss things over. "You're terrified of getting divorced. But terror can sabotage things. If you're that terrified, you can't relax," says Nina. You get into the pattern of paralyzing loyalty just to keep the peace. "If it's so paralyzing, you become a robot," she continues. You want to be able to say: "I'm going to be loyal but in a free way."

Eventually John and Nina reach a settling point. "It was a big readjustment. Our personalities had to take a new account of each other. We had to decide to be more tolerant of each other," says Nina, "more polite to each other. In a long-term relationship like ours, you have to see two sides of each other and of yourself . . . the weak, annoying side and the good side." Says John: "We are so fundamentally close to each other, we have to protect our boundaries with great ferocity."

Now they are contemplating what they will do in the years ahead. They like talking about different scenarios. John has started to do some consulting. Nina has cut back her practice to about twenty hours a week. Grandchildren live nearby. "I don't really know what I want to do. I want to be around the kids and grandchildren. For me, that's the future. I want to keep working for a while. It's interesting," says Nina. "I'd like to find a creative endeavor that's different." John is searching, too. Their exoskeleton is gone; they are both shedders. . . . They are vulnerable together and growing.

It takes time, effort, commitment, and vigilance on the part of both spouses to deal with retired spouse syndrome and regenerate marriage in this stage of life. As psychologist Erich Fromm writes in *The Art of Loving,* love "is not a resting place, but a moving, growing, working together." Out of this churning comes a new beginning for couples like John and Nina. Stepping down from the big job can eventually lead to closer and more joyful relations—not just with a spouse but with all those in your circle.

---

2. Erich Fromm, *The Art of Loving* ([Harper & Row, 1956] Bantam Books, 1963), p. 87.

3

In Sickness and Health

Modern fairy tale: Once upon a time in a land close at hand, a Great Wizard came to the people with a special gift: an extra ten years of good health! A biological bonus of time and vitality for the whole population! The period called youth would last until about age 60. "It's all good news," shouted the inventor of the new age measure. "The end is still bad, but it's being pushed out further." The Extra Ten "are good years."

But the people turned against aging and started an anti-aging movement. What would they do with the Extra Ten? Who would love them, feed them? Political leaders feared a tsunami of old folks washing over the land, bankrupting the Treasury, overwhelming health care.

The Wizard came back with a warning: don't squander my gift!

Reality: The fairy tale is true.

This is the conundrum of longevity. Americans are healthier at older ages than ever before. But they look on this gift with dread and denial. *Come grow old with me?* Forget it! Even the language of aging provokes a shudder. Labels such as "senior" and "elderly" have become dirty words.

You want to stay "young." You become more preoccupied with your health. You eat more fruits and vegetables. You exercise more. (Or you feel guilty.) As you pop vitamins and flex flagging muscles—or as you recover from surgery or from an injury—you keep coming back to nagging questions: How does aging affect your attractiveness to others? Your ability to make and keep close relationships?

All this has created a culture of body-madness, a preoccupation with looking "young." Yet, you're not hedging the truth when you take ten years off your age. Stanford University economics professor John B. Shoven has reconfigured the calendar of aging, based on mortality risk. Forget your date of birth! Your chance of dying within a year tells you your real age. "You're young if you have a lower than 1 percent risk of dying within the year," he explains. There is wide individual variation. If you have a life-threatening illness, your mortality risk rises. But for the population as a whole, people aren't "old" until almost 80, according to Shoven's measure.[1]

The Extra Ten amount to a huge gain in health span. Much like dollars, years of age don't have the same value as they did in the past. Today a man in his late 50s has the same mortality risk as a man in his late 40s would have had in 1940. More evidence for the ten-year health bonus comes from the MacArthur Foundation Study of Aging. All in all, the Wizard's gift is reshaping the population and overturning traditional concepts of growing old; now there are vast numbers of men and women who should be considered young. As a fashion consultant at the Saks Fifth Avenue department store in Boston told me: "You should see my 62-year-olds! They're wearing backless jumpers!"

At the same time you are entering mortality's red zone. You start going to the doctor more these days. Regular checkups: blood pressure, cholesterol levels, PSA count, breast examination. You start feeling it: stiff joints, back pain, leg cramps. You start dealing with it: dimming eyesight, hearing loss. After a certain age, everybody has got something.

You know a big one is out there. When it strikes, life turns upside down. Who will you be now that this unwanted stranger of illness has invaded your body? And who will be at ground zero with you when you get sick?

---

1. John B. Shoven, "New Age Thinking: Alternative Ways of Measuring Age, Their Relationship to Labor Force Participation, Government Policies and GDP" (National Bureau of Economic Research, 2007).

A relationship can suddenly change when you or someone you love—or both of you—are diagnosed with a major illness. Commitment to the other person and fear of abandonment are mixed up with rage, disappointment, and longing. Most likely you will survive your illness. But dreams of travel, creative pursuits, continued work, or leisure may get deferred or be deflated altogether. Longevity has postponed most fatal disease. That's why many people are caught off guard by a health crisis.

✦

The immediate challenge is to confirm the diagnosis and make arrangements for the appropriate medical treatment. For a while, life is suspended. Words like "normal" and "routine" vanish from the vocabulary. The danger is that couples become trapped in their different ways of coping and find themselves increasingly isolated and exhausted under the weight of illness.

You don't understand how things could change so fast.

Gil and Nelle Brown are celebrating their fifteenth wedding anniversary at their favorite restaurant in Great Falls, Virginia. The lights are low at L'Auberge Chez François. The menu is sumptuous: frogs' legs or snails? The waiters dance around them: roast duck breast? Perhaps the game plate of deer chop, bison, antelope? . . . But this evening, they are on edge. They start bickering, low-level stupid stuff. *Why did you park the car so far away? We always park the car there. . . . Don't use that tone of voice. Why are you yelling at me? . . . When do you want to leave? I told you I wanted to leave ages ago. . . . You aren't listening to me. Don't tell me what to do.*

This is not like them. Gil and Nelle are serial spouses: they've both been married before. When they first meet at a seminar at a church in downtown Washington, Gil is a widower and Nelle is divorced. Nelle works at the World Health Organization; Gill is retired from the World Bank where he focused primarily on the economies of South Asian countries. They quickly discover how much they share: an interest in economics, experience in foreign affairs, and, as they get to know each other, a deep faith in God. Nelle is twenty years younger, an independent career woman. When Gil at the age of 65 asks her father, who was then 80, for Nelle's hand in marriage, he comments: "I don't expect this to be easy but at least it won't be boring." And her father replies: "Being married to her mother hasn't been boring either!"

Not boring at all. Lively conversation, sparky debates, not a few disagreements. But no big fights. They are not relationship warmongers, the kind of people who need to fight to feel alive. Quite the opposite: they are too content, too rooted in mutual commitment and respect.

But suddenly they are off track.

A few weeks earlier, Gil notices a peanut-size lump under the skin of his arm. At his regular checkup with the dermatologist, he asks about the lump. Mmmm. Maybe a cyst. The usual steps: remove it, biopsy it. Probably nothing. More tests. Mmmmm. The lump turns out to be a rare aggressive skin cancer.

Gil and Nelle respond in different ways. When he tells her the diagnosis is Merkel cell carcinoma, "I went straight to the computer and started reading the abstracts," she says. Gil's first response is to reach out to people: he calls his three daughters, Nelle's two daughters, several close friends, including a woman who is a breast cancer survivor, and the retired pastor who stood by him and his daughters when his wife died.

Welcome to Diagnosis Shock. This is the immediate period after getting a life-threatening diagnosis. You are thrown back into your deep-seated preferences for dealing with a crisis. Nelle is a twenty-first-century data hunter, using all the resources of the computer to research the disease. Gil is a pre-computer seeker of information and support from people. Nelle tries to amass all the information she can. Gil wants the big picture. While he appreciates Nelle's efforts on the computer, he is not interested in reading esoteric medical journal abstracts. He wishes she were spending less time at the computer and more time with him.

Both Nelle and Gil realize that his cancer is very serious. The more she finds out about his cancer, the more alarmed and frustrated with him she becomes. She also senses—correctly—that Gil doesn't want to dwell on his cancer. Yet she knows he is praying for the proper care and a good outcome.

Gil enters a medical maze: the first oncologist, he feels, is worthless. A second oncologist inspires more confidence. Meanwhile, Nelle on the computer has tracked down a leading researcher on his cancer: Dr. Paul Nghiem of the Seattle Cancer Care Alliance. By this time, Gil is taking over more medical responsibility. He contacts the doctor and decides to go to Seattle for care.

But it's bad timing. Nelle is committed to flying to Geneva for a few days to introduce the head of the Komen Foundation—a major funder of World Health Organization breast cancer activities—to the director general of WHO. When she hesitates to go to Seattle, Gil is hurt. He wants her to come with him to provide emotional as well as practical support.

Nelle makes the choice: she goes to Seattle. The initial gap between them starts to close. They spend Memorial Day weekend at an island retreat in Puget Sound. When Gil begins his five-week course of radiation at the University of Washington Medical Center, he tells Nelle that it's time for her to return home and go back to her work. They part—closer together. "We have different strategies for coping with uncertainty," Nelle explains. These different coping skills create "a filter to communication that sets you at odds—but you are really not at odds."

Diagnosis Shock sets in motion a recalibration of all your relationships. You need to give yourself—and the ones you love—some slack in how you confront the crisis.

Ask yourself: How did you respond to crises in the past? When you lost a job or were dumped by a lover? When a parent got sick, or a child? You know how your child reacted to new or unwanted events—going to the first day of kindergarten, not getting into a first-choice college. And how has your spouse reacted to previous crises? The past can give you clues to how you will behave in a health crisis.

Nelle has already ridden the roller coaster of illness. At age 15, her daughter was jabbed in the head in a basketball game. Two days after the injury, her daughter loses feeling in some of her toes. A week later, she can't balance well enough to walk. The injury is strange; the doctors are confused. Nelle learns how to use the computer to research medical data. She learns to question doctors, to disagree with them. The injury has caused a blood clot that paralyzed nerves in her daughter's spine. Nelle lobbies for proper care. Today her daughter uses a wheelchair and is a medical student.

Getting medical information and questioning doctors are the ways Nelle shows how much she loves her daughter. When you're a parent, you take total charge and do everything you can to protect your child. Nelle is Super-Mom-on-Your-Side for her daughter. But the dynamic with a spouse is different. The relationship involves a more equal balance of power and experience and expectations. In most marriages you learn to share the controls. Unlike the dynamic between parent and young child, a partnership operates on a system of psychological parity.

"When you're dealing with a child, Mom is always Mom. Even when the child gets a little older, Mom sort of has the right to speak up," says Nelle. "When it's a spouse—and the spouse is clearly in charge of his own life and the ultimate arbiter of his own care—what is the spouse's role?"

With Gil, Nelle immediately slips into the role of Super-Spouse-on-Your-Side. Indeed, her research pays off. For months afterward, Gil tells everyone that Nelle has probably saved his life by pointing him to the most effective treatment—radiation—and sparing him more invasive surgery of his lymph nodes and a futile course of chemotherapy. But Gil wants a wife to share the challenge, not a mom-in-disguise to run the show.

Ultimately, if you are the patient, you have to get involved in your illness; it's your body and your life. Depending on your preference, you may initially delegate the responsibility of getting medical information to a family member—or delegate to someone else the task of reaching out to the people you love. Both tasks are essential.

After the initial crisis, you are likely to face a long period of living with an illness. Today, Gil is feeling very good. He does water aerobics and tai chi. He writes reports on national economic and budgetary policies. And he is eternally grateful to Nelle.

And Nelle is feeling good about Gil. "I'm a head person. That's my way to cope," says Nell. "Gil is a relationship person." As an only child "he developed a lot of skill in cultivating relationships because it was his survival strategy." Nelle is one of five children in a family where relationships are a given. Achieving in the marketplace is her survival skill. "His curiosity is in the context of relationships and people—and my curiosity is in the area of ideas and concepts," says Nelle.

They grow in respect for each other. Nelle is in awe of his talent for bonding with people. "What that has done for Gil is to give him a huge support community of people who care about him." When you feel uncertain or vulnerable, it's good to "let people know—to throw yourself into your world of relationships wholeheartedly," she says. "Other people want to be there for you, they want to be connected; it's a time that other people can really show that they are your community as opposed to your being a burden on them."

They learn from each other. "Now the rest is up to the doctors and to God," says Nelle. "Both of us are people of faith, so death isn't the worst thing in our way of thinking." Fortunately, they say, Gil's prognosis is quite good.

Illness becomes a long educational process. People can teach each other new skills. The rationalist can open up to emotions and learn to rely on others and nurture relationships. The relationist can learn to step back and use cognitive skills to solve problems and build up self-sufficiency. Both grow as individuals and as a couple.

✦

It is common for two people—whether partners, friends, or family members—to react to a life-threatening diagnosis with contrasting coping strategies. This kind of communication disconnect can cause a rift just when you need each other most.

"What happens when you get a diagnosis, you have no schema for it. You don't know how to behave," says social psychologist Jessie Gruman in Washington. "That is a source of incredible conflict in families." Gruman is president of the Center for the Advancement of Health and author of *AfterShock: What to Do When the Doctor Gives You—or Someone You Love—a Devastating Diagnosis*.

Research from the Fox Chase Cancer Center in Philadelphia suggests that people generally fall into two categories—*blunters* and *monitors*. Blunters keep anxiety at bay by blunting the deluge of new information and avoiding scary details. Monitors gain confidence and a sense of control by getting as much information as they can. Illness is a learning curve for both. In time, blunters have to learn enough medical details to manage the illness. Monitors have to learn enough about relationship needs to build emotional support.

The blunter-monitor spectrum crosses age boundaries. But since most illness such as cancer and heart disease occurs in older men and women, this may be the first time you've confronted a life-threatening health problem. When the diagnosis comes down, you find yourself on one or the other end of the spectrum.

Part of it depends on your situation: Are you the patient or the loved one?

Jessie Gruman has a PhD in social psychology from Columbia University and has worked in health care all her life. She is also a veteran survivor of cancer and heart disease. You would think she'd be a demon for medical data. But when diagnosed several years ago with colon cancer, she is the blunter; her husband, the monitor. At a meeting with the team of doctors to discuss the diagnosis, her husband, a medical scientist, starts asking questions. Could he see the pathology report? *What?* Feelings overwhelm her. Her husband is challenging her doctors—the ones she is counting on to make her well. How could he? She is furious at him. Maybe the doctors would punish her now.

In hindsight, she knows her husband was absolutely right to ask questions and get a second opinion. Patients and their families must seek the best information to decide on a strategy for treatment. That means questioning doctors, marshalling your own expertise, researching the disease. But in that period right after the diagnosis, coping strategies are likely to be at odds. The risk is that blunters may actively resist learning about their illness, while monitors spin out on a glut of information. Although both approaches to crisis are "correct," integrating different coping styles into one strategy is essential.

It's important for everyone on your team to understand this dynamic and come to a resolution of coping styles. At this point you have some experience with rough times—as Nelle did with her daughter. When a jolt hits, you can fall back on this learned resilience. Indeed, from past setbacks, you remember the dual challenge of gathering support and taking action—all the while grappling with rogue feelings about yourself, about your future, about those around you. You recall how long it took to confront the crisis, deal with it, and move on.

✦

Illness lays bare the bones of a marriage. It's hard to keep your mind clear when so much is happening around you: Is this conflict a superficial, communication problem? Or something deeper, more difficult to contain? A diagnosis can unleash long simmering problems in the relationship. It can also be the crisis that leads to a renewal of the bond—as it did with Nelle and Gil.

"The meaning will spread out over time. It intensifies a lot of things. It shows you so much about yourself and your partner. What you're made of. What's there, what's not there. What do you have here with each other? You see commitment. You see desertion. You see doubt. You think: Am I ready for this? Everything comes to a head," says Jessie Gruman.

Maybe you get caught up in the Lance Armstrong mystique of turning illness into a heroic triumph through the right attitude and strength of will. But illness, like other crises, brings out what is already there. "This is a time when people are going to behave the same way . . . only more so," continues Gruman. You think: major illness is such a profound crisis, can't people rise above it? "They can't. They are not going to rise above it. This is how they are built," says Gruman. A diagnosis "makes everything more what it is. If you're in incredible strain, it will be more so."

Illness has no set timetable. It doesn't always pick a good time in a relationship to strike. Perhaps your spouse has let you down in the past. Or there are major problems that aren't being addressed: abusive behavior or addiction issues; or one of you is having an affair. A blanket of fear covers your hospital bed. Illness awakens you to a truth about yourself, about your marriage. Sometimes that truth is devastating.

✦

Winnie Fitzgerald Simms[*2] lies in the recovery room. Same-day surgery: a laparoscopic procedure with a small incision in the abdomen. Diagnosis: mass on the ovary. She opens her eyes. A nurse comes in. Winnie throws up. Her throat is sore from the anesthesia tube. She remembers the drive to the hospital this morning. Her husband, red-faced and the smell on his breath, the almond smell of booze. They pick up her sister, who has taken the day off from work to be with her. Who takes one look at her husband and quips: "Some things don't change." "Nice sister," he says with a sneer. Winnie remembers the cramping in her chest at this exchange. How she gently rubs her abdomen in the ensuing silence. Cancer? A possibility. Unlikely, the doctors said. Her fate would soon be decided.

Winnie throws up again. The surgeon comes in smiling. A cyst, he says, most likely benign. Not cancerous. A week for the pathology report to be sure. *You can go home now.* Home now? Tears fill up her eyes. Home to the red face and almond breath? Her husband was downsized five years ago. At age 58, he calls himself a consultant. She is the main breadwinner. She can't retire for another ten years. Her sister comes into the recovery room, pats her arm. Tells her that her husband has gone out for lunch. . . . For a drink, Winnie thinks. Something snaps in her. When her husband pulls up the car to the hospital door, Winnie doesn't want him to touch her. He is taken aback. What's happened to her? The doc says she's going to be fine. When they get home, he brings her a present, a little stuffed bunny he bought in the hospital gift shop. She starts to cry. "I can't do this anymore," she says. "I cannot live a lie." He's hurt, mystified. She pushes him away; she wants to be alone. That night, she crawls into a bed in the spare bedroom. And that snaps something in him. Early the

_____

2. Throughout the chapter, asterisks indicate that names, identifying details, and some events have been changed.

next morning, he gets in the family car and takes off—somewhere, anywhere, away.

Winnie recovers from the surgery. Her sister moves in with her for a few weeks. Her son comes home for a visit. The pathology report confirms that the cyst is benign. But the marriage is over.

Illness cracks the façade of relationships. Some marriages are already in serious trouble. Just as surgery excises the inflammatory cyst from Winnie's body, sometimes a divorce is the necessary solution to a painful or dangerous marriage. The experience of illness becomes the agent of change.

Whether you are married or not—whether you're in a strong marriage or an unhappy one—it is a challenge to hold on to your identity and recalibrate your relationships when your body and future are in flux. Berkeley psychologist Carolyn Pape Cowan remembers that when she was diagnosed with breast cancer, people treated her differently. "I wasn't the same person," she recalls. When you are sick, you "want to be cared for—but not treated as a frail person." But those around you may go into a state of paralysis and think: I better not say anything because the person is sick. Emotions go underground. It's psychological lockdown.

"Illness is not different from other stresses. The issues are the same: what gets in the way of communication?" says Carolyn's husband, psychologist Philip A. Cowan. Together they have conducted studies of couples under stress,[3] and they have some advice for those new to illness. Philip Cowan speaks from experience:

"Number one: The well spouse is entitled to feelings and to communicate these feelings to the ill spouse," he says.

"Number two: Talk about the illness and the fears," he says. Let the one who is sick express the feelings and concerns. Will I die? How am I going to get through this? Will I be less sexually desirable? Find a comfort zone to lay out mutual concerns and discuss different aspects of the illness and treatment.

---

3. Carolyn Pape Cowan and Philip A. Cowan, *When Partners Become Parents: The Big Life Change for Couples* (Basic Books, 1993).

"Number three: Unresolved issues could be addressed. The couple could become closer," he says.

✦

Some marriages drift into the doldrums. Maybe you are living parallel lives, going on auto-pilot. After many years together, you achieve a quasi-peaceful rhythm that hides emotional estrangement. You are too busy to notice. And then illness stops the clock. What happens next lays down the foundation of the rest of your life.

Jim Middleton and Lynne S. Wilcox have been married for thirty-two years. He is an information technology consultant and former photojournalist; she is a physician epidemiologist. They have focused on raising their two children and mostly avoid dealing with their own relationship. "I was clueless in a lot of ways," says Jim. "I had assumed everything was okay." But Lynne is feeling very alone. "I like to sit down and talk everything out. I was frustrated by his inability to respond to that," says Lynne.

They start to fight at the micro-level. With Lynne's demanding workload in public health, Jim becomes the primary parent at home. They argue about money, about how to raise the children. "There was a lot of anger and frustration," says Lynne. "We fought about day-to-day things. . . . I felt unsupported and I think he did, too."

They never get to the macro-level of their relationship. "In the early years of marriage and in our careers, we were both Type A personalities," says Jim. "One of the ways we avoided conflict was to avoid each other."

Illness wakes them up. In 2002, Jim is diagnosed with a severe form of hypertension. This disease without symptoms has already damaged his heart. He must take a menu of medications for the rest of his life. In 2003, Lynne is diagnosed with hepatitis C. Now they both have a chronic disease. They both must undergo intensive drug therapy with unwanted side effects. Suddenly the marriage changes.

"I realized I was vulnerable and that there was an end to everything," says Jim. Getting his diagnosis is the ringing of an alarm bell. He knows his heart condition can be treated, but he worries about his kids. "I didn't know whether I'd be around to help them out in the future."

Jolted by illness, Jim and Lynne change the way they relate to each other. Lynne's treatment with two antiviral medications—ribiviran and interferon—is a year of hell. She has nausea the whole time and her weight drops below 100 pounds. "I became very protective," says Jim. "She felt I was being more reinforcing." Lynne does the same for Jim. When his doctors struggle to find the right combination of drugs for him, Lynne is supportive and protective. She makes sure they alter their diet and lifestyle to reduce his risks.

As part of the treatment for heart disease, Jim is prescribed an anti-anxiety drug. "My stress level went down tremendously. I wasn't so much on edge," says Jim. Lynne, meanwhile, used to suffer depressive episodes connected to the winter, prompting her to wonder whether her sad and lonely feelings stemmed from the marriage or from lack of sunlight. Today, their moods have evened out thanks to medication. Jim is no longer Mr. Hypercritical; Lynne is no longer Ms. Hypersensitive.

They draw closer together. "We're not arguing so much anymore," says Lynne, 54. "We learned how to cherish each other and appreciate each other's company." The change is gradual, a bit-by-bit thing, she says. With the children away at college, they do couple things like go out to dinner. "We are able to start talking more about the problems we had—about what we want to do as we near retirement," says Jim, 55. "You have to open up to possibility. We're past the 50 percent mark: the percentage of years you have left is less than the time you've spent here [on earth.] It's not an end. We're looking at it as a beginning of another phase."

"In terms of how we feel about each other, the marriage is the best it's ever been," says Lynne.

The transformation of their marriage is part medical, part behavioral. Family researchers note a mellowing out that naturally occurs among couples—especially with men—in this stage of life. Illness is both an awakening and a softening. As with Lynne and Jim, many older men and women point out that their relationships in this period are the best they have ever been.

Illness has the potential to be a very rich experience of love—opening yourself up to those who care for you or giving of yourself to someone you care for. "People can grow beyond anything they ever imagined or experienced," says Washington psychologist Dorree Lynn, co-author of *When the Man You Love Is Ill*.[4] "They suddenly realize: this person is important to them. Once they get past the terror, a lot of the junk of life tends to fall away."

✦

You need loved ones by your side. If your partner is not able or willing— or is not the right person to be with you in this moment—you turn to others in your intimate circle: a friend, an adult child, a sibling, even a former spouse. You need people to stand by you in loving kindness. You also need an advocate to be with you in the hospital and at doctors' appointments. Married or single, you need a team. When you bring people into your life in this way, it is very intimate. It takes the relationship to a deeper level. It can be a gift to those you love. And you may be surprised who comes to the bedside.

Ginger Dunlop* gets the call at 4 P.M. in her cubicle in the back office at Macy's in Milwaukee. Her brother, 54, has to have colon surgery to remove infected abscesses caused by diverticulitis. He was divorced about six years ago—a shock to the family who are stalwarts at St. Mark's AME church, the oldest African-American church in the city. Who is going to take care of him now? Ginger picks up her mother and they rush to the hospital—only to find his ex-wife by his side. She is a surgical nurse at the hospital. Before the surgery, she accompanies her ex-husband to doctors' appointments and gets his prescriptions. She goes to his apartment and helps him administer intravenous antibiotics. At the hospital she comes into the waiting room to let the family know how the operation is going.

---

4. Dorree Lynn and Florence Isaacs, *When the Man You Love Is Ill: Doing the Best for Your Partner Without Losing Yourself* (Avalon, 2007).

Afterward, she coordinates his care; he will be out of work for three months. She is glad to do this for her former husband—and he is glad to have her support. After all, they loved each other. They share a history. "I know we're divorced but we're still family," she says.

"Why don't you get back together?" asks her former sister-in-law. "Oh no," she replies. "I don't think so and I don't think your brother thinks that way either."

They broke up for good reasons, she explains. They married in their early 20s, and he quickly started cheating on her. She was nursing their second child when she found out he had taken up with a neighbor. Her father was a womanizer and she grew up in the shadow of her mother's abandonment. She doesn't want to repeat that in her own life. But she likes her ex; he's been a good father to their children. Their postmarital connection is strong.

Divorced and estranged couples may come together in the course of an illness. The crisis forces you to get below the surface of postmarital politeness to the bedrock of your bond. This can be enriching to both partners.

Writer Robert Lipsyte chronicles his own and his wife's battles against different cancers in his book, *In the Country of Illness*. He also chronicles their divorce. But when her cancer returns and she is dying, he comes to her bedside. "And then I surprised myself. I told her I still loved her, and that I would see her on the other side," he writes.[5]

Over a long life, the tapestry of marriage is woven by all those who have been part of your life. You need all of them. And they need you.

✦

Some diseases are sneaky. You may not think you are sick. You just know something's not right. Your world starts collapsing. The illness comes on slowly, a silent invader of your health, a masked destroyer of the marriage. Those you love don't understand. What's wrong? They grow concerned;

---

5. Robert Lipsyte, *In the Country of Illness: Comfort and Advice for the Journey* (Alfred A. Knopf, 1998), p. 225.

you get frightened. These are usually the diseases of the brain, disorders of behavior.

A severe depression can occur for the first time in men and women in their 50s, 60s, and beyond. You have to be alert to the risk—in yourself and in those you love. Depression can be associated with other medical conditions—heart attack, a stroke, a fractured hip—and with neurological disorders such as Alzheimer's disease and Parkinson's. Depression may also be triggered by life-changing events such as retirement or the loss of someone close to you through death, disease, or divorce. It can be a side effect of medication. Or it just emerges, throwing its heavy net of despair or irritability over your head.

You're not expecting such slippery guests to get into your mind, to bunk in with you and your family. Maybe you never had a problem before. Why now?

Judy Mattoon of Loveland, Colorado, is a high flyer. With her mass of wavy red hair and pale white skin, her wide smile and bright eyes, she has the force. As though she were born with extra voltage. A high achiever in school and in her career as a teacher. In relationships, too. As a young girl, she dates a lot. "I was wild," she says. She falls in love at first sight with her husband and they've been married more than thirty years. Where she is noisy, he is quiet. Where she is edgy, he is solid. They raise two children and build a light, airy house by a lake. Both have careers and are leading very successful lives.

But here is Judy, sobbing in the car as she commutes to work, curling up in a fetal position and breaking into tears when she comes home. She is 50 years old and falling apart. She thinks her husband isn't there for her. He thinks he is losing her; he couldn't reach her, not at first.

As she looks back on her struggle with depression, she can put it in perspective: in the space of a couple of years, she suffers a cascade of jolts that turn her transition period of "middle-escence" into a medical crisis:

- *Her work changes.* She gets a new job—a promotion to start a literacy program in a new school. But that means leaving a comfortable position where she is a success. She would have to prove herself all over again. The job requires tremendous energy and interpersonal skills—but Judy is feeling exhausted and reclusive. In addition, her mentor of sixteen years has just retired and is unavailable to give her guidance.

- *Her father-in-law dies.* He was the father she didn't have. Her own father grew up in the coal mining poverty of Western Pennsylvania. Even though he was a hardworking provider, he remained emotionally distant and eventually became estranged from her. Her beloved mother had died many years earlier. Jim's dad became like a father to her. Now her supportive parent is gone.

- *Her husband is absent.* Jim the stable, hardworking, get-the-job-done kind of husband has to be away a lot—settling his father's estate and helping his mom cope, rotating twelve-hour, seven-day shifts at Eastman Kodak Company where he works, plus lots of overtime for special projects.

- *Her best friend dies of invasive breast cancer.* "I was with her when she died," Judy says.

- *She suffers a back injury at work* that leaves her in constant pain. She grapples with a workers' compensation system that discounts her claim; ultimately, she and Jim have to hire a lawyer to get help.

- *Their youngest child leaves for college*—creating a very empty nest as both children are now away at schools 1,000 miles from home. It marks the loss of her early-motherhood role.

All these events push her abandonment buttons. Judy slides into a depression, which doesn't seem right because she is the ebullient spark in everyone's life. She struggles with an aching pain, with chronic fatigue. "I'd cry all the way to work, teach half a day. I'd weep through lunch. Continue teaching in the afternoon, sob driving back, curl up in bed," she says. "I became very secretive. I didn't trust anybody at school." Of course she goes to the doctor, who "diagnoses" menopause and prescribes a little Prozac. "It turned me into a sack of cement . . . and squirrelly in the head. I was like a lizard lying in the sun while my head was going round and round in a squirrel cage."

She keeps up her high-flying façade but it becomes harder and harder. "I was a grease spot on the floor. I'd walk around like a zombie. What should take ten minutes took a half an hour. I'd be welling up with hysteria."

At first Jim is mystified. He knows something is wrong. This sobbing, this telling him "I don't know how much longer I can do this." What can he do? All of this because of a bad back? It is winter, crunch time at school with parent-teacher conferences. A snowstorm is predicted. They are sitting around the dining room table. She is holding his hand. "Sit with me and hold me," she pleads. But dinner is over. He knows Judy has a long commute in the morning. He says: "I'm going to clean out the garage so I can fit both cars in before it starts to snow."

To Judy this is abandonment; now she's losing Jim. In time, she comes to realize that he was trying to help the situation by doing something practical. "He loved me in his way," she says. But in the midst of her crisis, they are far apart.

The slow spiral downward continues. Judy keeps going to doctors. Finally she gets to a psychiatrist who evaluates her symptoms and her life. The diagnosis: a form of bipolar depression. "I have this huge sense of relief." For most of her life she has been "hypomanic," operating on the subclinical, energetic side of the scale, the doctor tells her. Her dips into depression were so minor that she paid little attention to them. Doesn't everybody get down sometimes? Sure, she took over-the-counter St. John's Wort. But the high always came back, lifting her on to greater heights. Being "on" is part of her personality.

This is the first time she has experienced a major clinical depression. The jolts have mounted up, creating so many stresses on her psychological makeup that she crashes. She feels that the main part of her life is over and she doesn't see any hope in a "second adulthood." "I had death-of-first-adulthood issues. My passion was dying. I didn't know how to function," she says. "I had pride. I didn't want to be rank and file; I wanted to do 150 percent."

The diagnosis galvanizes Jim. He goes to her doctors' appointments. He does the grocery shopping. He accompanies her to one last teachers' conference in Washington, D.C. He does the paperwork with the union to allow her to retire from teaching. Meanwhile, with proper medication, Judy starts feeling better.

And then the tables turn. Jim tears his rotator cuff in three places and needs surgery. Judy is there to tend him and tilt the balance of their relationship into a more equal position. "We're two 'crips' [as in cripple] together," she says. He comes down with hives, an allergic reaction. She gives him calamine baths; she takes him to acupuncture treatments.

In a curious way, they normalize illness—his and hers. They make love; it's been a while. "We're having crip sex," she says. They talk about what each one of them needs. . . . "I cry when we make love," she says. She cries and looks up and sees that he's crying, too.

"Jude," he says, "I thought I had lost you."

They get through the crisis of illness. "I feel such gratitude," says Judy. "Jim loves me as a human being. He takes me as I am." It's the depth of knowing each other—love based on the reality of vulnerability. They've always had an unusually close and committed marriage. This difficult time of adjustment forces a new way of seeing each other, of being present for one another. The marriage is enhanced. "There's an element of grace. We're in a really close chapter now," she says. "Our love is on a deeper level."

Sometimes, it's hard to figure out what's wrong. What's normal malaise and what's a brain disorder. A gray-haired person comes into the doctor's office with a flat voice and lifeless eyes and says: "I'm sad." Too often the response would be "Well, you're old. Of course you're sad." You have to fight the prejudice of ageism. Losses occur in these decades: grieving is normal. Depression is not. Just being old is not a cause of depression. Yet the toll is high. People over 65 have the highest rates of suicide. Depression and alcohol use are often factors in later-life suicides. But much is unknown about mental health issues in older people. "Ageism is one of the reasons we don't have better data," says psychiatrist Gary J. Kennedy, director of the Division of Geriatric Psychiatry of Montefiore Medical Center in the Bronx, New York.

The responsibility falls on you—and the ones who love you—to detect the early signs and get help as soon as possible.

◆

Chances are you will manage your illness. Most major diseases today are chronic: heart disease, cancer, and diabetes as well as depression and thyroid conditions. Surveys show that the vast majority of older people rate their health as pretty good—even when they are living with a variety of medical problems from arthritis and high blood pressure to hearing loss. For many people, a health jolt is one of several changes in this stage of life. The challenge is to make the experience of illness part of an overall transformation.

Nancy I. Stein* remembers how her parents shocked the whole family. The youngest of four children, Nancy, 38, is a graphic designer at an advertising company in Chicago. One day her parents announce that they are selling the family house in the northern suburbs, putting the furniture in storage, getting in the family car, and driving around the country for six months. They don't know exactly where. They are going to wander around, see the sights. "You don't know how weird it is for your parents not to have a permanent address," she says. She and her brothers grow concerned. "My parents fight all the time. We figured if they were cooped up together in a car for six months, they'd kill each other," she says.

What seems like a crazy idea to adult children is a logical strategy for her parents to jump-start a new chapter together. Her father has recently sold his business. Her mother is retiring from county government; a new administration has come in; she wants out. Meanwhile, they have both been diagnosed with life-threatening diseases: Her father undergoes emergency heart bypass surgery. Her mother is treated for thyroid cancer. After months of illness, they regain their health.

They are ready to focus on the time they have left. A dream takes shape. They want to take time out and just be together. And so they set out. Nancy remembers the postcards: New Orleans. The Grand Canyon. Bozeman, Montana. "It was just awesome," says Nancy. "When they came back, they were in a different place." Her parents don't talk much about his heart disease or her cancer. There's no bickering now, says Nancy. She loves to hear the stories about Dad in the jazz club, Mom seeing a grizzly.

And Nancy has a new appreciation of what is possible in marriage when you get older. *On the road again/Goin' places that I've never been/Seein' things I may never see again.* "I hope I can do that when I get to be their age," says Nancy.

Regenerating love in the face of crisis is a great lesson to pass on to adult children. It used to be said that the task for the old was to show the young how not to fear death. Today, the task is to show the young how not to fear growing old.

4

Sexy Beasts

You may be enjoying high-octane Hollywood sex with great frequency (probably not). Or you find yourself in the doldrums. You may not have a partner; or your partner is not willing or able. You may have some performance issues yourself. And perhaps you are not especially interested in sex.

Yet you have a sexual identity. You don't want to lose that. Your sensuous grasp of life is not fixed on a chronological number. It is more deeply rooted and it is present throughout life. As a Surgeon General's report on sexuality has pointed out, we are sexual beings from birth to death.

Stereotypes of age and sexuality are shifting. It used to be that older people were not supposed to be interested in sex, let alone having sex. Doctors never asked older patients about their sex lives. Researchers ignored sexuality after age 50. Movies rarely showed older couples in bed. But now stereotypes are swinging to the other extreme. Headlines suggest a new culture of randy oldsters having as much sex as young folks. Once perceived as totally sexless, older men and women are portrayed as lusty champions who aim to go on and on and on. All the hoopla coverage of sexy seniors and come-and-get-it ads for Viagra and Cialis run the risk of hyping sexual activity for those at older ages.

But sexual identity is not about what you do in bed. It's about who you are and what you feel about your body. Not about cosmetics, but about connection—to yourself and to others. Not defined by any particular sexual activity, but shaped by many decades of different experiences and feelings. Not about how often, but about how you fulfill your needs for physical intimacy and pleasure.

Some people have intercourse into their 80s and beyond. Others do not. Couples can have a very close relationship without intercourse. Both pathways are *normal*. Both allow for physical closeness. Both foster a deepening of love. Both involve struggle and anguish. Sex is a second language. How you express yourself with your body reveals a lot about you. Physical connection from cuddling to oral sex is a conversation. Think about the "words" you use in this conversation. Would you describe them as quick . . . funny . . . angry . . . tender . . . distracted . . . self-absorbed . . . caring? You don't have to have intercourse to "speak" the language. On the other hand, if a couple eschews physical contact because they have both shut down, that can be a red flag. What is going on in the relationship? What is going on with you?

You have a rich vocabulary by now. You've passed through the main reproductive years. The danger is that you get caught up in the mind spin: *I'm too old for that.* You let go of your sexual identity.

One way to awaken that part of your self is to examine the past. Memory is a source of vitality. The challenge is to transform different experiences into a coherent sense of your sexual self. Your story begins early—long before the age of intercourse.

Nancy Wilson[*1] stands on her deck in the cool lush air of early morning, looking down across the back lawn and gardens to a pond, dark and quiet and surrounded by wise old oaks in full leaf. June in Maryland. Everything is still. Except for the birth of a fawn. She's been watching for about twenty minutes: under the trees, a huddling activity. A deer bent

---

1. Throughout the chapter, asterisks indicate that names, identifying details, and some events have been changed.

over in an odd way, licking and eating something on the ground; then she sees the spindly little creature stand up next to its mother.

She smiles to herself: the nature of sex. How messy, mesmerizing, and in certain moments, miraculous. As she watches mama and fawn, so close together by the pond, she looks back on her sexual life. For the record: two children. A first husband, a live-in companion, and currently a boyfriend.

Nancy at 60 has earned her strong sexual identity. With her auburn curls, her humor, her Jane Fonda body, she has always attracted men. In her childhood, it was a mysterious dangerous force. For a long while, it was unknown, unknowable. Not until midlife does she embrace her sexual power.

Nancy grows up in Dallas, the oldest of three girls. No one talks about sex in her family, but it hangs out there. The looks she would get from boys ever since she was 5 years old—the 13-year-old with freckles and thin lips who kept trying to touch her, hug her, offering her a Hershey bar if she'd take down her pants. She remembers the shock of getting her period at age 12. The teenage years of groping and wet kisses in cars. The stories about "bad girls" and a classmate who had to drop out of school because she was pregnant.

Nancy comes of age feeling marked; sex is a darkness, and it lurks inside her. Looking back, she says: "I'm a sexual beast. Right from the beginning, there was an attraction to me because of my sexuality. I resisted it. I resented it." As a young woman, she hunches over to make her breasts seem smaller. At 24, she marries her high school sweetheart—a hormonal decision, she says. But she isn't happy. Neither is he. They have two babies in four years. Sex comes not to matter. "The moment I became a mother I was completely consumed by that. I wasn't thinking about sex," she says. They get divorced after fifteen years of marriage.

In her next major relationship, she discovers the joy of sex. She is nearly 40 when she falls in love with a biomedical engineer. She has always masturbated so she knows what an orgasm is. How to translate that into a relationship. He takes the lead as her sexual mentor: "I was able to abandon myself completely. That was his doing. He persuaded me how important it was for him. My pleasure was important to him," she says. And she comes to realize her satisfaction is important for her. "He knew how much of an effort it was for me to lose myself. All the way. . . . The talking: Go to the left, go to the right. Screw it—I'll do it myself. [Later] we got the toys, the vibrator," she says. "He was so uniquely un-disapproving. Nothing was disgusting, nothing was off the page. He didn't have standards you could go beneath."

They live together in Maryland for fifteen years. The relationship is close, but they never marry. It ends suddenly and tragically when her partner is killed in a car crash. Nancy is devastated. After his death, she lives alone for about five years. She dates several men, renews friendships, and stays close to her grown children.

Her current relationship is with a retired high school teacher, a widower who is a decade older. He is taking heart medications, which affect his ability to achieve an erection. He can't ejaculate. She has lubrication problems and uses a vaginal cream. He wants her to be satisfied. She wants him to be satisfied. They struggle with intercourse. When that can't be accomplished, "he's devastated," she says, and she becomes so anxious—for him, for herself—that she can't respond to his love-making. They start down the slide into sexual angst.

Except that they are talking. They both have strong sexual identities built up over decades of experience. It's not as though he or Nancy has missed out on sexual activity. They are able to break down their inhibitions, confront their limitations, and explore different ways of making love. "It's tough," she says. "We really care for each other."

A strong sexual identity is an asset in this stage of life. As you confront changes in your body and in your circumstances, it is a resource you can draw on. Memory gives context to the present and enhances your hold on vitality as a sexual person.

✦

With all the cultural pressures, mostly aimed at youth, to have extraordinary sex, you may look at your past with a pass-fail mentality. How good was I/am I? Sexual activity becomes a test. But your sexuality is not static.

"Sexual identity changes through the phases of life," says physician Stacy Tessler Lindau of the University of Chicago, author of a major study on sexuality and older people.[2] "There are moments when it's pleasurable, moments when it's not." Where you end up on the pleasure-pain scale most of the time is what matters, she says.

Memory, says Chicago's Lindau, is a recurring theme in research on sexuality. "For those who are sexually active and those who are not, their memories of their sexual lives continue to be an important part of who they are. Memories are part of current fantasy, part of their identity," she adds. Recalling your sexual history "gets to the heart of who you are, what your body is all about."

Dr. Lindau remembers that in medical training, when physicians asked patients about their sexual history, "nobody had a shortage of things to say. I was struck by the transformation in the patient," she says. "I'd watch people transform from a sick older person in a hospital gown to someone with a real story. They had memories to tell."

For couples who have been together a long time, shared memories can help create a comfort zone of physical expression. With so much combined experience, you have probably gained some proficiency with the language of sex; you've built up trust in each other and are more likely to take changes in love-making in stride.

For new couples, finding a comfort zone is more complicated. A relationship often starts with sexual attraction. A new lover is sexually exciting. In the phase of romantic discovery, you may have fewer arousal and

---

2. Stacy Tessler Lindau, L. Philip Schumm, Edward O. Laumann, Wendy Levinson, Colm A. O'Muircheartaigh, and Linda J. Waite, "Study of Sexuality and Health Among Older Adults in the United States," *New England Journal of Medicine*, August 23, 2007 (hereafter referred to as the "Chicago sexuality study").

performance issues. At the same time, you're nervous. Perhaps you've not had much sexual pleasure in your past. You hear a lot about "technique" and being a "good lover"; you're afraid you're not going to measure up. Especially if a new partner has more experience than you.

The danger is that your anxiety may cause you to avoid new relationships altogether. Or to resist learning some new skills and stay blocked in your own insecurity.

"I've always been shy with women," begins Mike Hoffman.* He sits in an outdoor café in Galveston with his wife, Sally.* "I'm very male. I don't think I'm a bad sexual partner. I'm not great."

His wife breaks in: "I think you're great."

He goes on: "I'm not over-driven sexually. I'm not obsessive."

Mike and Sally are serial spouses. When they meet nearly twenty years earlier, Mike is coming out of a long moribund marriage in which sex had dimmed decades ago. Sally, married briefly in her 20s, has been single for fifteen years. She remembers the sexual freedom of the 1970s—before AIDS—and has had a variety of experiences. They bring different histories to the bedroom.

Sally, a nurse, is working in a health clinic in Galveston. One day early in their marriage, she comes home with a basket full of different condoms and dumps them on the kitchen table. At first Mike doesn't know what to think. Is something wrong? She gives him that vampy look and kisses him on the lips. Then she lays out her plan: he is to be her guinea pig to test all the different brands. They are going to do it for science—test out every position, every maneuver . . . so she can advise the kids, of course.

They look back at their in-house condom experiment and laugh. "Sex is very important," he says. "In the beginning, I was afraid. Here was a woman with more experience. There were questions about my performance."

His wife breaks in: "When the floodgates opened, they opened in pretty dynamic ways."

Her practical approach eases his fears and gives them confidence in each other. The experiment becomes a mainstay of their sexual history—a memory they talk about and enjoy. Now they are both 70. "Sex has cooled off some. I don't feel it's a driving force in my marriage," he says.

In love-making, old dogs can always learn new tricks. Often it is the man who has more experience. The cultural stereotype of marriage is for the husband to lead the wife. But by this stage both women and men have a sexual history to share. The key is to be open to your partner who may need guidance—or who can lead you to discover new pleasures.

For many people, the most satisfying sexual chapters come later in life, once you get past the pressures of child-rearing and can focus on the immediacy of enjoyment and connection. You can explore different ways of love-making. That is true of long-married couples as well as new couples.

✦

You wonder: What is normal as you get older?

The 2007 Chicago sexuality study was the first major study of sexual activity in older men and women. It found that, while sexual activity declines with age, many people have rich and varied sexual lives well into their 80s. The study surveyed 3,005 men and women, ages 57 to 85, in communities nationwide. Three-quarters of those with partners said they were sexually active—defined as genital contact with a partner.

According to the study, intercourse is the usual sexual behavior. Oral sex is frequent among both men and women. So is masturbation, and those with a partner and those without report equal rates of self-stimulation. The study also documented a significant amount of variation in activities and desire. About a quarter of the men and more than 40 percent of the women reported a lack of interest in sex. Overall, women reported less sexual activity than men, mainly because they were less likely to have partners—or to have healthy partners.

The gender partner gap is a feature of longevity. In part, it reflects the gap between an entrenched mating culture and the new biology of aging. Both men and women benefit from the Wizard's gift of a ten-year bonus of good health. But there's a catch. The Extra Ten favor women. In this phase of life, they are biologically younger than men of the same age. According to calculations by Stanford University economist John B. Shoven, a woman is "young" until she is 63. But a man loses his "youth" at age 58. This is the five-year aging gap. Generally speaking, a woman at 65 is the biological equivalent of a 60-year-old man.[3]

But culture is at odds with the new biology. Since women tend to marry older men, the health differential between partners becomes even wider in the later decades. A five-year chronological difference becomes a ten-year biology gap. It's a challenge to "age" together sexually when biology is pushing you further apart.

There is enormous individual variation. Personal health status is the critical element. But gender stereotypes perpetuate mixed images of the older man who retains sexual power (because of the ability to reproduce) and the older woman who is stripped of sexual power (because of the inability to reproduce). Celebrity headlines of powerful older men and much younger fertile women reinforce the mixed image of aging sexuality.

On dating service websites, older men state a preference for increasingly younger women. On eHarmony, men 50 and older are looking for women who are between six and twenty-six years younger. On match.com, the average 50-year-old man is seeking a 46-year-old woman; a 70-year-old wants a 58-year-old woman. A four-year difference widens to a twelve-year gap.

Evolutionary psychologists point to reproductive hard-wiring to explain the male preference for younger women. For example, they cite recent research on marriages in preindustrial Finland suggesting that a man should marry a woman nearly fifteen years younger to maximize his chances of having the most offspring survive to age 18. But that was then. In the United States today, couples not only have fewer children but the vast majority survive to adulthood. In contrast, life expectancy in the 1700s was about 35. (Besides, only 10 percent of the marriages in

---

3. John B. Shoven, "New Age Thinking: Alternative Ways of Measuring Age, Their Relationship to Labor Force Participation, Government Policies and GDP" (National Bureau of Economic Research, October, 2007).

the study's reindeer-herding community had the "optimal" age gap; the average age difference between husband and wife was three years.)

All in all, the new biology of aging is challenging evolutionary mating theories. The Extra Ten have created an unprecedented stage of sexual expression that is no longer linked to the urgency or ability to reproduce.

In a break with the older man/younger woman tradition, older women are turning to men their same age and younger. On match.com, the average 50-year-old woman is seeking a 48-year-old man; a 70-year-old woman wants a man who is 66. On eHarmony, older women are looking for men who range in age from one year older to eighteen years younger. In the past, "there would have been an advantage to older husbands. Women may be evolving more rapidly out of that than men. They are more accepting of equal-age partners," says Galen Buckwalter, vice-president of research and development at eHarmony.

But mating patterns change slowly. What women want and what men want seem to be on a collision course. If they both seek younger partners, they will miss out on each other. For an older woman, finding a much younger mate is relatively rare. Managers of dating websites point out that there is a difference between wishes and reality. As Buckwalter says: "Age in and of itself is not a factor in compatibility." Online dating, moreover, is a process. "Everyone would like to find someone smarter, better looking, wealthier . . . and sure, younger. Why wouldn't you start there," says Craig Wax, senior vice-president and general manager of match.com North America. In the next step, once you see who is out there, "you're willing to make a number of different trade-offs. In the end, it doesn't matter what a person's age is. It matters how well they connect." Or as a man who remarried an older woman puts it: "You have to shed your delusions."

Where there is agreement among older men and women is on the importance of sexuality. That is another finding of the Chicago sexuality study. Even those who are not engaging in sexual activity want to talk about their experiences and their feelings. They welcome questions about their sexual behavior and outlook. A very high percentage—76 percent—of those randomly contacted responded to the study's survey. "Sexuality is relevant. We did strike a chord," says the study's Stacy Lindau. "There is no reason to think that there is some number where we become sexually retired. That's a silly concept."

✦

In a long marriage, couples go through three general phases in their sexual narrative: the early honeymoon phase (bliss); the children-rearing phase (sex and marital satisfaction usually decline, according to most studies); and finally, the liberation phase—the period when it's just the two of you and you have all the time in the world to make love.

In general, if two people enjoyed sex together in earlier parts of their lives, they are likely to continue . . . in some fashion. If sex has not been very interesting for a while, retirement or a move can stimulate a new tack in love-making. For many couples, sexual activity is a happy habit. The desire for sex may persist even in unlikely circumstances.

A woman, 60, tells me about her husband, who is about to undergo a major treatment for a cancer. They have been married for thirty-five years. He is feeling good, though his prognosis is not favorable. In the morning before they are to go to the hospital, he pulls her to him. Yes, now. One more time. "You sure want to go out in style," she quips.

Long-married couples benefit from decades of experience. New couples also benefit from experience—but with different partners. It's a truism that when you make love to a partner, you are making love with your partner's past and vice versa. Rather than suppressing the past, you want to put it in perspective and take advantage of the experience you've both had before you met.

A woman, 81, falls in love again. "It's a surprise that we still have good sex, because I think a lot of people think: *oh if you're over 80, you're not having sex anymore*," she says.

She sees how her previous chapters—and his chapters—play out in their current relationship. She and her partner are both widowed. In her sexual narrative, each relationship has paved the way for the next. Not that she hasn't had her share of heartache. But her sexual identity has been strengthened through these different relationships.

- *An early marriage* that produced two children and ended in divorce: "My first husband, he was a wonderful lover. We were kids together. He's the first man I ever slept with. And we experimented, you know? And with youth and vigor and so forth, there were no problems. He was such a good lover because in the beginning I was very inexperienced and he had to find ways to get me turned on."
- *A second marriage* to a man fifteen years older: In the beginning, the marriage is successful, but the age gap becomes more difficult as he gets older. He died after a long illness: "He could have been made to be a better lover, I think," she says. His first wife confessed after their breakup that she hadn't had an orgasm in two years. "So I think he just kind of got away with a lot of things," the woman explains.
- *Her current relationship* with a man about her age: "A wonderful lover," she says. "He had a wife who he had to work like anything to turn her on, so I guess that's how he got so skillful."
- *His* past, *her* past: *their* new relationship.

You may not be aware of this vault of experience inside you. Maybe you ignore those issues that still smolder and need resolution. Not all the chapters in a sexual history will be pleasant or satisfying. But this period is a chance to sum up your sexual identity—to integrate fantasies of good sex with memories of past experience. You can turn to the past, like credit in the bank, to take into account the changes that occur in body and mind—and calibrate desire with opportunity.

✦

Problems also increase with age. In the Chicago sexuality study, about half of the men and women who are sexually active reported a "bothersome

sexual problem." For men, the main difficulties were achieving or maintaining an erection, climaxing too quickly or not at all, anxiety about performance. Women reported difficulties with lubrication, inability to climax,
and pain, commonly felt at entry.

You may need some extra help to continue. Sales of Viagra, used to
treat erectile dysfunction, topped $1.7 billion in 2006. Its rival, Cialis,
brought in $971 million. On drugstore shelves, meanwhile, in the "femi-
nine" section, vaginal creams and lubricants are edging out home preg-
nancy kits as the population gets grayer.

Some couples take the changes in performance in stride—his limpness,
her lagging arousal. "Viagra, oh yes. He uses Viagra," says a woman who
has been married more than fifty years. They didn't really talk about it.
"Oh, you just do. When you know each other, when you trust each other—
when you've had good sex and want to have more good sex—you just get
Viagra. It takes longer to get aroused, to get enthusiastic. I tell him: 'Put on
some Barbra Streisand and slow down. I'm not feeling so hot just now.'"

There are some generational differences, especially among women, according to the Chicago sexuality study. Women born before 1940, who
came of age before the sexual revolution of the 1960s, are more likely to
say that sex is not pleasurable or satisfying. A greater proportion report
pain with sex but feel it is their duty to "do it." "They welcomed
menopause as a reason to discontinue sex, as a time to stop sharing the
bed," says physician Lindau. Women born after 1940, she adds, tend to
have a different outlook, and not just about sex. They are more likely to
be engaged in careers; they tend to exercise more. "They want to maintain
sex as an active and satisfying part of their life," she says. "I do see generational differences."

For men, one issue crosses generational lines: erection. According to
the study, nearly 45 percent of men 65 and older reported problems
"achieving or maintaining" an erection. Men's problems are also a
woman's issue: the most common reason why a couple does not engage in
sexual activity—cited by 60 percent of women in this situation—is the
physical limitations of the male partner.

I am sitting in a private dining room with fifteen business leaders and their wives. They are having a retreat at a sumptuous resort, where I have been invited to talk about the impact of longevity on people's lives. The men are in their 50s. They run small businesses. They are successful. Their wives are attractive, energetic. They all look like models in glossy magazine ads for choosing a mutual fund, taking a cruise, or buying a Volvo. They are living the dream of *new stage—not old age*. We talk about community service and giving back. We talk about getting the kids through college. We talk about playing the drums again and forming a book club. We talk about the Red Sox—rising up from failure to score the winning run. Ah, sports! A couple of women roll their eyes. Another round of cocktails, the laughter gets louder; we sit down to dinner, the waiters start pouring the wine. What's next? Our voices rise. What is it all about—living longer, healthier lives?

Finally a woman at the end of the table breaks in. *Uh!* Then she giggles. *Uh! What about. . . .* She looks around the table. Then she puts up her index finger and then slowly folds it down. After a few seconds of silence, a rush of laughter. Some red faces on the men. A little grumbling. She holds up her index finger again and repeats the exercise. The other women join in: What about it? What about *it*?

Erectile dysfunction. Soothing television advertisements to treat ED have brought this sexual issue into the American family room. Former senator Bob Dole has made the male problem trendy. But the causes of ED are varied, and so are the remedies. It's important to have a thorough medical evaluation. And the solutions have to involve your partner. One of the accomplishments of the longevity revolution is to break the silence around sexual problems related to aging.

✦

But talking is probably the most difficult sexual activity for many couples. Especially if there are problems. "Couples don't know how to talk to each other about their concerns. They had never learned to talk about preferences or fears," says clinical psychologist Martha Gross in Washington,

D.C. A surface problem with intercourse goes deep into a nexus of blame and shame. A desperate dynamic is set in motion when partners personalize the problem. They blame themselves and sink into a sexual paralysis. Or they blame the partner. If the man is having trouble with an erection, it's the woman's fault; if a woman is having a problem with arousal, it's the man's fault. "It's your fault and you're unlovable. My problem is attributed to you. Then you distance from me. You get mad at me," continues Gross. "Talking about sex is so much harder than the act."

Sometimes the problems are mechanical. She uses too much lubrication. He can't get friction. Or an injury or disease gets in the way. Gross describes a client with severe arthritis in the knees. He and his wife had been having intercourse in the missionary position for forty years; now it hurts his knees too much. Or maybe you're bothered by a noisy hip—an artificial joint made with ceramic materials that squeak when you walk upstairs or make love.

Problems can also be emotional—how you feel about sex and your sexual identity. How you feel about your partner. Are you angry? Resentful? Suspicious? Frightened? What is going on in the relationship?

Denial is an effective defense. Talking opens the way to places you may not want to go. Does a sexual issue mean there is something wrong with the relationship? Maybe it will blow over. Yet you think you have to talk. . . .

✦

It's snowing hard as they stumble into a Dunkin' Donuts off the highway, a quick pick-me-up on their way into the city. They started out about five years ago with a big KAZZAM! Just thinking of him could bring a flood of desire. The kiss. The touch. The look. How he pursued her. The different places they would make love: in the woods behind a tree, at the beach, in hotel rooms with paisley down comforters. They have a history now. Both are divorced, both in their late 50s. She wants this to work out.

She hesitates. "But there's a problem: off and on. He can't maintain an erection," she says. She lubricates, she stimulates herself to be ready for him. Sometimes yes, sometimes no. She gets frightened . . . doesn't want him to feel bad. Is there something wrong with her? It builds up in her: they've got to talk about this. Not in bed; that's what all the sex manuals say. Go to a safe neutral place.

Like Dunkin' Donuts. "Ten-thirty in the morning," she continues. Filling up with regulars—the seniors who live in a retirement community nearby, the truck drivers passing through. They get their donuts and coffee—a jelly donut for him, a glazed donut for her—and sit down at the small square table by the window. How does she start? *Ummm, I was thinking.*

She gets it all out. *What about Viagra? Have you been to a doctor?* No, she thinks she should have said—let's both go to a doctor, don't make it just his problem; *it's our problem.* He takes a bite of his donut, a red glob appears on the side of his mouth. *Really,* she goes on. *We should have a sense of humor about this,* and she bites into the glazed donut, white flecks of glazed sugar sit on her upper lip. *A doctor,* she says, *to make sure your heart is okay.* He looks away, takes a sip of coffee. "I keep at it," she says, shaking her head, until he says: *I don't have this problem with anyone else.*

Another sip of coffee. *Oh. . . .* She picks up the rest of the glazed donut in two hands. White flecks float onto the laminate tabletop. He takes another bite of his jelly donut. *Not a problem. . . .* She's about to press on: *yes it is a problem . . . for me . . . for us. . . .* She wants to say: *I love you; we have something great here.* But someone bumps into his chair. Getting crowded. Sorry, 'scuze me. She doesn't get to: *for me, for us.* He takes a few more gulps of coffee and looks around: people sitting at other tables, right next to them. And she's saying *penis* and *vagina* and *entry* and *masturbate.* So like her. Talk about anything. Nothing is too shocking. Once he loved that about her. Now she makes him feel impotent. Grabbing at him in the morning. Something about her, he's resistant. His fingers are sticky with powdered sugar. Where's a napkin. *Let's get going,* he says. She thinks to herself: *At least I had the guts to bring it up.* He wipes the last of the jelly off his cheek and hands her a napkin to get the flakes of sugar off her lips; too thick, he thinks: Her lips are too thick. Too much.

He gets up from the table. "I followed him out into the snowfall," she says.

Over the next months, they drift apart. The inability to talk about their sexual life expands into a difficulty to talk about anything substantive in the relationship. They pull back on their thoughts, their feelings. It's not long before they stop seeing each other altogether.

There's no one right way to have a difficult conversation about sexual intimacy. So much depends on trust—trusting yourself, trusting your partner. So much depends on really knowing each other and feeling secure enough in the relationship to navigate the shoals of vulnerability.

◆

There is mourning to do. Mourning what has been lost, what cannot be in the future. Every year, nearly 220,000 men in the United States are diagnosed with prostate cancer. Many of them have difficulty with erection and ejaculation after treatment. Other medical conditions also affect sexual performance. Certain common medications for heart disease, depression, and other disorders suppress libido. These drugs also affect women. What is "normal" with respect to aging? A man, 80, says with a sigh: "I have a hard time bringing a woman past menopause to orgasm." A woman, 70, wails: "I want penetration!"

It's difficult to let the past go—parts of the past, anyway. But that doesn't mean you can't have a rich sexual life. You just have to write a different sexual script.

Keith and Virginia Laken[4] of Winona, Minnesota, have reformatted those old tapes of sexual performance into a new tape for sexual pleasure. As they chronicle in *Making Love Again*, Keith, at age 50, is diagnosed and treated for prostate cancer. Because of his young age and good health, the doctors reassure him that he is unlikely to suffer from ED. But that turns out to be a false hope.

---

4. Virginia and Keith Laken were profiled in *My Time: Making the Most of the Bonus Decades After Fifty*. They are the authors of *Making Love Again: Hope for Couples Facing Loss of Sexual Intimacy* (Ant Hill Press, 2002), and they give workshops on sexuality and aging.

The old tapes are running in his head: sex is a straightaway, three-step process of intercourse—arousal, insertion, and orgasm. Hallelujah, I'm a man! But with erection problems, the three-step process breaks down. He sinks into a depression. Virginia, ever the pleaser, tries to prop him up. *Don't worry about me, I don't care. It's all about you.* They try a range of remedies from drugs to devices. With the pump, he learns how to fake an orgasm, just to be done with it. As Virginia keeps trying to satisfy him, he feels hunted. With the old tapes running in his head—and in hers—they endure one humiliating failure after another.

Until they get rid of the old tapes. One morning, they are lying in bed. More than thirty years of marriage. Two fine children. Grandchildren. A good life together . . . but not in the bedroom. Keith lies there, tight-lipped in rage and despair. Virginia starts to cry. Finally she acknowledges what they have lost . . . and what they are not going to regain. How sad she is to lose that kind of sex, how much she shares his sorrow. Suddenly a great weight is lifted off Keith.

They set new sexual goals. The old tapes were about scoring with intercourse. The new tapes would be about connecting with pleasure. They broaden their repertoire and both are able to have an orgasm without penetration or ejaculation. "We're talking about sexual intimacy and the role of intimacy in self-identity, in personal image. It reminds us—hey, we're still alive," says Keith, now 60. "It's this reaffirmation of strength and security in the relationship and renewal of who we are."

In the past year, even with injections, Keith and Virginia have had actual intercourse and penetration only three or four times. "But that doesn't mean we haven't had a lot of sexual times together," says Keith. "By this stage, we know ourselves pretty good. We know what our bodies are doing. We're more friendly. . . . We do what feels good. It's very comforting to have someone with you, who also likes you. We put a lot of stock in that."

These are the take-home messages: *Do what feels good.* Enjoy the comfort of being with someone who *likes* you. Know your body—and your partner's. *Be more friendly.* There are many ways to have a good sexual time together: *put a lot of stock in that.*

Keith remembers that when he was about to get married, he asked his father about sex. His father's reply: "Don't worry about it, son. Nature will take care of it." Forty years later, the situation is reversed. His widowed father, 84, has found a girlfriend. But he is worried about sex. He turns to his son and asks: "Is there anything to Viagra?"

Keith laughs. "I thought about saying: 'Don't worry about it, Dad. Nature will take care of it,'" he says. But Keith knows better. He can give his father good advice. Not just about getting checked out by a physician and obtaining a prescription. He also counsels his father: "Don't assume that she wants intercourse."

✦

Maybe you're not that interested. Not just because of mounting problems that make intercourse difficult. Research suggests that the impulse for sex becomes less acute with age. Hormone levels decrease in both men and women. A man tells me: "It's nice not to be led around by your cock anymore." A 72-year-old Harvard college alum put it this way in his biography for a fiftieth class reunion: "When it comes to sex, I just won't take yes for an answer!"

This shift occurs in women, too. The fire of desire dies down. Not that you don't enjoy sex. But you're not thinking about it so much. Sometimes this shift sneaks up on you.

Louise Bard* is coming home on the plane from a meeting of travel agents. She settles into her business-class seat with a David Baldacci thriller novel. A professional woman in a Gerard Darel silk jacket, highlighted hair, a chemical peel or two. She has to look good for her job, and she's always paid attention to her body. After a smooth flight, during which she enjoys a club soda and lime and a packet of mini-pretzels, the plane taxis into the terminal. When she gets up to retrieve her carry-on bag out of the compartment above, the man sitting across the aisle offers to help her. He has white hair, a good tan, and sparkling white-capped teeth—a golfer, she thinks, a retired CEO. He keeps looking straight into her violet eyes. She smiles back; this always happens to her—it's her funny eyes.

Then it dawns on her: she didn't notice him before. She hadn't spotted him across the aisle. Two hours in flight, and she hadn't struck up a conversation with the attractive man across the aisle. She hadn't checked out any of the men in business class. Something had changed.

She used to be a hunter. In the old days, she would have walked off the plane with the business cards of at least three men who wanted to . . . keep in touch. "I had an enormous sex drive," she says.

Louise is married to her boyfriend from high school. She bypassed college and now works for a travel agency. Her husband, who played the drums in the school band, is a pharmacist. A steady husband and they have two children. All the while, she keeps her job, developing a niche in business travel for executives. For decades, her work has allowed her to lead a double life:

"I hunted men," she says. "I could tell who was available. My job gave me access to horny men." She looks back: sometimes a different one every night. "I was really going through men. I wanted to have as many partners as I could," she says.

The stereotype of the sexual predator is male. But the flood of women into all corners of the workplace has created equal opportunities for sexual hunting. Women don't talk about this as much. Sexual prowling is considered a male thing. But lust—or the desire for a new relationship—is gender neutral. The risks are real—and they include more than just contracting a sexually transmitted disease. Louise gets involved emotionally a few times, but the affairs usually burn out after six months. She has never wanted to leave her marriage.

But now Louise is undergoing a significant change. "The fire is gone," she says. "I notice I'm not hunting anymore." She and her husband have sex once a week. She supposes she's lucky that he's got some of the randy drummer left in him. She enjoys their love-making. But she doesn't desire it. The frequency is going down. That's fine with her. She's not obsessed with sex the way she used to be. She gets obsessed about other stuff— about starting her own travel business aimed at women who take solo vacations. Her mind starts racing. The energy of the hunt is going somewhere else, she says.

She makes this observation about her female friends and the men she has known: "Something happens around the age of 59 or 60. Women—and men, too, I think—fall into two groups: those who continue an interest in sex—and those who absolutely lose all interest."

This is a time when you take stock of your sexual life. Even if your interest diminishes, you hold on to a sexual identity. It is a source of power. Many men and women, like Louise, find that their sexual energy gets refocused. They start projects, they fall in love with grandchildren, they work on a political campaign, they look at the sunset in wonder. Sexual identity fuels your passion for the messy, mesmerizing, and miraculous in many different incarnations. It is the vitality to live fully for as long as you can.

The hero in Richard Ford's *The Lay of the Land* confronts the uncertain future in this stage of life—what Ford calls "The Permanent Period." The hero is in his late 50s, walking around with radioactive seeds that have been implanted to treat his prostate cancer. His estranged wife has returned, but what their sexual activity will be is unclear. The day before they go to the Mayo clinic for a checkup, the hero walks out on the beach barefoot on a cool November morning. A quiet day as the tide washes in. Suddenly his body comes alive as the glistening wet sand clutches at the bottoms of his feet and a frothing wave closes about his ankles "like a grasp." It is a momentary embrace of his sexual identity, of his essence as a human being. He stands there, awakened, alert, and thinks to himself: "Here is necessity. Here is the extra beat—to live, to live, to live it out."

PART TWO

Surprise

5

Circus Act

Actor and playwright Gerry Hiken[1] and his wife, Barbara, meet in New York; she is a makeup artist on a television soap opera and he is an actor in the show. His character is supposed to look mean. As Barbara expertly pencils in a menacing moustache on his upper lip, he suddenly kisses her fingers. The attraction is electric.

One evening they go to the Moscow circus. In the center of the ring, two gymnasts meet and extend their hands to each other. The music is slow, their muscles on display. One leans back, pulling the other toward him until the man's feet are off the ground. The one underneath supports the weight of the other, who slowly rolls up until he is on the man's shoulders; then the one underneath bends down and the other rolls down his back until one foot touches the ground and then he lifts the other on his back. Round and round the ring they go, one up, one down, so effortlessly it seems, but you know how hard they are working. Round and round, slow and smooth, to the quiet rhythm of the music, until the end when they both stand up and shake hands.

---

1. Gerald Hiken has appeared onstage and in film for more than fifty years. His credits range from *Uncle Vanya* by Anton Checkov to the television program *Cheers*.

"That to me became the definition of a relationship," says Gerry. "As on a seesaw, very seldom are you both on the same level. It takes the role of one supporting the other wholeheartedly, and then the other doing the same."

Gerry and Barbara live in Palo Alto and have been together more than forty-five years: moving from New York to California, raising two kids, looking for jobs, living apart for eight years, coming back together: "It's a working relationship, 'working' being the operative word," he says.

A long marriage evolves like the circus act. Ask yourself where you are on the seesaw in your relationships. Are you in the lead and carrying the load—*wholeheartedly*? Then do you allow yourself to be supported—*wholeheartedly*? Most important is how you switch roles back and forth—*smoothly, constantly.*

Problems arise when the seesaw gets stuck, with one of you down, the other up—*all the time*. Not fair to carry the load all the time. Not fair always to submit to another's will. Inequality in the power balance of a couple can lead to disappointment, anger, and estrangement. In a successful relationship, you need to have enough seesaw motion so that both of you perceive the balance to be fair. In a long marriage, you have to learn how to keep the seesaw in motion decade after decade.

Barbara Hiken is a lovely, warm woman with dark blue eyes that say come and sit beside me. She is always reaching out—to the stranger sitting on a park bench, to a lost puppy wandering the neighborhood, to a host of lifelong friends. Gerry is the artist-hero who lives in the realm of imagination. He has an actor's commanding presence and rebellious mind. He grows up thinking he is gay—and then he falls completely in love with Barbara. After their electric beginning, she looked at him and said: "Are we going to ignore our fate?"

Two weeks after his proposal, they tie the knot. A month later, Barbara invites twenty-five people to Thanksgiving dinner in their small New York apartment. It's their first big dinner as a couple, and who knows how to cook? She asks him to read the recipe from the cookbook because she says she doesn't understand it. And he says: *"Well, I don't understand* recipes either. *Why don't you just read it?"* And she says: *"Why can't you just read it to me?"* Back and forth: the fight is not about the recipe for stuffing a turkey. It's about her neediness and his inability to meet her neediness. "It became crazy," he says.

That theme gets played out for the next twenty years—what he sees as unreasonable demands placed on him, what she sees as an unreasonable reluctance to meet her needs. The agenda for many young couples is to learn how to fight and resolve conflict. Gerry and Barbara develop a pattern for settling arguments. After a fight, she'd say: *"Well, I suppose this is the end."* He'd reply: *"Don't be crazy! We're stuck together for the rest of our lives."* As Gerry says: "I knew it, she was my fate! We always calmed down, we always got together afterward. The ice would break and it was like nothing had happened."

They also minimize conflict by letting the other be—*wholeheartedly.* It's a process of mutual acceptance. They survive their telephone wars, for example. When they move from New York to California, Barbara would talk on the phone to her friends for hours "in a chatty harmless kind of way that I found stupid. I held her in a certain contempt," says Gerry. The cost of long-distance calls in those days! The waste of time! But contempt is a toxin in relationships, according to psychologist and marriage researcher John Gottman of Seattle.[2] It suggests that the one partner is stuck in the lead position and is dismissive of the other.

But Gerry is able to let go of his command place on the marital seesaw and give Barbara her due. "I said to myself: *She's doing that so I don't have to,*" he says. Slowly he turns a problem into an asset: Barbara brings many friends to the marriage; talking on the phone is part of friendship. "You begin to understand how differences in your partner free you from the need to be like that. I gave up my hidden contempt," he says.

---

2. John Gottman is known for his work on marital stability and divorce prediction. He is an emeritus professor of psychology at the University of Washington; founder, with his wife Julie Gottman, of the Gottman Institute; and author or co-author of more than thirty-five books, including *The Seven Principles for Making Marriage Work.*

Barbara also changes. In the early years, she is very submissive and dependent on Gerry—and in a theater career, he is rarely home before 11 P.M. "I got kind of antsy and depressed taking care of the children myself," she says. "I used to try to do things to please Gerry. *Oh death! Oh death!*" She'd go out and buy what he liked for lunch, always thinking about what *he* wanted. "I was not free inside," she says. Barbara responds to the women's movement; encounter groups are all the rage. She also gets treatment for her depression. After a while, she becomes less dependent on Gerry.

Their roles totally shift when Gerry is out of work. Barbara finds a job in a bakery. She comes into her own as a chef. "Consequently, I was a much more interesting person—*not* trying to please someone, being myself, so he could react to something that wasn't dopey and boring."

Yet, the strains continue. "We got on each other's nerves," says Gerry. Like many couples, they fight about money. His fears of poverty are no match for her generous impulses to buy things for others. "I told her that I wanted to be her husband and I wanted to be her lover and best friend, but I didn't want to share the checkbook."

The marriage reaches a break point when they are both 55. Gerry is struggling to get ahead in his career. His agent tells him he has to go to Los Angeles or New York. The result is a kind of marriage sabbatical. Gerry finds work in LA and Barbara stays in Palo Alto.

Barbara fears this is the end of the marriage. But they stay connected through phone calls and weekend visits. Meanwhile, Barbara tends to her own life. Her mother, who's had a stroke, comes to live with her. "My mother and I fell in love during that time," says Barbara. The experience was like earning an advanced degree in loving, she says. "I felt that I learned to be a human being." Her son, a senior in high school at the time, tells her: *"Mom, this is your chance to learn who you are. Be yourself!"*

When Gerry and Barbara get back together, they are more equal as marital gymnasts. He's more secure in his work; she's more secure in herself. "She could grow up without me being around and watching it, and I had a chance to develop myself as a single human being. Those eight years really did us a great deal of good," says Gerry. They become a boomerang couple—spouses who renew their bond after a separation. "Little by little, we climbed that hill of healing each other over."

Empathy is a key ingredient in their renaissance. As they become more sensitive to each other, they fight less. Their tastes start to merge. Gerry has always been mad about Ella Fitzgerald. Barbara is crazy for Billie Holiday. By listening to the music Barbara loves, he learns what it is she hears in Billie Holiday. And as she listens to the music Gerry loves, she develops an affection for Ella Fitzgerald. It is a process of putting yourself in the place of the other. That way, you keep the seesaw in motion, which leads to mutual accommodation. This merging spreads out to other areas of their marriage. "It goes into food, it goes into friends, and it doesn't stop," says Gerry.

Illness also switches their positions on the seesaw: Barbara takes the lead when Gerry undergoes coronary bypass surgery. When she has a knee replacement, Gerry makes her breakfast as she used to make breakfast for him. She becomes the dominant one again when he falls off a stage platform several years later. His legs go straight down and he smashes his left ankle and heel. "I had to let Barbara do things for me. It was one of those transforming moments. . . . I had to let go of a certain independence because I no longer had it, and allow her to do what she needed to do to take care of me in the way she wanted to take care of me," he says.

Throughout their marriage, they keep shifting positions on the seesaw. Gerry sums it up: "There were times when Barbara's been ill and I supported her. And there have been times when I've been ill and she's supported me. There are times when I haven't made any money and she's earned; and there are times when I've earned and supported the family."

Over nearly five decades, they've gone from hard to easy, a mellowing-out as they defuse the combustible sticking points, a transformation that occurs in many couples as people get older. "It starts getting smooth. That smoothness becomes a pleasure. You don't want any bumps," continues Gerry.

Gerry and Barbara are now in a honeymoon phase. "We've seen how much fun we can have," says Barbara. When he performs shows in their living room, she bakes. Together they produce a kind of gourmet theater for their friends. He rewrites *King Lear* in iambic pentameter: an old man who has taken off all his clothes on a golf course in Florida in the middle of a hurricane; the authorities have taken him away, he has no money—the kids got it all—and he's explaining in a group therapy session at a Veterans Administration hospital that *sometimes when men retire, they lose their souls. It's as if in some way they had died a little and they feel as if they don't know who they are.* Or as King Lear really put it: *Who is it who can tell me who I am?*

Everybody in the room cheers. "You have to enjoy life! That's the way we feel," says Barbara.

Gerry and Barbara have had a long circus act—including an intermission. They are an example of how hard couples must work to keep a relationship in motion. As a result, they become happier with age. They sit and talk to each other the way they never did in years past. "We never had time to do that before. Now, the bonus years, we have that time," says Gerry. They renew their sexual life. "We didn't for a long, long time! But recently we've been sexual with each other again. I say it's a growth of love, a growth of acceptance. . . . [W]e accept each other. It makes us very affectionate," says Barbara. "Every morning when I wake up, I'm so happy to see him—*Hi, Honey!*"

"The image that comes to my mind is sitting on top of a hill," says Gerry. "You spend a lot of time climbing and making paths and hanging on to trees and pushing away the brambles. And now here you are in this lovely open space in the sunshine."

You want to get to the lovely open space in the sunshine. Couples who stay together for many decades like Gerry and Barbara tend to soften. "They accept one another. They stop fighting over issues they encounter again and again. They make accommodations," says psychologist Gottman. The transformation is biological to some degree. As you get older, there are physiological reasons why you avoid conflict. Part of it has to do with changes in the vagus nerve system, which helps regulate your cardiovascular system—a process that doctors call "vagal tone." You have less ability to calm down—to lower your heart rate and soothe yourself. "Small things make you upset," says Gottman. "You want a peaceful life."

✦

The challenge for many couples in this stage is to transform the relationship from a fighting dynamic to a pleasure agenda. In youth, the seesaw motion is greased by how you deal with negative emotions and resolve conflict. In later years, it is greased with how you use positive emotions and delight in each other. When you are young, you fight. When you are older, you have to enjoy.

Gottman has developed a mathematical model of negative and positive emotions—disgust, contempt, belligerence, stonewalling versus affection, humor, validation, excitement—that predict the stability of a marriage. In the early chapters of a relationship, you seek ways to overcome negative emotions. As you get older, the focus switches: you need to build up the positive expressions of love—play, humor, adventure, romance.

"A lot of couples—they don't know how to talk to each other. Their lives have been a to-do list. They don't interact very much. All of a sudden, they are faced with one another's company." If you don't have the facility to draw on a bank of positive emotions, you can get "lost and lonely and depressed," says Gottman.

"Most couples who have stayed together that long have been able to manage the conflict. The ones who couldn't—those people have broken up." But marriage survivors have to find positive reasons to stay together. "That becomes really hard. There isn't that spark anymore. They don't feel that attracted to each other. They are not having sex. You can rekindle that," says Gottman: "you start with affection."

To build up positive emotions, you need to pay attention to the seesaw dynamic in your relationship. What is your role in the marriage? Without some role flexibility and a perception of fairness, how can you be affectionate? Or funny? Or playful and sexy? If the seesaw is stuck, you're more likely to be angry or distant. Sometimes couples who are stuck have solved the problem of conflict by living separate lives. But a good relationship in this stage is not only about avoiding conflict. There has to be more.

Maybe you think that roles in marriage are about gender issues. You know all about the traditional divisions of power with men in the dominant position, women in the submissive position—an echo of the hierarchy between parent and child, employer and employee, lord and vassal. In this scenario, the seesaw is stuck. "Status hierarchy," explains Gottman in a research paper on relationships,[3] "breeds hostility, particularly from women, who tend to have less power than men, and who typically bring up most of the relationship issues."

Certainly the lord-and-vassal image captures how unequal—and ultimately unfair—a relationship can become. But roles in the marital circus act are more about psychological power. They are not automatically gender specific. Many women "wear the pants" in a family. There are "henpecked" husbands as well as bullied wives. And in gay and lesbian couples, there is no difference in gender.

In all kinds of relationships, the ability to keep the seesaw in motion helps couples achieve equity and a sense of fairness in the union. At this point in your life, you want to be a free citizen in marriage.

Jane Kittery and Beth Felderst[*4] have been a couple for thirty-five years. They first meet at a reception after a dance recital when they are graduate students at the University of California, San Francisco. "We really hit it off. We made a lunch date. Another lunch date and the rest is history," says Jane, 62.

Jane is an archeologist; Beth is a biologist. All through their relationship, they are constantly taking turns on the seesaw as they juggle their academic careers.

---

3. John Mordechi Gottman, Robert Wayne Levenson, Catherine Swanson, Kristin Swanson, Rebecca Tyson, and Dan Yoshimoto, "Observing Gay, Lesbian and Heterosexual Couples' Relationships: Mathematical Modeling of Conflict Interaction," *Journal of Homosexuality* 45, no. 1 (2003).

4. Throughout the chapter, asterisks indicate that names, identifying details, and some events have been changed.

When Beth gets a position at UCLA, Jane stays in San Francisco; they have a commuter relationship for ten years. Because of teaching schedules, the main travel burden falls on Jane, who commutes to LA on weekends. Though she dislikes the commute, she understands how much the LA job means to Beth. "She loved teaching there," says Jane.

And then when Jane is hired by the University of California, Santa Barbara, Beth gives up her job and follows Jane. It's a setback to her career. But she knows how exciting this new job is for Jane. After a frustrating search, Beth lands a position at the Marine Biotechnology Center.

In negotiating these moves, they are each sensitive to what the other wants and needs. While both are ambitious and successful academics, they put a priority on their relationship. "Especially at this point," says Jane. "There are life quality issues that are much more important than career advancement issues."

When Beth wants to buy a cottage in Carpinteria on the coast, about an hour's drive from Santa Barbara, Jane is not particularly interested. She's wary of taking on another house. She'd rather spend the money on taking trips, hiking in the mountains. But Beth, who grew up in New Bedford, Massachusetts, longs to be by the sea. If it means that much to Beth, Jane says to herself, well, sure. She co-signs the mortgage without having seen the house. Yes, it's been a financial drain, but now they walk along the gentle, sloping beach and look for sea lions together. The house is Beth's baby and Jane grows to love it, too.

They also allow each other separate spaces. When Jane goes on a dig in India, she wants to go by herself. At first Beth takes umbrage. But they have spent time apart before. Beth knows she wouldn't do well with India's humid heat and spicy food. She knows Jane will return and they will relive the trip together, sharing stories over a glass of wine. After many decades together, there's a granite level of trust between them and a bank of positive emotions. They each think the other one is brilliant and funny and kind. They've grown together so well that they've begun to look alike. The students at UCSB can't tell them apart.

For Jane and Beth, the circus act has been seamless.

Homosexual couples are generally more effective in resolving conflicts and showing affection than heterosexual couples, researchers find. They tend to use more positive emotions to repair and enrich the relationship. Those who bring up a problem do so with more kindness and humor. Their partners who receive the unwelcome news or frank criticism show less belligerence, less domineering behavior, and less fear. With a greater sense of equity in the relationship, couples like Jane and Beth have a more positive influence on each other.

"Thus, based on our results, heterosexual relationships may have a great deal to learn from homosexual relationships," conclude Gottman and his colleagues in their report.

✦

Many marriages evolve along traditional gender lines. But in this stage of life, roles start to blur. The man is freed from the bread-winning role; the woman is freed from the child-rearing role. In popular lore, he discovers his "feminine" side and becomes more sensitive, more accessible. She discovers her "masculine" side and goes trekking in the wilderness. The gender switch makes neat headlines. He takes Italian cooking lessons and bakes bread; she runs for mayor.

On the psychological level, the changes may be less visible, but they are significant. Sometimes it takes a surprise move by one partner to remind the other that the seesaw is in motion.

Marilyn and Alan Webber of Middleton, Massachusetts, describe their marriage as traditional. "I'm the alpha male," says Alan. He builds up a successful antique business; she stays at home and cooks the meals, making sure their four children are fed and happy. When he turns 51, he tells her that he is going to retire. *"Good,"* she says. *"I'm going to retire, too."* He looks at her—stunned. Retire from what? From the job she's had for the last thirty years. "I had raised four children," she explains. "I decided not to cook anymore."

Alan reminisces: in Maine on vacation, Marilyn used to bake his favorite—blueberry pies. Now he has to check out the bakeries in town for the best blueberry pie. On one occasion, he offers a woman $50 to bake him a blueberry pie. He's still the alpha male. He has the dominating personality. Mostly he calls the shots.

But not always—that is the key. Marilyn smiles at him. "He's into control," she says. "I'm improving," he says, "slowly." She nods. He says he's grateful that she puts up with him, adding: "She's a completely different person from the woman I married." Marilyn, so pretty with her white hair and gentle manner, beams at her husband.

The balance of power may not appear equal, but the seesaw is in motion. Marilyn has her way, too, and Alan responds to her influence. They have empathy for each other and they both think the marriage is fair. They've just celebrated their forty-ninth wedding anniversary.

In successful relationships, it's the mutual perception of fairness that matters. Absolute equality may be illusory, but equity with a just exchange of influence from one to the other is a realistic goal. How open are you to what your partner is thinking and feeling? Is there a fair give-and-take? Sensitivity to each other often leads to greater appreciation and affection—as in the case of Alan and Marilyn.

✦

You may not be aware of your circus act. Perhaps the music has stopped and you are frozen in one position. You don't know why you're feeling so frustrated or so empty. You start to think: I'm not up for this.

"We would have broken up if we were 40," says Carol Smithen* of Tucson. She's finally making it as an artist. Good commissions to go to LA or Seattle to paint portraits of CEOs, one to hang in the boardroom, another to hang in the dining room—the trophy wife in a Gainsborough background of hunting dogs and weeping foliage. All the New Money! But at last, she's earning enough from the portraits to support herself, help out with the grandchildren, and paint what she likes. She's preparing a new show: abstract paintings of red-rust landscapes, bent Mexican workers, bitter Native Americans.

Carol grows up in Philadelphia, where her mother has seated dinners for twelve. She bolts from all that—heading west to the University of California, Berkeley, marching against the Vietnam War. With long straight black hair, she looks like a Flower Child, but she isn't really because she is too practical, too ambitious, and too talented simply to go with the flow. She marries another artist, Jack Smithen,* who quickly becomes successful as a kind of New Age Jackson Pollock whose splats of shape and color are said to carry a political message. Who smokes dope and leaves dirty underwear in the front hall. She loves him very much and they have two sons together. No question, he is impossible. They break up; she needs a more stable household for her sons, and she remains single until the boys are grown.

When she is 55, walking through the Denver airport, she spots a young man who looks just like her old boyfriend in Philadelphia. Could it have been his son?

She tracks him down: Mark Dubsky,* funny, warm, quirky—a combination of Old-World Charm and 1960s rebelliousness. A Marine who goes to Vietnam and comes back a Vet against the war. No, not his son— he has no children, he tells her. He and his wife are divorced. He's become a stockbroker, not a particularly successful one. He doesn't really care about money. His family has roots in the Austro-Hungarian Empire. She remembers their romance: after graduating from Amherst College, he wanted to marry her. He called her his Indian Princess. But she was a senior in high school and she freaked out—too young.

Now they are in their 60s. They have been a throwback couple for nearly ten years. They are not married. He lives around the corner, in a falling-down, one-bedroom house. Carol has her own place with a studio, a small inheritance from her mother, which she wants to pass on to her sons, and a busy schedule of painting jobs. Mark has congestive heart failure. He goes to the doctor every few months for a checkup. He takes medication. All he wants to do is be with her and enjoy the world. She worries about the future—because she's always had to worry and make plans. Mark doesn't worry. He doesn't make plans.

He makes jokes. He loves her and he loves life. But she wishes he'd find a way to make some money. They take a job together delivering newspapers to a new upscale subdivision. Two hours in the middle of the night roaring around under the stars in Mark's beat-up 1986 Toyota wagon. Throwing newspapers at the McMansions with addresses like Camelot Court. "We were extremely snobby about this," says Carol. They'd turn up the radio and listen to oldies: Mama Cass singing *Dream a little dream of me*. Thwack, as the newspaper hits the steps. *Night breezes seem to whisper "I love you."* Another McMansion and another, thwack, thwack. *Sweet dreams till sunbeams find you*. Thwack. "It was romantic. We were laughing and hooting. They had the McMansion. We had the newspaper route. The sun was coming up. It made you feel twenty years younger."

But the work is hard. Mark isn't fast enough: roll the newspaper, put it in plastic, throw it at the McMansion. They start getting complaints—the newspaper is late, it's in the flower bed, under the car. Then the rules change. No more throwing; the newspaper has to be put in the box.

They give up the route. Carol is glad to get some rest and get back to painting. But Mark is becoming more problematic. His house is a mess. He sleeps more. Where is this heading? "He's been a wildly generous boyfriend. Presents, perfume, dresses," she says. But in the last year, his extravagance has a sting. Why is he spending so much money when he has so little? How is he going to make out in the future? Does he expect that she will automatically pick up the slack? She is thinking: Don't give me presents. Pay attention to your own life.

He doesn't. His health deteriorates. He tires easily. Shortness of breath. Palpitations. Sometimes he's not so alert. He's supposed to watch his weight. But he loves to eat.

His situation gnaws at her. "He was running out of money. He wouldn't go on disability. I couldn't support him. I wasn't up for that. I didn't have the money," she says. "He's in denial in my perception. The whole thing is impossible unless he will take half the responsibility for his illness."

What's fair here? In this circus act, she is feeling like the one on the bottom supporting the other on her shoulders. And they're stuck in this position. Resentment boils up in her. He's had heart failure for years. "It didn't happen on my watch," she says.

They start to have regular battles. She slips into the role of a nagging parent: Are your clothes clean? You can't go out in the clothes you've slept in. What are you going to do with your life anyway? Sex goes to hell. She doesn't want to touch him. "Resentment kills sex," she says.

It's not long before they have the big blowup. "I can't be your girl-friend," she tells him. All the while she's feeling the guilt. How can she do this? *You can't break up with some old guy with heart failure!*

But she does. She cannot carry the load any further. She thinks they're done. "It is sad. I've put in my sad tears. My vision is to have a tranquil end of life. If he was a conscientious partner, we could have worked it out. To take on an invalid person and become the caretaker—there has to be a reason to do it."

But Mark doesn't follow her breakup script. He says: Fine. You're not responsible for me. I'll deal with it my way. It's my heart failure. Don't worry about me. Loosen up and let me deal with the future. . . . I love you. I don't want to break up. . . . Let's enjoy each other.

Mark has sad gray eyes. He remembers the siege of Khe Sanh; all the killing and dying, so pointless, so inevitable. One of his buddies looks out one morning and repeats the warriors' cry: "It's a beautiful day to die." In-deed, a beautiful day. The combat soldier's mentality. Death sits on his shoulder. What's the fuss about—succumbing to heart failure? Running out of money? Wearing dirty clothes? Eating too much? What about—telling a few jokes? Making a toast? Listening to music? Hey, it's a beau-tiful day. . . .

It takes some shuffling in Carol's head to stay in the relationship. She has to give up control and the feeling that she is the one responsible for his fate—and theirs. She has to push her end of the seesaw off the ground and let Mark be Mark.

"It means I don't have to solve his problems. I feel I don't. When we meet, we have a good time," says Carol. "We've had the conversation: *I cannot be responsible.* He says: *Okay; I'll take care of it.*"

They get unstuck and resume. They see each other four times a week and are constantly on the phone. They spend the night together and snuggle up. As she says: "He pitches woo." They go out as a couple. They host family vacations together. Gathering up the children and grandchildren and camping out in Colorado's Estes Park. "Mark is part of it. He makes a tremendous effort. He gets up and gives a big old sentimental toast. He makes everyone feel good." Positive emotions take hold, smoothing out negative ones. "It feels okay. What the hell: Live in the present. He's a gracious person, perceptive, sweet," she says. "He is very accepting and appreciative of me. It's a lovely thing to have a companion."

A great weight has been lifted off her shoulders. She is lighter, more flexible—and happier. She realizes that she was the one who had put the weight on her shoulders—because that had been her role in her family: going back to Philadelphia to nurse her mother through Alzheimer's, taking care of her son after he is injured in a car accident and has to learn to walk on an artificial leg. Care-taking is her default position. Rescue and control—control and rescue. This breeds a rumbling resentment. In confronting Mark, she lays the burden down.

And he is delighted. Who wants an angry mother type on their back?

He hasn't changed. His house is still a mess. He gets distracted: she asks him to get a bottle of milk and he comes back six hours later with a chair. She can't live with him, but she can love him. They are a living apart, loving together couple. The relationship goes deeper. The future is uncertain, but the present is a beautiful day.

In the process of shifting roles, Carol gains back her independence. She can spend more time on her painting, on her assignments, on her grandchildren. She doesn't feel guilty about leaving him when she goes on a trip. And Mark has gotten back his playful Indian Princess.

She could not have renegotiated the relationship like this if she were younger, she says. Not with young children to raise and educate, not with a joint mortgage to pay. The rules of survival are more rigid in earlier years. But she's free of those responsibilities now. There's a tempering of her sense of ought and should.

Mark has given much to her. He's taught her not to be so afraid of the future. "He is very alive. He's had many losses. He never complains. He is very loving," she says. "There is wisdom in him. It's got to do with the importance of life and death. You enjoy what you can in a free and generous way."

Recognizing your role in a relationship is a way to reframe problems and take steps to resolve them. How important is it for you to be in control? How easily do you let go of control? How strongly do you hold on to expectations—that may not be realistic? You think the problem is with your partner. And sometimes there are insurmountable problems involving abuse or neglect. But poisonous feelings are often prompted by how you interact with each other about a problem. The difficult issues between you may remain, but how you address them—and how you feel about them—can change. Like Carol and Mark, couples can reach a settling point and accommodate. This often opens up the flow of positive emotions.

✦

Sometimes there is a quiet competition between partners—status quo with an edge. You may not realize it but you have been stuck in opposing positions on the seesaw for decades. You are both committed to the marriage, but it's not a satisfying relationship. You operate out of habit. Then one or the other of you gets a life-changing jolt and the dominant-submissive axis is broken.

Illness, for example, is a jolt that directly affects the balance of power in a relationship. "Sometimes it can resolve conflicts over dominance and collegiality," says Garry J. Kennedy, a professor of psychiatry and behavioral sciences at the Albert Einstein College of Medicine in New York.

For many couples, illness that disrupts the power balance is also an opportunity to renegotiate the relationship—for the better.

John Humboldt* grows up in Cincinnati and he dies in Cincinnati. His family comes to Ohio in the railroad boom of the Gilded Age. He chafes under the small-town atmosphere of a city long surpassed by the bigger rivals of Cleveland and Chicago. Yet he would never leave his hometown, and after he retires from the Taft museum, he plays golf with the friends he went to school with.

But there's another side to John. As a young man he wants adventure, surprise. Yet he hangs back, especially with women. He dates waves of eligible brides as they graduate from high school and college. At 37, he is still a bachelor. And then at a party in Cleveland, he meets Mary Kate O'Reilly*: wild brown hair and a face of freckles. She looks at him and says: *"No one as cute as you is still unmarried."*

John finds his surprise. He pursues her and nine months later he brings her back to Cincinnati as his bride. Mary Kate is different from the other wives: A career woman. A decade younger. And originally from Vermont.

Suddenly, Mary Kate is the young wife of an older, settled man. And suddenly, something very curious happens to her: the independent go-getter vanishes. "I collapsed on him totally," she says. "I became this needy mush. I was willing for him to do everything. I was afraid to make a decision. I didn't want to do the wrong thing. I seemed so incompetent. He was so confident."

This dynamic doesn't budge for thirty years. John is dominant, she is dependent. At first, it doesn't seem odd: he's older, this is his town; what does she know? She also brings her past to the marriage. She was 9 when her father died. "The attraction to older men kept cropping up in my dating history," she says. Her mother is distant. What does a little girl do to protect herself from having to depend on unreliable loved ones? She becomes a go-getter! All the while, she keeps an eye out for the older man, for Mr. Reliable. When she finds him, she does a role switch: she doesn't have to be the independent go-getter anymore; she becomes a needy (almost childlike) submissive wife. "John said I was the most dependent liberated woman he knew."

Two years into the marriage, she gives birth to a boy with a severe heart abnormality. He lives eight years. Mary Kate devotes herself to the boy. After their son's death, it is just the two of them. She believes in the "if I have to, I can do anything" liberation message of the women's movement. But in the face of such overwhelming loss, she hangs on to Mr. Reliable. Looking back, she says: "He was thinking: *When is she getting out from this dependency stuff?*" But the seesaw never budges. He becomes a curator of the museum; she does volunteer work, mentoring preschool children. "We led parallel lives," she says.

He is a Cincinnati Elder Statesman. Domineering, yes, but also benevolent. He encourages her to go back to school and she gets a master's in education. Once he retires from the museum, he is happy for her to go to work as a high school guidance counselor. Now she is on a double track. "I was leading two lives: a subsuming-type wife and a very competent guidance counselor."

John does not invite her into his world. "He did not share his thoughts with me. He was stoic and self-contained. He could be critical. I was very defensive." She turns to the church and starts going to mass again. "I knew that my Savior loved me," she says.

And then John suffers a stroke. Over the next ten years, their relationship changes dramatically. He breaks down the self-containment wall around him and lets her in. Not as a subservient follower but as a strong advocate and partner. She takes over the medical details. "I was not afraid of doctors. I did not kowtow to anybody," she says. She had been through the medical maze with her son, pushing for better treatment, advocating for "special needs" children, fighting with bureaucracies, pressuring legislatures. She does the same for John, who rediscovers the liberated woman he fell in love with decades ago.

At first, it is hard to shake this habit of subservience. "He could always do things better than me," she says. Down she had stuffed herself over the years into Little Ms. Nothing. The dynamic had been frozen so long that they'd come to accept that he was the competent one, she the incompetent one.

But the stroke blasts away the old roles. John makes an impressive recovery: he can speak and walk with a cane. But one side of his body is weakened and his words are halting. Mary Kate becomes the competent one—in the management of the disease and in the running of the marriage. She goes to every doctor's appointment. She takes him to rehab.

When he comes down with pneumonia, she makes sure he gets properly treated.

She isn't leading a double life anymore. She is her competent self, getting the praise and respect she deserves. And John isn't carrying a subservient wife any longer. The seesaw begins moving now in a quiet rhythm. She is supporting him—wholeheartedly. And he in turn is supporting her—wholeheartedly. Instead of being critical, he is grateful. "Anything that would make it easier for me, he wanted to do," she says. Instead of feeling resentful and alone in the marriage, Mary Kate feels emboldened and embraced.

One afternoon, she is sitting quietly in a chair, humming the love song from *West Side Story*: "There's a place for us, a time and a place for us." He listens and calls out to her: *"Mary Kate . . . lovely voice."* His words are slow. *"You . . . sing."* She guffaws at that. What—me sing? Yes; please sing. So she sings the song again, louder: "Take my hand . . . almost there." She welcomes his encouragement; maybe she should take singing lessons.

After nearly a decade of quasi-normalcy, John suffers another stroke and dies three months later. In the end, "I was sleeping in a bed next to him in the hospital. I was seeing to every need he had. That was my need as much as it was his," she says. It's ultimately "a person's need to be accepted and loved and cared for," she continues. She never had that growing up. "When it didn't pay off to invest heavily in a relationship, you learned not to. That was what was so intense, to finally be drawn into the relationship with John. Finally I was needed. I was able to fill a real need for him. It was such a high. I was really needed."

The last years of her marriage are the best, she says. Illness brings them together. "It peels away all the pretensions. All the superficial crap. It peels it all away," she says. "I'm so blessed."

Meanwhile, singing has become a vital part of her life. After John's death, she takes lessons and joins a theater group. Next month she will be in the chorus of *The Music Man*.

It's never too late to change the dynamic of a relationship. Sometimes it takes a major jolt to reframe the marriage. You have to let go of old habits that no longer sustain the relationship—that may even have been eroding the bond over many decades. It is a dramatic turnaround.

✦

The French say there is always a kisser and a kissee—one who sets the agenda for a relationship and the other who implements it; the initiator and the follower, the dominant one and the submissive partner.

The roles are not set in stone. You can switch from kisser to kissee and back again. You may be the kisser with one person, the kissee with another. In a long relationship, you switch back and forth to keep the seesaw in its rhythmic balance.

My friend Barbara Youmans of Newport, New Hampshire, tells me how she played different roles in different marriages. In her marriage to poet Raymond Holden, she is two decades younger, the student bride, the kissee. "It seemed an obvious thing to me," recalls Barbara, 92.

After his death from leukemia, she marries David Youmans, whom she had known in high school. With David, she is the kisser. "A lot of women were interested in him. That made me more the pursuer," she says. They are a throwback couple. "He claims he loved me when we were kids and I won out over those other ladies," she says. "I was the pursuer as far as getting married. He didn't resist very long."

After they marry, they take turns setting the agenda—where to live, where to go on a trip. The seesaw becomes more balanced. They are evenly matched—in age, in shared experience. Now Barbara is a widow. She smiles. "I look at that marriage as very successful," she says.

6

Breaking Up

The shoe drops.

I don't love you anymore.

I can't go on like this.

I've met someone.

It's better this way.

Why now?

Most divorces occur within the first ten years of a marriage. By the time you celebrate your twenty-fifth wedding anniversary, you're probably in the smooth zone. Most of the conflicted marriages of couples who married when you did have already broken up. But time is no guarantee. Neither is age. Couples continue to break up across the life span.

It hurts. No matter how old you are. Or how long you've been together—or whether it's a marriage or a significant love affair. You sit there, steeped in the familiar. You numb each other with habitual chit chat. *Nice scarf you're wearing. . . . Can you believe this president?* . . . You know things haven't been so great, but what's great? You're having a nice dinner in a restaurant. Your spouse is talking very fast and you think, *He's sure in a good mood tonight.* You order linguine and clams. The food comes, you start to eat, and then he says: *I can't go on like this. . . . I've met someone* . . . and suddenly your stomach is in your throat and you can't breathe.

You know it's over. The bottom falls out of your life. Or you are the one who says: *I can't go on like this,* and suddenly silence blocks your ears and your heart pounds. The truth is: *I don't want you anymore.* Time stops. Two people suspended in the breakup scene, you wait for the noise to come back, the tinkling of glasses, the rushing about of waiters. You wait for the first waves of emotion: relief or disbelief—depending on who initiates the break. You think: finally it's out in the open. Or you're a deer in the headlights—this can't be happening; not here, not now. *How's the linguine?* Over: it's over. Six months? Two years? Twenty years? All over!

Every breakup has its own scenario. Maybe you're screaming in the kitchen, and smashing the cereal bowls that were a wedding present from Aunt Lucy. Or you don't really have a conversation. You just go. Or your partner does. Whatever the circumstances, the end of a relationship is a savage loss. Back to square one. French torch singer Edith Piaf sings for you in her classic: *Rien de rien. . . . No, nothing at all; I regret nothing. . . . I begin again at zero.* That's the point, you have to start over. As the weight of the breakup sinks in, you think: I'm too old for this.

But you're not too old.

Longevity changes the rules of "sticking it out." You may live in good health for another twenty or thirty years or more. That's a long time to stay in an unrewarding relationship. It's enough time to seek a different future. The major threat to marriages in this stage is burnout. Simmering problems have never been adequately addressed. Instead, you disengage, perhaps without realizing it.

Scott Jones*[1] follows in his father's footsteps. He grows up in the Napa Valley and goes to Swarthmore like his father and starts a business like his father—and marries a college classmate like his father. His mother is the one who believes in Great Love. She reads Baudelaire in French. When Scott is 20, his mother runs off with a French count—he claims he is a count, "count no account," says Scott's uncle. It is a family scandal. After the affair ends, his mother, divorced and alone, moves to San Diego

---

1. Throughout the chapter, asterisks indicate that names, identifying details, and some events have been changed.

with her French poetry books. Scott ends up supporting her. Meanwhile, his father quickly remarries a nurse who is passionate about homeopathic medicine.

As a boy, Scott is caring and cheerful; as an adult, he is the same. He makes his mother happy; he makes his father happy—he makes his step-mother happy. He makes his wife happy. He has a talent for anticipating other people's needs and turning a potential nightmare of a family gathering into a happy occasion. For his twenty-fifth college reunion he writes: "The best thing I did was marry our classmate—the beautiful and intelligent Angeline Whittle."*

"I truly loved Angie," says Scott, 55. "She was my best friend. She had a great sense of humor. I bonded with her family. I loved her mom and dad." They flesh out the marital dream: a nice house in the Berkeley hills, two nice children, and the son would go to Swarthmore, too. Family Thanksgivings are perfectly prepared, with the turkey set on a Tiffany silver platter.

But behind the dream, a different reality is unfolding. Angie is moody, irritable. Everything has to be just so. She feels that other people aren't measuring up—the neighbors who let their dog bark outside, Scott's cousin who becomes a Buddhist and makes wind chimes for a living. But her husband just keeps smiling, a kind of belligerent optimism that leaves her to hold the line.

She rides the children hard. Everything depends on their doing well. She goes over their homework every night. She worries about their safety. She doesn't want her daughter to play soccer in high school—too dangerous.

Scott usually works late. He travels to meetings. Meanwhile, Angie becomes something of a hermit. She refuses several jobs that come her way. When their son goes east to college—*"like cutting off my right arm,"* she tells him. He tries to comfort her, give her a back rub. Angie's bouts of weeping, bouts of rages—what are they about? Any little thing: eating some pizza while watching a football game on television—*how can you eat pizza? It's bad for you! It's going to drip on the sofa! How can you watch that awful game?*

But Scott is brought up to make people happy. His self-esteem is built on that role. So he keeps trying to calm the waters. He never confronts her. "I don't like to get into fights," he says. "If I know I'm going to lose—or if I know I'm going to win—why fight? That philosophy did come back to bite me. There were many times she said I should tell her to buzz off. But I'm not comfortable doing that."

To Angie, Scott sometimes seems like the inflatable vinyl clown that pops back up smiling. She keeps pushing at him: Why won't he take a stand? With his weird family? His dreary colleagues? Take a stand with his children? With her?

Scott and Angie are stuck. Without realizing it, they have slipped into the fatal submissive-dominant dance: Scott the submissive pleaser will do anything to make her happy and keep the family together—Angie, the dominant one on the pedestal, will have to do everything to achieve their dream of perfection. They both throw themselves into their roles. For a while, it is a terrific dance. While other marriages are breaking up, Scott and Angie are firmly together.

But there is not a lot of joy in their life. The burden of perfection is getting so heavy, Angie thinks she might break. And once again, her husband is gone, another meeting. Alone; she is very alone for many years—consoled by the fact that she is doing the right thing: protecting her children from harm, running a good home, being faithful to her husband.

And then one day, Scott comes home and says they should go to marital therapy!

Scott describes the decades of marriage as Chinese water torture. "It was a cumulative effect," he says. And then after thirty years, he has a kind of epiphany and says to himself: "Wait a second. My whole way of being is not making it better. It's making it worse. By being kind and helpful and understanding, I'm contributing to this," he explains. By being the soft one, he turns her into the hard one. He starts thinking: *I'll confront her.*

Angie refuses to go to a marriage counselor. Everyone she knows who went into therapy ended up getting divorced. No, she tells him. The habit of control is entrenched. Meanwhile, Angie and Scott haven't had any sex for years. The distance widens between them. Not like two leaves on a pond that drift apart, but more stark: two branches on a tree trunk that grow in opposite directions.

The confrontation scene takes place in the kitchen. He stands there in his bathrobe. She thinks he should get ready for work—he's already late. No, they have to talk, he says. Really talk. He sits her down and tells her he wants to end the marriage. Then he packs up a few things and goes to a hotel. He has no plan.

The breakup is devastating for Angie. She is unprepared for the emotional and practical consequences of divorce. Momentous tasks lie ahead: to reestablish her sense of self, to get a job, to build an intimate team of friends and family, to gain insight into her marriage and her role in its breakdown. The children—now away at college—are caught in the middle. Scott, after an initial period of relief, plunges into a chaotic period of self-examination.

"I'm the poster child of someone who waited too long, who waited until the last second," he says. "I had a hundred opportunities to give her more straight feedback," but by the time he began to be straighter with her, "she wasn't hearing it." They have both been in their separate boxes too long, stuck in place and finally exhausted. It is like the moment in a wrestling match when one taps the other on the shoulder: "I give up. It's over," says Scott.

Marriages in this stage tend to end with a whimper, not a bang. Just how a relationship unravels is unique to each couple. Breakup tales are full of bastards and bitches. But the underlying structure of the relationship provides some clues to why a marriage comes apart. When two people are stuck on a seesaw, mutual engagement stops. They may stay together for many years, but unless there's some movement in their marital circus act, the countdown to a breakup has begun. The ones stuck in the dependent position finally get sick of the complaints and the bullying, and they rebel. Or those stuck in the dominant position get so filled with disappointment and contempt that they can't go on another minute.

What took you so long?

You don't want to let go. As Scott says of Angie: "I loved and cared for her." You want to keep your family. You want to hold on to the safe harbor of home that protects you from the outrageous fortune of the outside world. Even when home is no longer a safe or welcoming refuge, you stay. No one wants to give up on the dream. Yet, holding on to the dream may be dangerous.

You don't realize how shut down you are. "Some of the participants in empty marriages are themselves unaware of the emotional bankruptcy of their lives," writes psychiatrist Ethel S. Person in *Dreams of Love and Fateful Encounters.* "To preserve such a bond often requires the deadening of one's general emotional availability and the suppression of one's imaginative life. Many people die psychologically decades before their biological deaths."[2]

You don't want to die psychologically. How *alive* are you with your partner? Can you be your true self in the presence of your mate? A tip-off to burnout is when you go out by yourself and someone says: "You're a totally different person when you're not with your spouse."

✦

Overall, both divorce and marriage are in decline. Divorce rates peaked in 1981.[3] In 2005, there were 3.5 divorces per 1,000 people—the lowest level since 1970. Among those who were married as of 2005, the divorce rate has also declined—to 16.7 divorces per 1,000 marriages in that year down from 22.8 in 1979. At the same time, marriage-like relationships are on the rise, with an undocumented record of beginnings and endings.

A generation ago, it was very rare for older people to get divorced. That appears to be changing. Family counselors and lawyers are noticing an

2. Ethel S. Person, *Dreams of Love and Fateful Encounters: The Power of Romantic Passion* (American Psychiatric Publishing, Inc., 2006), pp. 311–312.

3. Betsey Stevenson and Justin Wolfers, "Marriage and Divorce: Changes and Their Driving Forces," *Journal of Economic Perspectives* 21, no. 2 (Spring 2007), pp. 27–52.

uptick in men and women in their 50s and beyond who are divorcing. "Now it's happening. It's visible. It's new," says sociologist Andrew J. Cherlin of Johns Hopkins University.[4] "Older couples are waiting until kids are out of the house. Some have been unhappy for years. Others become more unhappy when the kids leave home."

In part, gray divorce reflects the changes in the institution of marriage that put a premium on happiness and intimacy. "The meaning of marriage has shifted to being about personal satisfaction," continues Cherlin. "People are suddenly allowed [to contemplate divorce] in a way they weren't before."

Vast majorities of Americans believe that divorce is "preferable to maintaining an unhappy marriage," according to a 2007 telephone survey of more than 2,000 men and women conducted by the Pew Research Center.[5] This attitude increases with age: more than 65 percent of those ages 50 to 64 favor divorce over an unhappy union—compared to 54 percent of those under 50.

Later-life divorce is making headlines. Mostly it's rich executives who are leaving their wives for younger versions. Viacom CEO Sumner Redstone was 81 when he divorced his wife after fifty-two years of marriage. International financier George Soros was 74 when he separated from his wife after twenty-one years. Former General Electric CEO Jack Welsh was 68 when he left his wife. This is called "CEO-itis," writes Deirdre Bair in Calling It Quits.[6]

You hear about the couple down the street, a colleague at work, your old college roommate. And it's not just the stereotype of the aging lion who leaves his wife for arm candy. It's also women saying they can't stay in an unsatisfactory marriage any longer. They'd rather be by themselves.

---

4. Andrew J. Cherlin is the author of Marriage, Divorce, Remarriage.

5. "As Marriage and Parenthood Drift Apart, Public Is Concerned About Social Impact" (Pew Research Center, July 2007). Interviews were conducted under the direction of Princeton Survey Research Associates International.

6. Deirdre Bair, Calling It Quits: Late-Life Divorce and Starting Over (Random House, 2007).

Divorce among older adults is also often about re-divorce—remarriages that end in divorce. (Both the recent exes of Soros and Welsh are second wives.) Since divorces generally occur within the first decade of marriage, people who remarry at 40 or 50 are at higher risk of splitting up in this stage than those in marriages of many decades. Besides, if you have already been through a divorce, you may be quicker to end a relationship that is not working.

Gray divorce is also generational. People born between 1950 and 1955 are more likely to exit their marriage than older—and younger—generations. Among marriages that occurred in the 1970s, 48 percent dissolved within twenty-five years, roughly confirming the popular claim that half of all marriages end in divorce. And divorce is a transition. Most people re-couple after a breakup. About 70 percent of those who got divorced and are in their 50s and 60s today went on to another marriage. These men and women have grown up in a culture of serial marriage. There is no reason to think that they will change as they get older, researchers say.

Gregg Herman, a family attorney in Milwaukee, remembers his oldest client: a 96-year-old man who divorced his 89-year-old wife—a second marriage of nineteen years. They were living in an assisted-living facility and when he was hospitalized, he felt his wife let him down and didn't visit him. "He got very angry," says Herman. "The marriage was not so great. The hospitalization was a catalyst for action." The man said to Herman: *"I don't want to live the rest of my life being married to her."*

✦

Many breakups later in life are deferred divorces. The overwhelming reason why people postpone ending a troubled marriage is concern about the children and fear of being cut off from them, according to the AARP survey of divorce in older adults.[7] The study is based on surveys and interviews with 1,147 men and women, ages 40 to 70, who have gone through a divorce in their 40s, 50s, and 60s. Nearly 58 percent of men

---

7. "The Divorce Experience: A Study of Divorce at Midlife and Beyond" (AARP, 2004).

cite children as the top reason why they put off a divorce for five years or more.

Once the children are grown, the lid is off. But in gray divorce, there is a wide gender gap. *Why* couples break up is different for men and women, according to the AARP study. Women report physical or emotional abuse, infidelity, and drug or alcohol abuse as the top reasons. Men cite "different values or lifestyles" and "fell out of love"—which may be code for falling in love with somebody else, thus jibing with women's concern about infidelity.

"Infidelity at that age is by far the most precipitating factor," says Sharon Kalemkarian, a California family lawyer. Usually, it's the men who have marriage-breaking affairs, she says, but not always. Alcoholism and prescription drug abuse are also factors for both men and women. In her practice, gray divorce tends to occur for hard reasons—infidelity, domestic abuse, addictions— rather than for softer reasons of incompatibility. "People don't say: we're not getting along—not like younger people," continues Kalemkarian. "With older couples—there is something that happens that makes them no longer able to tolerate each other."

Mental health issues come into play. "You see a lot of people with mild depression issues associated with aging," says Milwaukee lawyer Herman. The marriage is not healthy to begin with, he explains. You may be unhappy for many reasons, but you can do something about marital doldrums. "Inertia is a reason for divorce. Maybe, if you change the inertia, you'll change how you're feeling," he says. (That doesn't always work out. A clinical depression requires therapeutic attention.)

How you break up is also different for women and men. Women are the most likely to initiate a divorce, according to the AARP survey. (They usually are. But a woman may be forced into taking that step if her husband has found someone else or is trapped in the downward spiral of alcohol or drug abuse.)

More interesting in the AARP study is that husbands are more likely than wives to be caught off guard by a marriage meltdown. One in four men whose wives initiated the divorce didn't see the breakup coming. Only 14 percent of the wives were surprised when the husband walked.

Women generally are more attuned to what's going on in their relationships—and more bothered by a dysfunctional marriage. In the classic scenario of female-initiated divorce in this stage, the wife has faced emotional abuse, constant infidelities, or alcoholic behavior on the part of her partner. Denial is common among people with addictions and those who have to be in control. You may not realize how your behavior affects your spouse. Hey, she put up with you for decades. But like a rubber band pulled too tight, the marriage finally snaps.

"I was in a terrible marriage, and I was absolutely dreading the thought of going through retirement with him," says Marcia Verdon,* 53, of Cleveland. Twenty-eight years together. For the last ten years, it's been a one-sided war and they no longer have the buffer of children at home. He is a kind of bully, she is the bruised survivor. He never hit her, but he crushed her psychologically, she says. He'd come home from work at the Ford dealership and take out his frustrations on her. *Fucking meat loaf— can't you even cook a steak?* Maybe he doesn't realize what he is doing. She glosses over it in front of the kids. She drags him to two separate stints of marriage counseling. Therapy doesn't help the relationship— but the sessions lay bare her unhappiness. So many years of Kleenex and tears. What is the matter with her? He thinks it must be a woman thing; always was a Broody Trudy. Not a lot of laughs, that's for sure. The kids are grown. Things are going well at the dealership. But look at her— sourpuss!

She starts thinking about what it would be like not to be married to him. Little thoughts coming into her head as she drives down the freeway. A studio apartment where she could eat a salad for dinner and play her own CDs at night. How to support herself? She has a job at Verizon Wireless. She doesn't have to worry about the kids. March, April. She tiptoes around her husband. But one night she tries to get him to talk about their problems—his putdowns, his lack of help in the kitchen, the jokes at parties at her expense.

She says to him: "In order for a marriage to succeed, we have to work at it." *Oh for Chrissake!* He blows up. Sick of all the talk. *Can't you just leave it alone?* Then he turns on her in a nasty voice: *After this many years of marriage, I shouldn't have to work at it at all!*

Those words deal the fatal blow to the marriage. "I knew it was time to throw in the towel," she says. But she waits until she is strong enough to live alone. "I made every effort to increase my income until I felt comfortable enough to survive." At last she is ready. Suppertime, she cooks him a steak, baked potato. *Nice*, he says. But she has made up her mind. Halfway through the steak, she breaks the news. "When I finally told him I wanted a divorce, he looked stunned, like he never saw it coming, despite the years and years of problems we'd been having," she says.

The divorce evens out the power balance between them. For once, he has to listen to her. For once, she gets her way. The marriage is over.

When there are hard reasons to break up, divorce can be a healthy option to make the most of the time left. But in the crisis of separating and starting over, you need to muster your resources—not just inner strength but outside support from your team of colleagues, neighbors, and family members.

What happens after a breakup also reflects the gender divide. Older women are "more fragile, generally speaking," says California lawyer Kalemkarian. They worry more about money and the prospect of being alone. "The men are more confident. They want to move on. They think they can get another relationship and take care of themselves."

The culture is shifting as more women hold jobs and gain financial security. "There's going to be a huge change," says Kalemkarian. "Once women can make their own money, what is the reason to stay together unless there is a romantic emotional bond or a solid friendship? Why wouldn't you live on your own?" Especially since you can find companionship as a single woman, if you want to. Kalemkarian is 51. "My friends are not remarrying," she says.

◆

Maybe you're not thinking divorce. Then you glimpse an alternate scenario for the future that is more meaningful. Like other jolts, it changes your life. But unlike illness or a blow at work, this kind of jolt is not a crisis of loss. You experience it as a positive change.

Sheila and Fred Castilani* of Bloomfield, Michigan, meet on campus at the University of Michigan. As children, they were each forced to go to Sunday school. As an adult, she likes all the Christmas rituals—singing carols, decorating the tree, setting up the crèche. But he doesn't. He always says: bah humbug. Nevertheless, she's made sure they always celebrate Christmas with the trimmings. Their marriage is like that, each one pushing against the other. But she usually has the last word.

And so, the marriage becomes a subtle war game that neither recognizes; after all, they never raise their voices. Everyone says they are so similar: same backgrounds, same college. Both are neat and organized. He crunches numbers for a utility company; she is a personal home manager: she goes into clients' houses and organizes their closets and drawers. They have two grown children. They have been married for thirty-five years.

But they are stuck in a flat-lined marriage: "We didn't have an outwardly fighting marriage . . . but it was quiet and empty," says Sheila, 60.

Sheila's family is rooted in the red soil of Alabama, and her father gets as far away as he can from cotton and soybeans when he joins the Navy in World War II. After the war, he brings his childhood sweetheart to New London, where he works in the shipyard. He is as determined as any immigrant to make a better life. His wife is intimidated. His sons don't amount to much. Sheila is the one who does well in school and never misbehaves. Her father dotes on her.

But behind her good-daughter exterior, she is scared. She needs a Great Man like her father to dote on her. And here she is at the university—one of thousands. "I was terrified of being alone," she says. By her junior year, she had a purpose: "I had this 'Desperate to Get Married' banner on my forehead." A classmate tells her that all the science majors take a general literature class and that's where the boys are. She takes the class. She drowns herself in *Anna Karenina*. The chemistry major sitting next to her nods off. She helps him study for the exam.

They marry soon after graduation. In the beginning, she looks up to Fred for "doting," as she had looked up to her father. But once the children are born, she focuses on them. Fred rises slowly and predictably up the ladder at Detroit Edison. Every year she brings out the Christmas decorations. Every year, he rolls his eyes. When the children are in middle school, she gets a job with a company that helps families move. She finds that she is good at organizing details, good at relating to people, good at being a success. But the marriage has changed. She and Fred are spending most of their time and emotional energy in different worlds. "I had a life that was very separate," she says. "My life was really with my kids, and my work, and my community." And Fred doesn't really like her community. Her parents, obnoxious hillbillies, he calls them. Back and forth: He complains. She criticizes. He complains about her criticism; she criticizes him for complaining. "I was forever overriding him, which wasn't such a great idea. We were not a united front," she says.

They do marriage counseling, but the therapy never addresses the power struggle between them. She decides to make the best of it and move on: "If I wanted my life to be fuller I was going to make it fuller myself," she says. Sheila starts her own home consulting business and pulls away from her husband even further.

One Saturday, she goes to a church workshop on helping adults with disabilities find jobs. The speaker describes how his daughter was paralyzed from the waist down in a car crash; now he has turned his personal trauma into a calling and started an organization to open up opportunities for people who are disabled. And that includes older men and women, too, he says. Don't we all have some disability? Everybody in the audience nods.

Sheila is mesmerized. "He's just speaking eloquently and his energy is good, and I love what he's talking about," she explains. "He has a presence—his hair, his bearing; there's a look about him and I thought: oh what an interesting-looking person." After the lecture, they gather in the common room for more discussion. Everyone exchanges cards. A few days later, he asks if she would speak at a group home and give the residents tools to manage the running of the house.

She is happy to help. It goes on like this for a while. He is a retired CPA. Divorced for more than a decade. Later in the year, she's invited to a two-day state meeting of social service agencies in Detroit, and they end up together at the disabilities table. "During that dinner, you know, I didn't know him that well but I felt we were functioning as a couple. It was the oddest thing," she says. And a flooding starts in her chest. The next day, they attend all the sessions together. "I never felt so much myself—it makes me teary—ever in my life," she says. "There was something in the way we connected that just felt natural." Coming back in the car to Bloomfield, all she can think about is that feeling. What just happened? "I wasn't thinking: *I'm leaving my husband. I'm falling in love.* I wasn't thinking that at all," she says.

But the marriage is shattered. She has a glimpse of what a fulfilling relationship could be. The final break is over money. Fred reneges on a promise to build a deck. "For me it was kind of a last straw," says Sheila. "Probably within a day or two after that, I made up my mind that I was going to get divorced," she says. "There was no looking back. I had no regret. It had nothing to do with the other man. What it did have to do with was my life."

She describes herself as a romantic. All her life, she has daydreamed about a transcendent connection with a man. The two days at the conference—"just talking, and again, nothing happened"—affirmed her fantasies that, yes, "a connection like that exists in this world," she says. "If nothing more ever happened beyond that—that was enough. It was like the universe saying: yes, everything you've longed for, everything you've dreamed of—it does exist. It's true."

(Sheila is also practical. She calls an attorney. What would happen to her if they broke up? They would split the house; she is earning money from her business. She could leave him.)

Flat-lined marriages can go on for years. With the breakup scene, spouses often become unstuck. When Sheila tells Fred that she wants a divorce, he throws her a curve ball. He acknowledges that he has put up a wall against her. He tells her what a good person she is. He asks her to give him another chance.

But it is too late. Some couples can renegotiate the relationship after many years on separate tracks. The danger in flat-lined marriages is that the emotional deadening has gone on too long. By the time you confront each other, at least one of you has already "left" the marriage. "Once I'd reached the point where I was really ready to go, I couldn't wait to live a life that was really reflective of me," says Sheila. "I knew we could never be good together. It just wasn't going to happen."

Emptiness kills love. A positive jolt—a different job, new friendships, even a romantic crush—shifts your focus to what is possible in the future. In good marriages, positive jolts can be reinvigorating. In empty marriages, they often strike a mortal blow.

✦

The marriage-breaking affair is a cliché for good reason. Generally, there are pole-vaulters and featherbedders. The pole-vaulting affair wakes you up. Sometimes it develops into a deeper bond. Other times, it fades once the initial intensity is over. Or you meet someone else. You need the pole to leap over the wall. And you may go back to your marriage. Whatever the outcome, a pole-vaulting experience shatters the status quo.

The featherbed affair gives you a nice, warm, comforting place to go to once you leave the marriage. These relationships have usually gone on for a while. By the time you officially separate, you have been essentially living with someone else for years in a marriage-like relationship. Without the new relationship, you might not have left your marriage. The problem is that featherbed breakups can lead to very messy (and expensive) divorces in this stage of life.

"If I hadn't met Carol, I would still be married," says Blake Rendel,* 60. A contemplative man who teaches American history at a boys' school in Baltimore, Blake leaves his marriage after thirty years. "We went on in our own way. We had our roles. We sort of let go without examining it," he says. Not like him to let go. He isn't a roamer. He's been a responsible husband and father to their son. His wife, Kitty,* is the flamboyant one. She has become a successful real estate broker. A haughty pretty woman, she enjoys the social whirl of Green Spring Valley in the suburbs. Blake does not. What Blake likes to do is go to the Eastern Shore, to the property his grandfather bought long ago near Ocean City, and get in his boat. Or to Assateague, wandering the sand spit of land and following the wild ponies. "We were leading parallel lives. We were very committed to our professions. We were intersecting mostly with our child." Should the boy go to camp or work in a nursing home? "My wife was the dominant one. She was always making the decisions. I'd say 'okay,' rather than fight it."

He is 55 when he takes a leave of absence from the school after teaching the same course for twenty-five years. He heads to the Eastern Shore with a carload of books to redesign the history curriculum. Kitty comes down from time to time. Off-season isn't so interesting. Blake starts looking like a crusty old fisherman with baggy overalls and a sun-wrinkled face. "We began to drift further and further apart. We were going through the motion of marriage," he says. Yet, they are very bonded after so many years of marriage, starting out so young, making it through ten years of miscarriages before their miracle son is born, encouraging each other's careers, being a popular and successful couple.

Blake doesn't care about social success. He likes hanging out with the fishermen. At a community meeting to debate waterfront development, he meets Carol,* who wears blue jeans and no makeup—a refugee from Washington where she had worked for a senator who lost his seat. She is renting a place not far from him. They talk about politics, about the Chesapeake Bay. They fall into seeing each other. She offers to help Blake draft a letter to Congress about pollution of the bay. "That became a real crutch. Carol was the person I could go to, the person I could talk to," says Blake.

He tells his wife he's met this wonderful person who has invited them to dinner. And Kitty immediately gets suspicious. Being a woman in charge, she delivers Blake an ultimatum: no more meetings with this woman.

Something snaps in Blake with Kitty's ultimatum. His pattern of going along with his wife's decisions abruptly stops. But he does not tell Kitty about this. Instead, he turns to Carol. They go from being friends to lovers; from discussing politics and pollution at the kitchen table to making love in the bedroom.

When it's time to return to school and to Kitty, Blake refuses. The affair explodes. Kitty is furious. She says she would take him back if he ends the affair. "I couldn't say that I was through with Carol," he says. "We went to a counselor. That didn't work. I was mentally out of the marriage." The day comes when he says to his wife: *I'm afraid . . . I don't want you anymore. I don't want to be here anymore.*

It's a tumultuous divorce. Two people are rarely in the same place in the breakup. Kitty is still rooted in the marriage. Their son turns against Blake. His financial resources are drained in the divorce settlement. (Kitty does have a good case against him.) For the one who is left, rejection is compounded by replacement. Blake sees his wife go through a very painful period. The woman who was always in charge collapses physically and emotionally. She develops allergies and leaves her job. It takes her several years to rebuild her life. Blake knows that he has caused a lot of suffering.

"I can't say I ever felt guilty," he says. But there is "reasonable guilt," an honest review of the past and acceptance of responsibility for the heartache caused by divorcing so late in life. "I had screwed up with my son. I had been the one who walked out of the marriage. It was unfair. You can do crazy rationalizations when you're in love with someone else. You say to yourself: better for her not to be married to me. I'm a stick in the mud. But the truth is you've disrupted people's lives. You're not the person they thought you were," he says. "That undermines your self-appreciation."

There is no going back to the old marriage, however. "It wasn't going to work. I didn't want it to work. I burned out on the job. I burned out with my marriage," he says. "Being with Carol was so wonderful. The other was full of dread. There was no fire on the other side. The comparison was there. It took a catalyst to make me aware of it."

In a burned-out marriage, there aren't enough positive elements to rekindle the fire. Relationships in this stage need playfulness, humor, enjoyment. That's what the featherbed relationship provides. Think: How much do you laugh together? A sense of fun is a precious part of love—with a child, with a friend, as well as with a mate. If you shut down in a marriage, you're probably not having a lot of fun. It's a sign that something is not right—with you and/or the relationship.

◆

Sometimes you and your partner are so out of sync that you don't really know when the breakup starts. It is such a long rollout to the separation, you almost miss that it's happened. Only in the aftermath do you unravel the story.

"It was a long-term death," says Josh Edstrom,* 67, of Stamford, Connecticut. There is a kindliness about him, a needy softness. His life was not supposed to work out this way. He is a Dartmouth man. His marriage to Virginia* begins on the high of love at first sight. He is on leave from the Army. Four days after their first date, he asks her to marry him. Ginny replies: "What took you so long?"

He looks dashing in uniform. He has a degree in philosophy. After the Army, he lands a job with a major advertising agency in New York. Along the way, they have four children. "We continued with the normal ups and downs of marriage," he says. A white clapboard house in New Canaan. "We loved entertaining. We loved raising the children." As the oldest approaches college, his wife goes to work. They need the money. First she works in a clinic for at-risk kids in New Canaan. Then she gets a state job in social services and is offered an internship in Hartford. He says okay. His job is getting more difficult. He isn't bringing in the business that is expected of him. He switches to a smaller agency and less money. She gets a promotion. "My career was not going well. Hers was going very well. That created unaddressed tensions," he says.

Unaddressed tensions: a difficult balancing act for couples when the wife overtakes the husband in the workplace and becomes the main breadwinner. But that is a reality for many couples in this stage: husbands—who are generally older—are winding down in the workplace, while wives who may have started work later are now surging ahead. Rationally, you're fine with it. But how do you feel about yourself if you are being supported by your wife? And how does she feel about carrying you?

Josh and Ginny stay off the subject. But thoughts keep gnawing at them: Where is that dashing Dartmouth man? Where is that woman who couldn't wait to marry him? They muddle along until he gets the velvet pink slip: an early-retirement package. He's glad to leave work behind and end the humiliation of dealing with those bottom-line bastards. But now what? He volunteers at church. Ginny nags him about getting his résumé up to date. But he knows he'll never get a high-paying job.

Josh and Ginny are trapped in the out-of-sync retirement quagmire: he is technically retired and she is working. He makes jokes about being unemployed; she withdraws in simmering disappointment.

The gulf between them is exacerbated when Ginny lands the big one: executive director of a private nonprofit foundation in Chicago that supports programs for children. She takes the job . . . and tells Josh not to follow.

"It was devastating," he says. They sell the house. She moves to Chicago and he moves into a condo. "I can't explain it. The separation had occurred," he says. He talks to the kids and gets another shock. They are not surprised. *We think you'll be happier apart, Dad.* "They really accepted that we were separated." He thinks the whole world is crazy.

It takes Josh several years to understand the long unraveling of his marriage: how each clung to an image of the other, but could not accept or even know who they had become—Ginny wanting a dashing tycoon, Josh wanting an adoring supporter. Settling in marriage doesn't mean settling for the status quo of a static or empty relationship. Settling involves accepting the other person as she or he really is—and finding a comfort zone of closeness and pleasure together.

✦

To be "left" is a devastating rejection—whether it's a long marriage or a short romance. But as you review the past, you may see the breakup in a different light. If you are in shock at being "dumped," you may have put on blinders as to what has been going on in the relationship. Perhaps you were more obsessed with your partner's behavior than with your own— more focused on what could be than on what is. You haven't accepted your mate as he or she is (and maybe that person is fatally incapable of deep love). Rather, you've settled into a difficult or vacant relationship.

Two sisters are having their weekly lunch. The younger one, 58, is divorced and involved with a married man. Every week she complains to her older married sister: the guy is selfish, he forgot her birthday, he cancels a weekend. He doesn't seem to hear her when she says: *Are you going to make a commitment to me?* She thinks she'll have to break it off. And then, flowers on Valentine's Day, great sex in a motel room. But after five years of listening to these tales of anguish, the older sister, 61, is fed up with this relationship that she can see is going nowhere.

This lunch is different. The younger woman is sobbing into wads of Kleenex, then shaking a knife in rage. The guy has dumped her. Bam! What a shock! How could he do this? She replays the video of the breakup scene. More tears, more anger. After a while, her sister says: *You're just mad you didn't break up with him first.*

The splash of cold reality.

You may be shocked when a relationship ends, but once you process the experience, you're not so surprised. Disappointed, angry, saddened— yes. But so are most people confronting loss. In time, it matters less who initiates the break. More important is what you learned and how you move on.

In the heat of breaking up, the history of a relationship gets rewritten. Sometimes it takes years to retrieve the memory of love and commitment. But in time—and you have time—you gain perspective. You remember falling in love at first sight, the vacation in Colorado. You may have children and grandchildren together. Sharon Kalemkarian tells her clients who are getting divorced: "You are going to be at each other's deathbed." Indeed, when photojournalist Dith Pran, survivor of Cambodia's Killing Fields, was dying at age 65 of pancreatic cancer, his first wife was by his bedside, bringing him rice noodles in his last weeks.

What endures is the legacy of the relationship. Everyone you have ever loved becomes part of you. Even the ones you come to hate. They didn't just hurt you. They loved you and you loved them.

7

Romantic Adventures

You know what falling in love feels like: the pull in the stomach, the tingling in the arms and lips, the fluttering in the lungs. You remember those moments of youth: the obsessive longing, the wild bouts of fantasy. Whether the romance lasted for a night or launched a fifty-year relationship, the experience stays with you forever.

Then it happens again. You've got crow's-feet around your eyes, an extra inch or two around your waist. Cupid's Arrow still finds it mark. How could this be? You are hardly a teenager. Yet you feel like one. This is what the French call a *coup de foudre*—a bolt of lightning—out of the blue: BAM! And at your age! History has a few names for you: *dirty old man ... merry widow.* The social grapevine gets to work. *You must be demented. ... Certainly you look foolish.* Adult children get worried—and protective. *Has Mom lost it? Is Dad being taken for a ride?*

Longevity is opening up a whole new culture of romantic adventures for older men and women. There is more opportunity to pursue different kinds of relationships. It's also a time to review old loves and ponder the role of romance in your life.

You think it's all about the other person. But the real source of passion is within you. "Love arises from within ourselves as an imaginative act," writes Columbia University psychiatrist Ethel S. Person in her groundbreaking book: *Dreams of Love and Fateful Encounters: The Power of Romantic Passion*. Love "aims to fulfill our deepest longings and our oldest dreams, that allows us both to renew and transform ourselves."[1]

The imperative of living longer is renewal. For many, love is an agent of transformation. You can love in many ways. You may be in a thirty-plus-year marriage, or in a new relationship. You may be staring into the face of a newborn grandchild. Or entering a different phase of love with a grown child. Or rediscovering an old friend. Or going to church. You find renewal through love in all its forms.

The classic *coup* is a distinct experience: overpowering, ecstatic—and temporary. A *coup* can metamorphose into attachment, stumble into friendship, turn into hate, or dissipate. Science tells you that the infatuation phase lasts from about eighteen months to three years.[2] The intensity of a *coup* is matched by its mystery: Why do you fall in love *when* you do? It feels so spontaneous.

For older men and women, the answer is found in the link between love and loss. As Person explains, people tend to fall in love after they experience loss or are separated from the familiar. Teenagers fall in love as they "lose" childhood and separate from their parents. Shipboard romances flourish, and so do conference flirtations and travel trysts, because people are away from home—they have "lost" their moorings. Wartime love explodes in the urgent shadow of separation and death.

Longevity creates another kind of urgent shadow. This period that promises vitality to many men and women is also a time of losses. Death and disease are constant realities. Your readiness to develop new relationships is often in response to mounting losses. As you get older, there is a

---

1. Ethel S. Person, *Dreams of Love and Fateful Encounters: The Power of Romantic Passion* (American Psychiatric Publishing, Inc., 2006), p. 31.

2. In particular, note the research carried out by psychologist Dorothy Tennov at the University of Bridgeport, Connecticut, which is written up in *Love and Limerence: The Experience of Being in Love* (Scarborough House, 1999). Tennov found that the duration from the moment subjects fell in love to the moment when they began to feel more neutral about the love object was most often between eighteen months and three years.

reduction in hormonal drive but an increase in losses, which sets the stage for connecting with others.

It's glorious to know that you are never too old to fall in love. And wise to remember that you are never too old to fall apart in love. Maybe you aren't thinking too straight right now. You live in the moment. Colors are sharper. You're more attractive; smarter, wittier. You don't eat. You wait for the phone to ring—you pick up the phone and call. You take the chance. The Nike ad speaks to the swelling generation of older lovers: *Just Do It!*

At the end of a two-hour lunch, she looks at him and says: "Do you think you'd be ready yet for dinner parties?" It has been a year since his wife died. Bob Butler,[3] physician, author, and godfather of gerontology, looks at her and says: "Yes, I think so."

And so begins the transforming experience of falling in love. "I really had no interest" in finding someone, says Bob. "It was out of the blue!" One dinner leads to another and another. Soon they are enmeshed. The deep sorrow and depression that embraced him after his wife's death begin to lift. He is smiling again. Making jokes. The twinkle is back in his eye.

Falling in love at 80 is reminiscent of falling in love at 18. "There's excitement and admiration," he says. There is an intense desire "to get to know the person." At the same time, there is the feeling that you already know the loved one—that you are soul mates. "I think I know her quite well. She is very open. Very direct," he says.

It is a new life for Bob. But the difference between having a *coup* at 80 and having one at 18 is the weight of the past. Bob's regeneration in new love is rooted in old love. Unlike teenagers, you bring a rich and complex past to a new relationship. In many people, losses soften a rigid heart and

---

3. Robert N. Butler is also president and CEO of the International Longevity Center in New York and founding director of the National Institute on Aging. In 1982, he started the first department of geriatrics in a U.S. medical school at New York's Mount Sinai Medical Center. He is the author of *The Longevity Revolution: The Benefits and Challenges of Living a Long Life* (PublicAffairs, 2008) and the Pulitzer Prize–winning *Why Survive? Being Old in America* (Harper & Row, 1975; Johns Hopkins Paperbacks, 2002).

deepen the capacity to love. For older men and women, loving anew is an alchemy of love lost and love gained.

Bob looks back on his long marital narrative: A first marriage that ended in divorce. A second marriage to psychotherapist and social worker Myrna Lewis "was made in heaven," he says. When Bob and Myrna met in Washington in the early 1970s, he was a divorced father of three. They worked on a book together on mental health and aging, and after a few years of courtship, they married and had a daughter. "She was miraculous at forging the blended family," he says. Professionally and emotionally they grow together. Myrna earned a PhD at age 62 and built up a thriving practice on women and aging. They were co-authors of *The New Love and Sex After 60.*

They were separated only by age. Myrna was more than a decade younger. In their marriage, when Bob thought about death, he figured he would go first. But fate intervened. Myrna was diagnosed with an aggressive brain tumor and died seventeen months later at age 67. "I could hardly stand it. It was just awful. I was determined to find the best care," he says. "I was a little bit in denial. I had the feeling we could somehow beat this thing. We whistled in the dark." Myrna continued her therapy practice. She wanted to do international relief work. They went to the theater. They went to restaurants. They saw friends. But dying was in the atmosphere. They would sit side by side in the evening. "I'd rub her feet until I could not rub them anymore." As the future vanished, they focused on the moment.

Bob and his daughter cling to each other in the cataclysm of loss. After Myrna's death, grief overwhelms them. Bob plunges in to write a book on longevity; his daughter plunges in to write a memoir of her mother. They write and sob together. For many months, writing and sobbing. The two of them, bound together in sorrow, transforming their loss by writing about it, each in a different way.

And then Cupid intervenes. "Out of the blue," Bob repeats.

Perhaps it takes the thunderbolt to make you receptive to new love. It's an instinctive, physiological process rather than a conscious decision. In a long life, you grow accustomed to the alternating faces of love and loss.

Wisdom comes alone through suffering, in the words of Aeschylus. Bob has earned his wisdom and is ready to love again.

Another part of the mystery is *who* you fall for. Chemistry and physical attraction are perennial forces. Sexuality fuels desire and desire can empower love. But the other big draw in this stage is commonality—shared values and common interests. While younger people seek novelty in romance, older men and women look for familiarity.

Bob falls in love with a lively attractive woman who is similar in political views, similar in social values. They admire each other. They are also about the same age. As a result, they quickly develop a bond of shared memories. They remember gas rationing during World War II and the first black-and-white television sets. They know the songs in *My Fair Lady*. They have witnessed with the same eye the advent of the modern world, its burst of innovation and cornucopia of benefits, as well as its tragedies.

Shared memory reinforces the sensation of being soul mates. Couples who have been together for many decades have a built-in memory box of shared experiences from the wondrous birth of a child to the terrible Thanksgiving when Aunt Marcia threw a drumstick at her drunken husband. New couples have to create a memory box that can sustain the relationship over the next decades. In finding common threads in your separate pasts, each of you brings a dowry or treasury of shared experiences to support the new union. Where were you when *Apollo 11* landed on the moon? "This is shared memory," says Bob. "It's cultural. It's historical. It's shared experience, shared people, shared music." Shared memory holds "the significance of life," says Bob.

You want a partner who truly knows you. That is an advantage of finding someone of similar age who shares your historical trajectory—because there is not that much time left to build up a memory bank. In youth, you meld visions of the future. In this stage, you also join pasts.

✦

Sometimes, new love starts slowly. History has made you wary. There can be less emotional intensity and more congeniality, less turmoil and more comfort, less obsessive urgency and more confidence. It can be the kind of love that arises out of friendship, out of the slow knowing of each other rather than instant passion. It has a softer rhythm—and sometimes a surer outcome.

My friend Becky Lescaze remarries at age 56. It starts with a blind lunch date. And then another lunch and another. "We weren't ready to be intimate with each other right away," she says. That day would come, but they take their time.

Becky has suffered in the course of loving: a glamorous first marriage that ends in divorce when her husband leaves her. And then the death of their son from injuries in a car crash. Her grief is raw and palpable. After the marriage breakup, she is single for almost fifteen years—raising two daughters, working as an editor for *National Geographic*, cementing friendships, exploring new relationships. But she is very cautious about falling in love again.

Becky remembers how her first marriage started with a *coup*. Her husband was a journalist of great charm, warmth, and talent. Three months after they met, he proposed. Two months later they got married and went to Vietnam, where he made his name covering the war. Everyone said they were so much in love. But the romantic high is lost after the initial wave of passion gives way to the realities of raising small children. Becky loses herself in the crumbling relationship. What happened to that smart, sexy woman who fell in love with a dashing foreign correspondent? Starting a marriage that way ultimately led to a shutdown of herself and finally to her abandonment. She is not going to do that again.

Step by step, she gets to know this new and engaging man who grew up on a farm in Iowa and is a specialist in Asian politics and economics. Mark Borthwick is several years younger, divorced with a young son. When he hears about Becky from a mutual friend, he wants to meet her. She has space in her heart torn open by loss. His son is about the age her son was when he died five years earlier. Mark and Becky make lunch a habit. And dinner. They travel together. The flood of excitement takes hold of them. If they are to marry, his son would live with them. Some 50-

plus women might balk at taking care of a 10-year-old child. But for Becky, it is a blinding click of connection. As Mark says: her son brought them together.

After a two-year courtship, Becky and Mark get married. On a very deep level, helping Mark raise his son opens a way for her to share the memory of her son with him on a daily basis. Through their sons, one in memory, the other in their home, the emotional links between them grow tighter. The years go by: the weddings of her daughters, the death of his mother and then the death of hers, the graduation of his son, the births of grandchildren. They celebrate their twelfth wedding anniversary.

It is a slower, surer pace of passion that allows Becky and Mark to fall in love more firmly, more deeply. That allows her to let her heart go and not to be afraid anymore. That makes it easy to light up at the sound of his voice, to feel secure in the soft look in his eye.

There are many routes to a loving relationship in the Indian Summer of life. You can fall fast or slow. You are guided by previous experience, so it helps to understand your personal history in love—the heartbreak as well as the joy. Wisdom gained from suffering often points the way to how and who you love again. The goal is not speed or dazzle, but depth in a meaningful romance.

◆

Older lovers may be just as star-crossed as younger Romeos and Juliets. Yet, a situation that would have been untenable in youth may be possible now. New love in old age often has a forbidden edge.

Cindy Wells,[*4] 84, confides in her daughter . . . there's a man in her life. Cindy has been a widow for five years. In the exchange of sympathy notes and Christmas cards, she reconnects with a friend she and her husband knew decades ago. Cindy lives in St. Louis. He lives in Atlanta. The throwback romance develops with letters, phone calls. And then he comes to visit her. They take the tram ride to the top of the Gateway Arch

---

4. Throughout the chapter, asterisks indicate that names, identifying details, and some events have been changed.

over the Mississippi River. They go to the Mardi Gras casino and she wins $150 at blackjack. She brings him back to her apartment and they make love. As she tells her daughter: *"I went to the moon and back. I never knew it could be like this before."*

To the moon and back. Her daughter stares at her—her fluffy white hair, her graceful hands. Her daughter is married with two children in high school. She tries to take this in: *the moon.* Her mother! In love at 84! As the story unfolds, her daughter realizes that the future is not to be theirs. The man is married. His wife is ailing, with a dementia that has robbed her of consciousness. She is pulling away from him, no longer recognizing him, not even his voice. He would never leave her. He is loyal to the woman he's been with for more than fifty years. Yet, he has fallen in love with Cindy and Cindy has fallen in love with him. They talk on the phone every day.

"I think they are having phone sex," says the daughter, somewhat bewildered but also in awe of her mother. *The moon* . . . to experience that for the first time in your 80s! Her mother has a glow in her cheek. Her father's photograph remains on the table in the living room, along with photographs of children and grandchildren.

Cindy and her lover meet in secret. The fact that they cannot marry doesn't bother Cindy the way it would have if she were young and ready to start a family. She was raised to be a good girl, and for more than fifty years she was a good wife and mother. She has paid her debt to society, and so has he. Now it's *their time* to be together as best they can. They reinterpret the old rules.

Cindy explains all this to her daughter. She wants her daughter to understand this bolt of love, this gift of ecstasy that has finally come to her. She wants her not to be judgmental of her "illicit" love affair. How different the culture of romance is in this time of life, she says.

Her daughter understands.

✦

Romantic adventures have a dark side, too. The potential for heartbreak is part of the *coup's* flaming intensity. You see the destructive power of passionate obsession in friends and colleagues. You may worry about it with an adult child. You read about it in Proust. You've probably experienced it yourself—the crushes of old, a calamitous romance or two, a fatal flirtation.

When you're older you don't have as much time to recover from a fatal *coup*. But here you are, about to receive Social Security and behaving like a lovesick puppy.

She knows it is wrong by the standards she was brought up with, but she can't stop. She is 53 and has inherited a broken-down cabin in the Minnesota woods from her mother. Her second marriage has ended, and she feels adrift. She decides to fix up the cabin, an escape from her job in New York. She hires a local contractor who also manages the hardware store. He is married with children. "There was all this attraction between us and I hadn't felt anything like that for a long time and I thought: *well, I'll just let him kiss me,*" she begins. "And then it became much more. . . . I mean he's just an incredibly attractive guy. I remember thinking: *this is so wonderful; I know I'm going to have to pay.*"

What is it—"his unavailability, but he was also a really nice guy," she says. "It got out of hand. . . . We tried to break it off and we couldn't and then he couldn't stand up to his wife." Instead he lets his wife find out, and it becomes a public scandal in the small town. In retrospect, it seems to her that he used the relationship to get his wife's attention. "A major heartbreak. It hurt me so badly."

But longevity brings a measure of tolerance. About five years later she makes friends with another man in the town, a retired schoolteacher. On their first date, she says to him: *"Look, I want you to hear the story from me. . . ."* He smiles. After all, he's had a few *coups*, too. The two start seeing each other. It's the beginning of a longer-lasting love.

Another danger is recidivism. At this point you know that falling in love is a prelude to something else, hopefully a deeper relationship. Perhaps, without realizing it, all you really want is prelude. You're stuck on the high of a *coup*. When things get too routine, you get edgy for a hit. Again and again all through your life.

Charlie Bremmel,* 74, is slowing down. He has a reputation. Four marriages, countless romances, children with different wives. *Play with him, don't fall in love with him,* chants his Greek Chorus of friends and family in Georgia. He's always loved women. He knows how to make them happy. He knows how to feed them in the beginning to get them to fall in love with him; he knows how to water them to keep them on the side. Sometimes he gets involved and doesn't really know why. *What am I doing at Disney World with this woman and her children?* Sometimes it's a challenge flirtation—can he score? Sometimes he's just lonely and she's there.

There are plenty of women to choose from. That's the male advantage. Among those over 65 who are widowed, divorced, or separated, there are about 10.7 million women compared to 3.5 million men. For Charlie, playing the mating game is like being in a candy store.

But he wants a wife. His knees are shot. Who will take him in for his doctor's appointment next week? He owns a landscape nursery. He enjoys planting trees, especially evergreens: Juniper Spartan, Southern Balsam, Cedar Green Giant. Long-lasting, he thinks. He wants a long-lasting woman. And so he falls in love. It's been fifteen years since he flipped over a woman like this. She is a perfect match, he says. Over the wall he leaps into another marriage.

Two things can happen in this stage of life. Either you mellow out and break the passion-seeking habit. Indeed, energy and libido wane with age—you're more likely to stick with your partner. Or you keep repeating the pattern. You remain a passion addict.

The rebound *coup* is another danger—especially if your losses are laced with rejection. Your spouse dumps you. You are pushed out of the workplace. The children ignore you. Your shoulder freezes up. You're 60 years old and down. One risk is that you get stuck in a rut of bitterness and regret. The other is you let Cupid do your dirty work. You fall in love and avoid mourning your losses.

Gilbert ("Bert") Sawyer* of Hightstown, New Jersey, gets the double boot. He loses his job reviewing claims for an auto insurance company.

Then his wife leaves him. He is unemployed and alone. He thinks about driving a cab. Instead, he hangs out at the watering hole for politicians and government workers in Trenton. Good talk, good laughs. Some good male bonding in the bar, he says.

He also gets in touch with Nina,* his wife's best friend in Baltimore, the godmother to their daughter. *"We could see this coming,"* says Nina, who is divorced after a twenty-five-year marriage. Nina has done all kinds of therapy and spiritual retreats; she encourages him to talk. *"How could I have been so blind,"* he cries. Nina comforts him. He falls madly in love with her—a real *coup.* "It was immediate," he says. "Terrific sex."

Now, he's got some confidence back. He's also got some leverage with his departed wife. After some months on her own, she suggests that they try to get back together. But he's in love with Nina! What better way to settle the score with his wife? To get back his pride, his dignity. He is too kind to be overtly nasty. "It just happened," he says to his wife. *Out of the blue!* She is outraged. Who is leaving whom? The marital battlefield gets leveled and the march to divorce speeds up.

All through the breakup with his wife, Nina is his romantic solution. Nine months into the new relationship, Nina suggests that he get some counseling. Bit of a shock; things are going so well, aren't they? Bert asks Nina to marry him. "I was convinced she was right for me," he says. A few days after he proposes they have a big fight. He gives Nina advice on how to deal with her 28-year-old son, who doesn't have a real job and sponges off her. She blows up and ends the relationship. "I had overstepped the boundaries. She wanted me to leave," he says. He's a little bewildered. He carries the torch for a year. When his divorce becomes final, he calls Nina and invites her to visit him; maybe they'd go to Atlantic City. "No, Bert. It's not going to work," she replies.

The *coup* is over. The marriage is over. It takes the breakup of a short romance to force him to come to terms with the end of a long marriage.

A *coup* can give you a needed break. Maybe you're just too beaten down by a cascade of blows to cope right now. Falling in love builds up your strength and fires your imagination. But it is not necessarily going to lead to permanent love. Yet, even when romances end in heartbreak, they leave a lasting imprint on your life. You can learn from them. They are part of your intimate education.

◆

Sometimes it takes a *coup* to wake you up.

Maria Jackson* speaks with a soft Spanish accent from her childhood in Peru, where she was the daughter of a businessman. Her parents divorce when she is 6. At age 18, with no real home of her own, she is sent to New Orleans to Newcomb College. Her contact is the family of her father's business associate: the Jacksons. They live in a large house in the Garden District. Mrs. Jackson is from Biloxi, a grand old broken-down Southern family with all the charm, gradations of mental illness, and sense of entitlement typical of American gentry. She gathers into the living room a constant parade of cousins and connections. Mr. Jackson leads debates at the dining room table: Watergate—burglary or treason! The noise level is high with much argument and laughter, along with bowls of gumbo.

Maria falls in love with the family. The Jacksons represent what she lacks: a large loving family, secure in the social establishment, where sorrow is covered up by a code of optimism and constant celebration. Maria is pretty with her almond-shaped brown eyes. At age 21, she marries the second son. "I was madly in love with him," she says.

But when he dies of colon cancer after thirty-five years of marriage, she is not devastated. She is numb. As she explains later, she had shut down long ago. "I had run out of steam. I had run out of energy. I just didn't care that much," she says. At the funeral she wears a trim black suit and Cole Haan black patent-leather heels. She keeps her hair jet black. All the Jacksons are there—more scattered these days, less sure of themselves but just as warm and boisterous as always. One of Maria's sons is in Los Angeles, the other in Washington. She decorates the living room with pink-and-white azaleas and brings out a white linen tablecloth from more prosperous times. She greets the guests . . . and then she spots him:

Jacques Boulang,* the college roommate of her husband's brother, a scholarship boy from Lafayette. How they all used to laugh together. Mrs. Jackson had pegged him as someone who would go far in life.

Lightning strikes somewhere between the cocktail shrimp in the living room and the gumbo in the dining room. "There was an attraction. I never forgot it. Somehow he had this power," she says. He is skinny with black eyes; his hair is bushy and gray. When he leaves, he squeezes her shoulder, says he'll call, check in to make sure she's all right. A week goes by. She drives her sons to the airport. Another week, then another. Every time the phone rings, she thinks it might be him.

Six months later, he calls her. How are you? What are you doing? He tells her he owns a trucking company. Maria recalls Mrs. Jackson's words: Jacques—a winner! Please stop by when you're in town, she says. Next week? Maria's heart is pounding. She adorns Jacques with magical properties—handsome, successful, bright, sexy. Just talking to him makes her feel like the bubbly girl who dazzled the Jacksons with her foreign accent, her romantic turn of phrase—oh, the little notes she used to write as a young bride.

He pulls up in an eighteen-wheeler. What's going on? *"I own a trucking company. Actually I own one truck and I drive it,"* he says with a laugh, that racy laugh. He walks toward her . . . and stays the weekend. "It was like a dream come true. The weather was perfect. The house and the yard were perfect," she says. He tells her: *"When I walked in the front door I felt I had come home."*

In the rush of romance, reality is suspended. They are young again, free and in love. There's no question, she tells her sons, this was meant to be. *Awfully quick, Mom,* they chant. Yes, but. When you get to this age, you don't waste time. The days are caught up in a swirl of plans. Jacques has asked her to come on a truck run from New Orleans to Los Angeles.

"I drove with him for two weeks," she says, a glorious adventure, taking showers at truck stops with marble bathrooms, "no different from traveling by stagecoach," she says. The truck has leather seats, a double bed, microwave, sink. "It was very comfortable. We talked the whole time. I had so much fun. It was like being on a safari. Beautiful. Go to bed at six or seven, get up and drive at 1 A.M. Breakfast in the dark at some truck stop. I had him all those hours a day. I thought: We were an amazing combination. Our values were similar. Our personalities meshed. It seemed fine."

A week after the trip he sells the truck and tells her: *"I'm going to come and live with you."*

Maria is taken aback. "In my heart, I didn't like that idea," she says. "He didn't have any money. He lost it to his wife in the divorce. I knew this is not a good thing." But she says to herself: he's a winner. Somehow, it escapes her that his nostrils are red and beer is his constant companion. Instead, she is determined to make the man bloom. She buys bright-yellow napkins to cheer up the kitchen when they have breakfast and a new set of fancy sage-green striped sheets for when they make love in bed. "Everything should have been wonderful, but it wasn't," she says.

Sex stops. After such a passionate beginning, nothing. He explains that he needs to find a job first. She doesn't really buy that, but she swallows her thoughts. "I'll do it his way," she says, "see how it goes." When it doesn't go anywhere, she asks him: *"Why aren't we having mad sex the way we did in the truck?"*

The answer unravels the dream: *"Oh, I wasn't in love with you then,"* he replies. Not in love with her? She stares at him. How to explain it? He likes sex on the trashy side. The Madonna-whore syndrome. Out of the truck and in the house, she's someone to admire, but not to touch. *"I want to be your whore,"* she tells him. He shrinks away from her. He cares about her, cares a lot about her, he says; that's the problem. He gets another beer.

Reality breaks through. The winner who graduated in the top of his class has become a self-made loser. He has a drinking problem, a cocaine problem. He has no job, no purpose. He retains a certain swagger—a remnant of his having once been a successful man. But he knows he can't live up to the person Maria has fallen in love with. His body knows that and so does his wavering libido.

The *coup* is over. "This is never going to get better. Even though my heart and soul loved that man—much as I loved him—he could not stay here," she says. He packs up a few things. He says: *I love you*. She says: *I love you*. "He left. I cried all that day."

How could she have made such a mistake? She wakes up from her psychological slumber. Alone now, she can see the pattern. After the loss of her homeland, she falls in love with her husband. The *coup* is her pass back into the Garden of Eden with the Jackson family where everything is possible and everyone is adored. In her marriage, when she is inevitably thrown out of the Garden—there's no going back to the Garden of Eden: to be human is to be thrown out of the mythical womb—she shuts down. The fluttering excitement she once felt for her husband becomes a choking sensation in her throat. After the death of her husband, she uses the *coup* as a pass again: this time with Jacques and his steamy swagger and throwback link to the Jacksons.

She has no model in her parents of an enduring or satisfying relationship. How to go beyond the *coup* and forge a deeper bond that allows loving and hating all at once in the tangle of attachment—the double mix of fury and anguish, longing and delight, boredom and respect, forgetfulness and forgiveness? For decades, she's been stuck in the swept-away scene, another way to sleepwalk in a relationship.

The Jacques disaster blasts her psyche open. That changes the way she looks back on her past—and what she does in the future. First she rewrites in her own mind the story of her marriage. She remembers how one side of her husband's mouth would pull back in a smile, how he could imitate every kind of Southern accent from Charleston to Beaumont. After so many years together, they had a bond. She begins to mourn the loss of her husband. Who was he really? Who was she? Who were they? She finds patches of warmth and pleasure. She reminisces to the boys—*remember when we took the trip down the Mississippi?*

Slowly Maria rebuilds her life with less fantasy and more humor. She goes to Peru and visits the apartment building in Lima where she grew up. She connects with some distant cousins and with the musicality of the Spanish language. When she returns to New Orleans, she feels lighter. Her friendships deepen. Her links with the Jackson clan become easier, tighter. She dances at the wedding of her older son. She takes a course in interior design. She is 61 and feeling good. Perhaps she'll go online and see who might be out there.

A catastrophic love affair is like a healthy forest fire: it can clear out deadwood and choking underbrush so that new life can grow. It is a high-risk awakening. You have to pay attention to the reality clues coming from the loved one—and guard against making fatal decisions.

✦

As you review the past, you can probably point to half a dozen major *coups:* some before marriage and, if you've been married many decades, maybe a few during marriage. A man, 68, married for more than forty years, tells me: "It's amazing how you can find yourself attracted to others. That's all I have to say about that." As a safety net around your marriage, you may keep the *coups* free of sexual involvement, protected from becoming a threatening affair. You remain attached to your spouse. But the obsessive intensity in a new relationship is significant.

A 64-year-old professor of music at a conservatory has been married to a chemist for thirty-five years: "I love my husband," she says. "Our love has grown over the years. But I have never been in love with him. I've been in love about five times in my life—two times after I was married." Her most recent *coup* is with another musician a decade younger. "He lives on the piano," she says, "not in the real world." She is careful not to cross the sexual line and they become friends. Her other coup occurred fifteen years earlier with a colleague who was married. "We were soul mates," she says. They stop just short of intercourse. Instead, with both *coups*, she channels passion into her music—all that mysterious, wondrous, transcendent power of being in love is given over to creativity.

She can separate the in-love experience of *coups* from the attachment experience of marriage. Not like people in conflicted or flat-lined marriages who are awakened to the possibilities of a meaningful relationship by a *coup*. She points out that the amount of energy and turmoil it would have taken to break up her marriage—and the harm she would have done others—would have been too much: (a) the love object was not good marriage material; (b) she had a good marriage; (c) she would have missed out on the creative boost from a "pure" *coup*. What's more, the chaste *coups* have become long-lasting friendships. And the *coups'* sensuous awakenings have made her sex life better with her husband, she adds.

Not everybody can make such a clear distinction between a *coup* and attachment. Falling in love is an involuntary act. But how you respond to the *coup* is voluntary. In a long life, you learn that there are many different ways to respond, and you are better able to navigate choices in the gray zone of nuance. As you review those romances before marriage, you see how they now fit into the narrative of your love life. It's a way to gain mastery over this involuntary, irrational aspect of love.

◆

For many long-married couples, how they fell in love becomes their marital "creation myth." Every relationship has its own love story, sometimes moving slowly, sometimes rapidly. You turn to the story in crisis and celebrate it at family reunions. The way you were when you started out often bears little resemblance to the present. The quiet girl now runs her own insurance agency. The high school track star gets arthritic knees. Yet part of you is securely fixed in a distant time when faces were smooth and bodies were limber. You remember how you met, what you wore, who said what.

Memory is creative. People in long marriages cherish their love story. People who get divorced tend to say there were problems from the beginning. Certainly, in the pursuit of love, "mistakes are made." You want to clarify the story of romance so that it fits with the longer narrative of your intimate history. If you've been married many decades, you keep refreshing the story so that it remains an essential part of the current relationship.

Gordon and Sharon Bower[5] meet in 1952 at a summer camp for citizenship in New York City—two of about a hundred college students

---

5. Gordon and Sharon Bower live in Stanford, California. Gordon won the Presidential National Medal of Science in 2007 for "his unparalleled contributions to cognitive and mathematical psychology." Sharon is president of Confidence Training, Inc., and has written three books, including *Asserting Yourself: A Practical Guide for Positive Change* (Da Capo Press, 1991), which she co-authored with Gordon.

drawn from across the country to study grassroots democracy. Both are 19. They arrive at the welcome mixer and lock eyes across the room. Gordon is a baseball pitcher, tall and sinewy, with aspirations for professional baseball, studying at Case Western Reserve University on an athletic scholarship. Sharon is an actress attending a small Minnesota college. She's a Norwegian blond—very blond. "I saw him. He saw me," she recalls. He walks over to her; then they role-play one of those cool 1950s movie scenes:

He: *"Where did you get the peroxide bottle?"*
She: *"Why don't you stick around and find out."*

After all, they have grown up on the sarcastic, snappy repartee of Humphrey Bogart and Lauren Bacall.

Bogart: *"What's wrong with you?"*
Bacall: *"Nothing you can't fix."*

Baseball Pitcher meets Minnesota Actress. Gordon comes to her Minnesota hometown during summers and pitches for the St. Peter Saints semi-pro baseball team. Following the college-students' script of the 1950s, they write hundreds of love letters throughout a five-year, long-distance courtship. In this pre-email ritual of correspondence, they share dreams and reveal personalities, before they eventually marry. "Our behaviors were controlled by traditional scripts—we never lived together until we got married. But there were many exchanges of plaintive, yearning letters," says Sharon.

Fifty-two years. Three children, five grandchildren. Long dual careers, many adjustments. Gordon doesn't become a professional baseball player; Sharon doesn't go off to Broadway. He becomes a leading experimental psychologist in a forty-eight-year career as a professor of psychology at Stanford University. She becomes a counseling psychologist and uses her theater background to develop programs for training assertiveness, public speaking, and legal testifying. Now, both are retiring, heading into the churn of uncertainty and change. As Sharon says: "We have to decide: What are we going to do with all this free time? We've never had to decide that before—previously, our jobs and family determined what we had to do."

They keep returning to that crowded room in New York where they first locked eyes. "Even today a strong attraction pulls us toward one another. As in a time warp, Gordon remembers me as his 'Aspiring Minnesota Actress' and I remember him as my 'Powerful Baseball Pitcher,'" says Sharon.

"I am now more than an aspiring actress and he is far more than a baseball prospect," Sharon continues. But they remember each other enshrined in nostalgic memory. "While we know we're not the people we used to be, we carry each other's history, and we can't imagine a better 'Field of Dreams.'"

The glow of the *coup* has been transformed into shared memories. In a long marriage, spouses bear witness to each other's personal development. No one else knows them so deeply or remembers in so much detail the way they were. For the Bowers, their story of origin has always been an emotional magnet that keeps them attracted to each other. Sharon uses certain images to glide over the rough spots. Just remembering what he looked like at 19—or what he wrote in his first love letter—trumps momentary displeasure. The marriage evolves into deep attachment and mutual engagement. "We now find it hard to imagine life without each other. We can get irritated, we can get mad, maybe even embarrassed, but we never get disappointed with one another," she says.

When the children are 6, 8, and 11, Sharon returns to graduate school to earn a master's degree in counseling psychology—with Gordon's enthusiastic support. "Unlike husbands who wanted stay-at-home wives, Gordon encouraged me to develop this second career. He was my cheerleader. He got our young children 'onboard' in supporting my decision," says Sharon.

Their independent growth and shared parenting have been as essential to their relationship as their passionate connection. "Our marriage matured as Sharon developed her own business and could have supported herself and our children independently," says Gordon. "I realized we were freely choosing to be together because of love, not because of financial insecurity. The framing of that old marriage script was revised. We were together simply to enjoy the pleasure of each other's company."

The aspiring actress and promising baseball pitcher have come a long way. They agree: "We're both still crazy about each other—still in love," says Sharon. It takes imagination and effort to stay on the daily road of a marriage. "At heart, we are both romantics and there's nothing better than seeing each other's smiles and feeling that a warm hug can last all day— only to be repeated thousands of times through the years, no matter how we feel at the moment." The warm hug no matter what can protect a marriage. "Just do it!" says Sharon. "Carry on! Go for it! Life has a way of rewarding the effort and the caring and the holding back of those spur-of-the-moment, angry flashes."

"Most of all, we've been just plain lucky to have found each other when we were so young and unformed. We've had time and opportunities to help each other develop fulfilling lives," says Gordon.

Sharon and Gordon know they are in the mortality zone. News of friends and colleagues struck down by a fatal injury or terminal illness reminds them of life's fragility. "Every time I see Gordon carry a cup of coffee across the living room to his home office, I think: life can change in an instant," says Sharon. "That terrifying thought makes me cherish even more the opportunities we have had to revise and complete our history together. It's a gift to have one relationship for such a long time."

Holding on to your love story is a way to rekindle romantic energy— in yourself and in your relationships. The *coup* may be long gone, but the memory lingers on . . . and expands. It generates the spark of renewal as time goes by.

8

New Normal

By the time people reach 50, most are following one of two main pathways: the track of a long relationship with one spouse or the multi-track of sequential relationships with different partners.

The two tracks can go in very different directions—with different risks, rewards, achievements, and regrets. But what is amazing is the common ground between one-track couples and multi-track serial spouses. Both pathways are based on the same intimate contract of commitment. The same principles of ebb and flow. The same culture of kinship.

Barbara Probst Solomon[1] of New York City and Helen Dennis of Los Angeles live on opposite coasts. Their vital statistics are similar: Both are widows. Each was married only once. Each has two daughters and grandchildren. They both have careers: Barbara is an author, essayist, and journalist; Helen is a specialist in gerontology.

---

1. In 2007, Barbara Solomon received the United Nations/Women Together Award—for her commitment to her work and her "devotion to making the world a better place," in the words of the award. She taught for many years as a member of the Graduate Writing Faculty at Sarah Lawrence College and has been a visiting professor at the International University Menendez Pelayo in Spain. She is also the United States Cultural Correspondent of El Pais and editor in chief of the literary journal *The Reading Room*.

But they have taken different marital pathways—Helen, the track of one long relationship with her husband; Barbara, the track of a sequence of meaningful relationships.

Helen grows up in Lansdale, Pennsylvania, about thirty miles north of Philadelphia. Her parents fled Germany in the mid-1930s to escape Hitler. Helen, born in 1940, is the first in her family to be born in the United States. There are only about 100 other Jewish families in the Pennsylvania town of about 10,000 where the Mennonites and Amish flourish and Blue Laws order daily life. "For me it was a great growing up. I never felt like a minority," she says. Her parents work in a factory making raincoats. Her father then starts a furniture business. Her mother works for her father. He is autocratic, rigid, and entrepreneurial. "He could sell anything," says Helen. Even candy. "I remember weighing jelly beans to put in packages to sell at Easter."

She inherits the family's work ethic and drive for success: good grades at school, lots of friends. After graduating from Penn State, she lives with an aunt in Philadelphia and works in a psychiatric research department at the University of Pennsylvania. She meets her future husband on a blind date set up by a friend of her aunt's. It doesn't sound too promising, she recalls, but she goes to visit her aunt's friend and his wife in Baltimore. The man is involved in Republican politics and the blind date is to go to the inaugural ball of Maryland governor J. Millard Tawes. Her date is a neighbor, Lloyd Dennis, who is working the police beat at the *Baltimore Sun*. She and Lloyd literally dance all night. (She dances with the governor, too.) After the ball, she goes back to his apartment. "We did nothing but talk until 2:30 A.M.," she says.

It is not a bolt-of-lightning kind of love. In fact, Helen has never had a *coup de foudre* of madly and instantly falling in love, she says. She likes Lloyd—his angular face, his strong features. "There was a simpatico. We talked about our families. He had the Walter Lippmann test; he didn't want to date any woman who did not know who Walter Lippmann was. I guess I passed the test. I tried to turn the tables and talk about artists," she says. Later on, the Walter Lippmann test would become their private joke. "That is the most outrageous, elitist thing to do," she'd tease. But she understands what he is looking for. "He wanted a soul mate. A companion who understood and liked his world." Lloyd had been a copyboy for James Reston of the *New York Times* and he would read the *Times* all his life. Helen starts reading the *Times*, too. "There was an ease in being with Lloyd. He was great company—never a boring second. He was interested in a lot of things. That was fun. Exciting," she says. "I could match him. I was on the same level with him. I'm a good listener. There were mutual interests and a certain reciprocity—sense of humor and connection."

They date for about a year. In the summer, he gives her a jade necklace. "This could be an engagement present," he said to her. "If not, a birthday present." Helen consults her mother. She enjoys her freedom and doesn't want to settle down just yet. Her mother encourages her to accept the proposal. Helen is 23; Lloyd is 27. They marry in 1963 and are together until Lloyd's death in 2003. "We shared in each other's life. We had a good time," she says.

Over four decades, Helen's intimate life would ebb and flow through many phases: an initiation period of young love, a period of struggle and stress after the birth of children, a period of personal development and career building, a period of partnership and companionship with Lloyd, a period of care-giving when he became sick. And now a single period as a widow.

Her "relational" life can be broken down into about six different chapters over a span of forty years.

◆

Barbara's intimate narrative involves similar phases but with different partners: a young first love in Paris, a life-shaping relationship that lasts five years; marriage to Harold Solomon in New York, a period of family building—they have two daughters—that lasts fourteen years until Harold's premature death at age 43 in 1967. After that, Barbara has a series of important personal relationships—thus an intimate life of love and commitment adding up to forty-three years.

Is Barbara's trajectory so different from Helen's? "In my notion of marriage, I've always felt married," Barbara remarks with amusement.

Barbara is born in 1928 and grows up in New York City and Connecticut, the desired daughter in a family that until then included only males. Her grandparents come to the United States from Vienna in the early 1890s. Her mother and father are cosmopolitan Jews, shaped by World War I. Her father, Jack Probst, survives gas warfare in the trenches of France. He had been Woodrow Wilson's youngest campaign manager. After the war, he becomes a successful lawyer and industrialist.

Her father is the dominant parent because Barbara's mother, the artist Frances Probst, suffers from severe depressions and withdraws from the traditional maternal role. Barbara remembers going with her father to Horn & Hardart, the old automat. Put in a coin and the glass window would slide open: inside, a piece of apple pie or a plate of macaroni and cheese. Magic! Her father takes her behind the scenes to see how the food miraculously appears in the window. This is the larger world: predictable, productive—and magical! Her father holds the key. "He represented an outer world that seemed to me to be less threatening than the sometimes depressive atmosphere at home," says Barbara. "I lived in this world of successful men who were paternal and women who were problematic. I felt my true security came from men. I thought love came from men. I didn't know we were supposed to be afraid of men."

As far back as high school, Barbara has a definite idea of her life trajectory: she wants to be a writer; she wants to be a "witness to world events"; she wants to live in Europe in the aftermath of World War II; and she wants to understand the Holocaust. She follows her own compass. And all her life, Barbara has been involved with interesting, successful men—mostly they are writers on the political left. That these men could also be at times problematic as well as loving is part of the plot of her long "relational" narrative.

Unlike Helen's quieter beginnings in love, Barbara's first love is turbulent. The relationship is rooted in the political upheaval of postwar Europe and resistance to the repressive regime of Francisco Franco in Spain. It is also connected to Barbara's own idea of herself—making the relationship extremely symbiotic.

Instead of going to college in 1948, Barbara persuades her parents to let her live in Paris. There she meets Norman Mailer (he is not yet *the* Norman Mailer). Through him, she and Norman's sister Barbara Mailer make friends with Paco Benet, a young student exiled from Spain. The two Barbaras help Paco successfully rescue his student friends being held in a Franco gulag near Madrid for clandestinely printing the poems of Pablo Neruda. Paco, 20, and Barbara, 18, then settle into student life in Paris; they edit together the non-Communist leftist resistance magazine *Peninsula*, which they smuggle into Spain. Love and work are blended together, a major thread throughout her "relational" narrative. "We invented the wheel sexually like any young kids. I was totally part of his world." For all their differences in nationality, they also have similarities. Both learn to speak French in childhood. Paco's father, who was killed in the Spanish Civil War, was a lawyer, like Barbara's father. His mother, like hers, is involved in the world of art.

After five years with Paco, Barbara wants to return to New York. As a writer, she needs to hear English; she is ready to make a family and have children. Meanwhile, Paco has become a cultural anthropologist and is off to the desert on a dig. Barbara gets a job at the Spanish edition of *Life* magazine and quickly launches into the next chapter. She meets Harold Solomon, a left-wing Harvard star turned law professor. They are instantly smitten with each other and decide to marry. Soon they have two daughters.

Barbara and Harold are the typical intelligent, intellectual couple. They are also two very willful people. "Harold was the right husband for me and an extraordinary father. We had a good sex life—that wasn't our problem." But Barbara is used to a European café conversational style where people chatted on and on for hours. Harold is more remote. "He was great at talking to a crowd, but it was harder for him to sit around a kitchen table talking about nothing much," she says.

Meanwhile, she is trying to build a writing career—juggling her ties to Europe and the Spanish opposition with being a mother and a wife. Harold is juggling the demands of climbing the academic ladder with the responsibilities of family life. In that era, the professional workplace is largely a male province. There is little social support and few opportunities for the dual-career family. Academia is hostile to wives who are leading their own lives and following their own careers. This causes a crisis in the marriage. For a short period, Barbara and Harold separate. Then they come back together and the family settles in LA.

In 1967, her world crashes when Harold suddenly dies of a heart attack. Six months before, she learns that Paco was killed in a Jeep accident in the desert where he was studying the Bedouins. In addition, her father has been diagnosed with Parkinson's disease and suffers huge financial losses. Barbara returns to New York and takes care of her parents. Despite her success as a writer, she faces deepening anxiety about money. Her worst struggles are economic. But she is pragmatic and continues a basically "married" life with her children. "My habits were those of a married woman. Our apartment was run like a married household: daughters, their sleep-over friends, dogs and the rest," she says, pointing out that big apartments were cheap in the '60s. "I sent my kids to private school. I wanted them to have the same chances at life that I had had."

The contradictions begin to emerge in her story line: Protective Mother, determined to be homebound, versus Passionate Writer desiring geographical adventure. She has an intense love affair with a London-based American writer. "Of all the men I knew, I felt that he had the best emotional understanding of the parts of my psyche that were fragile. . . . To this day we are in constant communication," says Barbara.

After a while, she turns to a sort of father figure, a man nineteen years older. George Kirstein is a widower like herself, and longtime publisher of the liberal weekly *The Nation*. Barbara has written for the magazine; they have known each other for many years. Their backgrounds are similar. "My father loved boats, George adored boats," she says. She could take the children to George's house and the housekeeper would give them freshly baked brownies. "I was on that sailboat for weeks on end," she says. The relationship—on and off—lasts five years. "Though I never saw my destiny as living in the Virgin Islands on a Bermuda Forty, I was still furious when George abruptly married someone else."

Her next relationship is also a throwback, not to a father figure but to an earlier part of her life. The Spanish writer Juan Goytosolo, on a visiting professorship at New York University, looks her up. He's read her memoir *Arriving Where We Started*, about her years in France and Spain, and he identifies with Paco Benet. "That's what you call repetitive. We fall madly in love," she says. Like Paco, Juan is the son of an upper-class Catalan and Basque family. Like Paco, he lost one parent in the Spanish Civil War and is an exile in Paris. Juan asks her to join him in Paris; the Franco regime is crumbling, doesn't she want to go to Spain when Franco dies? She hesitates. Still, her daughters are in college; "there was no need for me to stay home." She knows Paco's friends would be returning to Spain. "I dreaded thinking that Paco would not be among them. Then I thought: If I didn't join Juan, would I regret the missed moment?"

Barbara joins Juan in Paris. They go to Spain. "Those were heady days," she says. Paco had become something of a legend. Crowds surround Juan on his first official return. She starts writing for the new Spanish press. They visit Marrakech and drive on the edges of the Sahara desert. She wonders: "How had I managed to find two half-Catalan, half-Basque exiled Spaniards in love with the desert?" The summer stretches to six years. "In many ways, Juan and I were playmates," she says. "We are still close. We never entirely let go of each other."

She returns to New York. "For a long time I didn't seek a new relationship," she says. "Then I became aware that I was lonely." She is nearing 60. "I felt awkward about admitting to myself that I needed a relationship." One evening she is joining friends at a Lionel Trilling lecture at Columbia University. It is raining, and she is wearing the usual dull Manhattan black outfit. She says to herself: *dress up as though you were in Paris or Madrid. Who knows? You might meet somebody.* She puts on a green silk Valentino dress that she bought on sale.

She is introduced to the artist Larry Rivers, who is about to have a show in Madrid. She mumbles that she could interview him for her Madrid newsweekly, *Cambio 16*. The next day, Larry calls her. She feels intuitively that they will end up having a relationship. Like Harold, Larry is seven years older than she.

"Larry and I really hit it off," she says. "I'm not saying it was a perfect thing. I never had the perfect thing."

Barbara and Larry make room for each other in a decade-long relationship that ends with his death in 2002. "On some level we were soul mates," she says. They travel together. They work together—he draws covers for her literary magazine, *The Reading Room*, while she writes essays for it. He dedicates his memoir about his early years to Barbara. His daughters ask her to speak at the headstone ceremony in Sag Harbor. As Barbara writes in a piece about Larry: "Put simply, we mattered to each other."

With Larry, the contradictions in her past ease up. There is no geographical problem; they both live in New York. Nor any career competitiveness, as Larry is super-famous. In an interesting way, Larry integrates the playmate–soul mate with the father figure. He is an artist like her mother—and he's surrounded by assistants like her industrialist father. "In Larry's studio, there always seemed to be people walking in and out, and children to be picked up from school. That sort of organized chaos reminded me of my own childhood," she says. This brings her back to her earliest beginnings, integrating the conflicting threads of her "relational" narrative.

"I mind Larry's death," she says. "He was a big loss in my life."

◆

Helen, too, talks about the empty spot left by the death of her mate. "The hard thing is, you come back from an evening—of theater or a concert, or giving a speech—you feel great, and there's no one here to share that with. The lack of sharing these kinds of moments is a real vacuum," she says.

She looks out the large plate-glass windows of her house with a view of the ocean, the mountains, and downtown Los Angeles. Most of the scenes of her marriage took place in this house. "We both grew," she says. "We were both grounded."

As Helen reviews her "relational" life, she can see the struggles and achievements in each chapter of their marriage. In the initial period of youthful love, Helen joins Lloyd's world the way Barbara joined Paco's world. Lloyd takes center stage with his degree in international relations and his career in journalism. She finds a job at a state psychiatric hospital. "We were getting used to each other," she says. "I was going to be the perfect wife." She reads everything he reads so she can be an informed conversationalist with him and his friends. She puts on special Sunday brunches. "I'd be the perfect hostess, I'd be the perfect wife."

She winds up in the office of a neurodermatologist; she has a rash across her body. The doctor asks: "Are you under stress?" It's a first step toward loosening the unequal dynamic of the marriage. She realizes that she doesn't have to know everything that her husband knows to be a good wife. Nevertheless, she remains in a supportive role at work and in the marriage. As she points out, in her job she is doing research for her boss so he can pursue his PhD. At home she keeps making gourmet meals for her husband. "I was very supportive," she says.

Meanwhile, they start a family. Their daughters are born in 1966 and 1969.

The middle period in the marriage is difficult. Helen is struggling to find her own way—to put the "I" back in her marriage. She and Lloyd move to Washington when Lloyd gets a job on *Congressional Quarterly* and then becomes a speech writer in the public affairs office of the Treasury Department. They are living in Bethesda with a baby and a toddler. Helen is working two days a week in a psychometric lab and looking for a part-time graduate degree program in psychology—with no luck. Back then when Richard Nixon was elected president, women's aspirations were more a quiet rumble than a movement; there were few opportunities for married housewives to work or to earn graduate degrees on a part-time basis. "I was getting restless. I wanted more than a job," says Helen. Her aunt tells her that being Mrs. Lloyd Dennis should be sufficient. "She didn't get it," says Helen.

Meanwhile, Helen is going to extremes to fulfill her role as a good wife and a supreme cook. She even makes Beef Wellington: take a beef tenderloin and coat it with pâté de foie gras and duxelles (finely chopped mushrooms, onions, shallots, and herbs sautéed in butter and reduced to a paste). Then wrap the whole thing in puff pastry and bake. (This was Winston Churchill's favorite dish.) "I remember rolling out the crust and thinking: *What am I doing?*"

Suddenly her inner world shifts with the realization that she needs a life. "That was my Beef Wellington moment," she says.

In the next chapter, Helen is able to break out on her own—with Lloyd's support. This period of "self-actualization" coincides with a move in 1970 to Los Angeles, where Lloyd gets a job in public affairs at a national bank. For both of them, California is freeing. "There was a prescribed way of doing things in the East. If you don't play the game well, you don't do it. Here in California everybody does everything. We took risks in doing new things that we never would have done in the East," she says. "It was as though someone lifted a curtain."

It is a spectacular growth spurt for Helen. She goes to graduate school at Cal State in Long Beach. Everybody is in tie-dye and sandals. She is the oldest in the class. She earns a master's degree in clinical psychology at age 36. "This was freedom and indulgence. It was egocentric. It was my time. This was just me and the noble pursuit. I didn't have to feel guilty about it," she says.

The critical piece in her story—and in Lloyd's story and in the story of their relationship—is her husband's attitude: "Lloyd was supportive. He wanted me to be the best I could be. His support of wanting me to grow was critical. When I finished school and started working, he was proud."

Helen builds up her career: a lecturer at the Andrus Gerontology Center at the University of Southern California; a consultant on aging and business to corporate clients; a public speaker on retirement.

As the decades go by and the daughters grow up, she develops a philosophy that helps her both at work and in relationships. When you get into a tough spot, "you didn't have to comply or walk away. You could modify. You could have an impact and start something new," she says. "You don't change people but you can change relationships. It's too simplistic: comply or walk. You're selling yourself short."

In Helen's narrative, she has the flexibility in her marriage (and at work) to *start something new* and to *change the relationship* with her husband. This is not always the case. Your spouse may not be supportive of your independent growth. The marriage may break down and end in divorce. Or you may become widowed. In these situations, to *change relationships* and *start something new* involves a change of partners (or jobs).

With Helen, the process of renewal takes place within the marriage. After a period of independent growth, she moves on to a new phase with an equal partnership with her husband. In this phase, the children are grown; Helen and Lloyd are supporting each other as they stretch themselves at work. She helps chart new directions at the Andrus Center, redesigning education programs and business strategies to keep up with the aging of the workforce. Lloyd develops a television documentary on water resources and pollution, sponsored by the bank. He becomes the leader of CORO, a national public affairs training program for leadership in business and government.

They draw closer together as their interests merge and their work overlaps. When they both attend a business meeting in Boca Raton, Lloyd is the one who introduces Helen as the keynote speaker on aging and business.

As in Barbara's relationship with Larry, Helen and Lloyd are on an equal plane. Her prominence is an asset to the marriage, not a threat. "Lloyd was secure in himself. He was the apple of his mother's eye. She really affirmed his self-worth," Helen says. "We shared in each other's achievements."

In the last phase of their marriage, Helen emerges as the commander in chief. Lloyd is in his early 60s when he is diagnosed with cancer and he battles the disease for five years. Helen takes over. She pays the bills and moves the trash cans to the street. She makes the doctors' appointments, gives him injections, dresses the catheter, and when he needs twenty-four-hour care, she gets a CNA (certified nurse-assistant) degree. They continue to make love and go out for ice cream cones. They celebrate Shabbat in the hospital. Helen doesn't think he will ever die. They walk on the beach and watch the dolphins play. "You can't live and die at the same time, so we lived," she says.

When the clock starts to run down, she turns to him: "Honey, do you have anything to talk about?" He says, no. "There are times when silence is more powerful than words," she says. "In our relationship, we didn't say *I love you* all the time. It was so clear. We had forty years together. There are no last words. We've lived them."

◆

Helen looks back on different relationships with her husband at different stages of their life together. Barbara looks back on different relationships with different partners. Both lived out their early love story when they joined the world of their partners. Both experienced a range of relationships from all-knowing father figure to playmate and equal partner. Both remain fierce mothers.

Both have created intimate circles that grow out of their relational narratives. Barbara has firm ties to Harold's family. She's in touch with Juan Goytosolo and his family, and keeps up with Paco's family. She remains close to Larry Rivers' daughters. Her own daughters live nearby. There are four grandchildren to love. It is the same with Helen. Her daughters live around the corner in Los Angeles. Helen, too, has grandchildren to love—along with a network of friends.

Both are looking forward. Barbara is a busy writer. Helen has started "Project Renewment," a program for women who are starting over after 50.[2] She has taken off her wedding ring. Her daughters have urged her to date.

---

2. Helen Dennis is co-author with Bernice Bratter of *Project Renewment: The First Retirement Model for Career Women* (Scribner, 2008).

Barbara and Helen are living the New Normal of "marriage," of long-lasting relatedness. Technically, they are both single. But they are living a "married" life of purpose, family, and relationships. Barbara speaks for both of them when she says: "I'm married. I just don't have a husband."

To meet the new imperative of aging, the definition of marriage has to expand. For most men and women, a long "married" life embraces many different configurations of intimate relationships over many decades. The legal bond between two people is the central definition of marriage. For many people, that is the only definition. But there are other definitions that transcend the legal parameters of any one particular marriage. These transcendent definitions define a state of "relatedness" that lasts 'til death—the New Normal of love and intimacy in a era of longevity.

In this expanded concept, the definition of "marriage" becomes:

- *The intimate contract*: a psychological and social framework for caring and connection, a moral code of commitment. It is a vow to love and cherish throughout the life span. This construct of committed relationships includes couples who are legally married and those who are not, as well as the formerly married. It embraces single men and women as well as couples.
- A *balance between intimacy and independence*: an ebb-and-flow pattern of closeness and apartness. The New Normal usually involves individual periods of development and multiple relationships over a long life—sometimes with the same spouse; other times, with different partners.
- A *culture of kinship*: a core of people whom you can't imagine your life without—relationships you create over the years. The circle may include grandchildren and even former spouses as well as an encompassing web of friends, colleagues, and other family members. It is your family of choice shaped by your relationship history.
- A *"relational" narrative*: a synthesis of your story, the partner's story, and the story of the relationship. The stories overlap but

are not synonymous. The narrative is your legacy of how you loved and were loved over a lifetime—a source of strength to draw on, consciously or unconsciously.

The New Normal validates the ebb-and flow pattern of relatedness that has become the reality of most people's lives. It elevates the importance of private space—psychological as well as actual—in the construct of re-latedness. In the traditional legal definition of marriage, the focus is solely on the couple. In the expanded definition, some (but not all) of the focus is shifted from the couple to the individual, bringing more bal-ance to the institution and putting the "I" into "marriage." The trilogy concept of "marriage" makes room for the entwining stories of individu-als along with the shared story of more than one "I" in "relationship" and "intimacy."

Instead of being a threat to marriage, putting the "I" into "marriage"—and two "I's" into "relationship" and "intimacy"—provides the foundation to preserve the institution as the basic unit of families and society.

✦

What is your "relational" narrative? Can you diagram the plot and identify recurring themes? By now you have a rich story.

There are trade-offs. The pathway of one long marriage may be more stable; the attachment deeper, the shared memory richer, the family bonds simpler and closer. The sequential track may be more exciting; in-dividual growth greater, passion more intense, family connections broader and richer. Or not. The single track can also be an avenue of great ex-citement; the serial track can also lead to deep attachment. The two path-ways are not set in stone.

How comfortable are you with taking risks? Do you have choices? Sometimes you are thrust onto the sequential pathway in the wake of losing a partner through divorce or death. Other times, you make the de-cision to end a relationship or to start a new one. The route of one long relationship also involves choices. On some level, maybe you realize that stability and security are stronger needs in your makeup than the desire for freedom or the drive for self-expression. Or you're just lucky to be in a relationship of mutual support that fosters personal development and adventure. Fate is as important as self-knowledge in determining destiny. "You can hit real bad luck. You can hit good luck. Not everything is psychologically explainable," says Barbara Solomon.

Love is about bonding, and the word—*bonds*—captures the ambiguity of relationships. You speak of bonds as in bondage, being tied down, incarcerated; you also speak of "pair bonding," family bonds, and love that binds—the ground zero of unconditional love.

Timing is important. Inherent in the ebb-and-flow dynamic is the notion of taking turns. When do the bonds of a relationship hold you back? When do they set you free to let you soar . . . and catch you when you fall?

For Helen, like many war-baby women of her generation, taking turns meant postponing her career ambitions until her children were settled in school and her husband was settled in his career. Helen chose to wait her turn. Hindsight has helped Helen understand her trajectory. "There are moments when two careers cannot be equally important," observes Helen. "We were completely equal in our later life. But it's hard to have total equality all the time. Somebody has to give a little. You take turns."

Many other women, especially younger women today, are more like Barbara. They follow a pattern of taking turns—simultaneously. Barbara pursues intimacy and career at the same time, giving full force to both parts of her life from the start. In some fields, you can't afford to miss out on the early years of building up a résumé. In most households, you can't afford to miss out on a paycheck. To keep the seesaw dynamic of a relationship in motion, both partners have to give a little.

There is a bonus in longevity: when you finally get to this stage of life, you may find that you and your partner are on a more equal plane—in work and play. It is part of the settling process. You realize that longevity gives you time to have it all—not all along, but now. That's the gift: enough time.

✦

In the New Normal, the walls break down between married, single, divorced, widowed. The different tracks of "relational" life begin to merge as time goes by.

I look at my own family: the cousin who recently celebrated fifty years of marriage with his wife; the cousin whose wife died after four decades of marriage and who is now remarried; the cousin who was divorced from his first wife nearly thirty years ago and then started another family in a second marriage; the cousin who never married. We gather at family reunions. We cherish the next generation of children and grandchildren. We know each other's histories. We support each other in crisis—enjoy each other at picnics and weddings. The New Normal is a broad institution of loving connections.

Perhaps this expanded definition of "marriage" is a way to break the cultural deadlock in the political battles over marriage. On one side are the doomsayers who look at the statistics on marriage, divorce, widowhood, cohabitation, and remarriage and conclude that the traditional formula of one-relationship-for-life is obsolete. On the other side are the advocates of "old-fashioned marriage." They call for tighter laws and social sanctions to enforce the legal bond between husband and wife forever.

The current generation of older people may be able to bridge the two sides. Many older couples can attest to the sanctity and glory of marriage. They also know that the focus of the old-fashioned marriage movement aimed at young couples who are raising children has time limits. After the child-rearing years, responsibilities change and so do the rules of a loving partnership. To try to enforce a one-relationship-for-life policy, when a life can last 100 years, is like King Canute ordering the tide not to come in. Yet to diminish marriage as the mainstay of society and the model of caring and commitment would be just as foolish.

Expanding the social definition of marriage creates a new framework for committed relationships that takes longer life spans into account. Older men and women—who are nurturing, cherishing, and inventing unprecedented richness and variety in relationships—are the ones spelling out the New Normal of relational life.

PART THREE

Truth and Reconciliation

9

Sticking Together

I t is late afternoon and a soft light is falling across California's Prairie Creek Redwoods State Park. Nell Hamm, 65, and her husband, Jim, 70, are finishing up their ten-mile hike. They are healthy and athletic. They scuba dive, they run. Every week, they take two or three long hikes along the trails. In a month they are to celebrate their fiftieth wedding anniversary.

Nell inches ahead on the trail. Suddenly, the mountain lion attacks from behind. She hears a strangled cry and turns around to see her husband's head in the jaws of the beast. She knows what to do: she faces the lion and screams. As Jim is dragged to the ground, Nell picks up a four-inch-wide log and relentlessly beats the lion on its back. "It wouldn't let go, no matter how hard I hit it," she says. Jim is pinned facedown on the trail. Nell tries to jab the beast in the eye with a pen. But the animal doesn't flinch. Nell picks up the log again and slams the butt end into the cat's snout. That gets the lion's attention. With blood on its snout, the cat lets go, steps back, glares at Nell with its ears pinned back. She continues to scream and wave the bloody log. The lion slips away into the woods and disappears.[1]

---

1. This anecdote is based on news reports and a website, maintained by Tom Chester, listing lion attacks (http://tchester.org/sgm/lists/lion_attacks_ca.html).

"We love each other very much. We've been together for fifty years," Nell explains later in media interviews. Jim survives the attack and is taken to the hospital for treatment. "We were fighting for his life, and we fought together like we've done with everything."

Fighting the good fight *together like we've done with everything* is the essence of a long, close marriage. Nell's words reflect a deep and secure—indeed fierce—attachment. That is what you want in a relationship.

When the lion attacks—whether the assault comes in the form of a diagnosis, the loss of a job, or a problem with an adult child or grandchild—you count on each other to fight hard, to face the truth together. This is the structural underpinning of enduring relationships. As the decades go by and the children grow up, the wrinkles get deeper and the libido weaker; no matter, you are in it together: you really know each other; you are completely there for each other. You would hang for each other.

I always wanted one long marriage like my Grandmother Trafford. The family portrait of the fiftieth wedding anniversary hangs in the hall: my grandfather stern with white hair—we called him Big Perry—and my grandmother, diminutive and dressed in satin—Little Granny—surrounded by their four adult children, spouses, and children. My sister and I, dressed in matching royal-blue velvet dresses with white lace collars, are relegated to the children's table with the other younger cousins.

The fairy tale went like this: she was a belle from New York; he was a freshly minted lawyer from Massachusetts. She rejected all the other suitors in favor of this "comer," whose favorite book was *Moby Dick*, whose career was based on order, and whose lodestone was good character. When Granny talked about my grandfather, her eyes would get that longing teenage look of adoration. We'd be having tea and lemon cookies on a summer afternoon. She was looking back; I was looking forward. We shared the same dream—she in memory, me in dreams.

Of course when I really got to know my grandmother, she was a widow. Her postmarriage life lasted nearly twenty years. (She lived to be 98.) And people say that she really came into her own after her husband died.

I remember my grandfather as a huge man with sensitive dark eyes. He was a football player in college (like his son, my father), and all of us cousins grew up on the code of playing fair and being a good sport. When I was 8, he announced that we would correspond by letter; usually he waited for grandchildren to be 12 or 13. For me, it was a special honor; for him, it was the rush of time. He died a year later.

I have the diary he wrote when he spent the year studying in Germany at age 17. He suffered from terrible headaches. He set for himself a rigid schedule of study and travel. I can see that he liked to be in control of the world around him. My grandmother was also looking for order. Her father had died when she was young; her mother drank. She grew up in the polite despair of money, privilege, and loss. I imagine their working dynamic: he controlled; she adored. He provided her with granite; she brought him silk. They gave each other the security they both craved.

I can only speculate on how my grandparents fought the lion together through two world wars, the Depression, the bomb—through illness and financial losses; through inevitable disappointments and family crises. How they changed as individuals and as a couple. How they guarded their secrets and stoked the fire of attachment.

A mystery! Yet it is the lens through which I look at relationships. I have followed a different trajectory in love: the pathway of serial relationships. I have known deep commitment and the rush of passion—like my grandmother. But my story is not wrapped around one person in one long relationship.

✦

Each person has a template of love and intimacy. The problem comes when cherished fantasies don't fit with reality. You're too mature to hold on to the wedding mystique—the romantic ideology of a permanent state of perfection in a partner and complete fulfillment in the relationship. But you have dreams and nurture an idealized concept of long-lasting love inside you.

It helps to understand the origins of your love model. You may be fortunate enough to inherit from your parents or other family members a working model of maturing attachment. The empathy and compromises necessary to sustain a long relationship seem to materialize—slowly and painfully—but naturally. The relationship has a secure base.

You may also inherit negative bits from unhappy relationships: perhaps your parents were dissatisfied, bitter. You come to marriage braced for trouble, in need of extra nurturing, unfamiliar with pleasure, and used to looking the other way. *The parents have eaten the sour grapes and the children's teeth are set on edge.*

A group of older men and women gathers in Greenville, South Carolina, for the regular weekly meeting in a continuing education program. Most are officially retired, but are working and engaged in public service or the arts. Some are married, some widowed, some divorced, some remarried, some single—all of them are part of the New Normal. They've been together for more than a decade and form a community of support.

The question is asked: *Looking back, what would you most want to change about your life?*

One of the most frequent answers: *parents!* Roughly 20 percent of the group replies that their parents are what they would like to change most in their lives. After more than half a century, the hurt is still raw. After successful lives as artists, teachers, business managers, ministers, government leaders, a sense of injustice simmers. After becoming parents and grandparents themselves, there is still a hole from love crushed. A man, long married, explains the situation: His father died when he was a teenager. His mother was needy, demanding, and bitter. Nothing he did was ever right. He left home at 16 and never looked back—except in anger.

In research on attachment, many people "describe their relationship with their parents as negative. That serves as a working model for [current] relationships," explains Berkeley psychologist Philip Cowan. Can you talk about a negative relationship and put it in perspective? If you can, that augurs well for your marriage. "These people do better with partners and with children than people who are still angry."

The same principles apply in a long marriage. Can you talk about painful subjects and put them in perspective? "If you were upset; did you get comfort? If you're still pissed off, you don't expect you're going to get what you need in the relationship. Nothing is on a secure basis," explains Carolyn Cowan, Philip's partner in research and marriage. "Can you go off [the secure base] and come back when you're scared or vulnerable or in pain? Do you expect someone compassionate? Or do you expect criticism or blame [or indifference]? If so, you are not in a secure place."

In their studies of older couples, the Cowans find gender differences. Overall, the more successful couples pair up with a secure set of expectations in both spouses. And if a woman who is vulnerable marries a man with a secure base, she is as likely to have as positive a relationship with her spouse and kids as those couples in which each has a secure base. However, if the woman has a secure base but the man has this vulnerability, the marriage is likely to be more troubled. Men who come to a relationship with a negative background tend to be angry. "Women have a hard time with these guys," says Carolyn Cowan.

It is possible to lay a painful past to rest and develop a secure base. You search for positive models—in relatives and mentors, in religion and literature, in movies and on television. Sometimes the model is so positive—or the concessions so well concealed—that no mortal can measure up. You can also develop a secure base with those in your intimate circle of friends and family. Therapy is another resource. In many instances, counseling can help individuals and couples get to a safe place.

You soon learn that behind fairy tales lies the much richer, edgier, more complex and challenging story of love. Life's task is to make peace with the modeling you inherit and then to forge ahead. The goal is to develop a secure base in yourself that becomes the platform for the relationship. In close, enduring unions, the secure base *is* the "marriage."

✦

All the while, the lion is lurking in the woods. Sometimes the most devastating attacks come late in life. Other times, they strike earlier in a relationship and set the tone for the later years. Learning how to face the lion is a critical survival skill in marriage. Fighting off the attack is how you build up a secure base. Although crises are painful, they turn up the volume in a marriage. They force you to confront the relationship and renegotiate the marriage contract. In the process you calibrate ideology with reality and create a working dynamic.

There is no shortcut to learning how to fight.

It is Christmas in Atlanta and Kathryn Wiedl Mettler, MD, is determined to go through the holidays as though nothing has happened. Christmas Eve with the grandchildren, midnight mass in the great cathedral where she graduated from high school, where she married Stephen C. Mettler forty years ago: Kathy, then fresh from St. Mary's College in South Bend—Steve, an Air Force Academy man. Tonight is bitter cold; the church is packed with worshippers. Kathy and Steve hold hands like teenagers. "A slow-motion movie," she says, ever since the lion attacked. Steve got the diagnosis that morning. They decide not to tell anybody. "I was determined to get through it," she says. The next day she puts on Christmas dinner with all the trimmings: a leg of lamb and a gathering of relatives—her 92-year-old mother, her brother's family and all the grandchildren again, running gleefully around the living room. "I found myself saying: *'Be quiet!'* and *'Time out!'*" she says. At one point during dinner, her son turns to her and exclaims: *"Mom—it's Christmas!"* "Everybody looked at me," she says.

The next day they break the news to the family: Steve has non-Hodgkin's lymphoma. They are sitting in the living room of their youngest son. They hug and cry. *"Don't tell me you're going to die,"* says the son. *"Honey, we're all going to die,"* replies doctor mom. "We played up the positive," recalls Kathy. A course of therapy, the likelihood of good years ahead; the disease is not curable but treatable. *"Enough of this. I'm going to be fine,"* says iron man dad. *"There are things to do."*

As they turn to leave, their son says: *"That was what was wrong yesterday. I had never seen you yell at the kids at Christmas."*

How hard it is to fight the lion and maintain normalcy. Kathy has struggled all her life. She goes to medical school at age 36 and battles the old boys' system to get a residency in gastroenterology. She builds up a practice. Determination and realism are habits. She keeps fate at bay through sheer vigilance.

At first, Steve's symptoms are slow and confusing: fatigue, swollen feet. She thinks it might be kidney failure and gets him to a doctor. Protein level up; he's anemic, losing weight. She knows too much, she fears multiple myeloma. She holds in her fears and screams in the lion's face: "No matter what," she says to her husband, "I want you to remember that this has been a good thing. We could have gotten hit walking across the street. This is a gift." When the diagnosis is lymphoma and not myeloma, she says: "I want to go Yippee!" A gentler diagnosis, she explains to Steve. *Yippee?*

For the next two years, Steve undergoes treatment with immunotherapy. "All I kept thinking," she says, "what was crystal clear—we've had a good marriage."

Their beginning love story is so quick, so romantic. Steve is a brother of Kathy's classmate at St. Mary's and he asks her to a party. "I looked out the window and saw a cute blond guy with blue eyes in a red Austin Healy with the top down," she says. The Air Force cadet, a jet-jockey pilot before the flyboys with the Right Stuff made history by landing on the moon. "It was so teenage-girlish to fall in love with a young tall blond athlete in a thread-bare blue shirt." They meet on April 13; he asks her to marry him on July 20. Their fairy tale is simple: *live happily forever after.*

In the early chapter, Steve is a pilot in the Air Force. He flies combat missions in Vietnam. They move around: North Carolina, New Hampshire. Steve is gone much of the time. Being a pilot is like that. Meanwhile, they have three children and Kathy is getting restless.

Steve asks her: *"What do you want to do?"*

"If I could do anything, I'd be a doctor."

"Why not? You can do it."

"He was the reason I went" to medical school, she says. By this time, they are living in Atlanta and their children are 12, 10, and 7. Steve has left the Air Force and is working for a technology company. When Kathy enters Emory medical school, their roles switch. Steve is the main one home with the kids. She is gone. Becoming a doctor is like that. Medical school is bad enough; the internship is 24/7 hospital hell. "You either get into the internship or not. The only way to go through it is to delve deep. You sleep it. He had the kids. I was gone." Not just physically but emotionally, too. Kathy is sucked into the maelstrom of medicine: the long hours, the life-and-death moments, the opportunity to make a difference—or at least, do no harm—always to comfort.

In early adulthood, you enter the zoom zone of getting ahead at work. Whether you're a fire fighter or a pilot, a teacher or a journalist, you are likely to go through a "greening" period that requires a total commitment to your calling. History is used to husbands turning away from their home life in order to pursue a cause: keeping the streets safe, starting a business, going off to war. And now more and more women are going through the same process. The high intensity of this early period eventually eases as you gain more experience; but while it lasts, adrenalin is pumping, nerves are on edge, and every day is exciting, even dangerous.

It's also a phase when the lion is likely to attack the marriage. When the relationship gets ragged and distant. When one or both start thinking *May Day! May Day! May Day!* The marriage is going down.

Kathy and Steve look back on her internship as that kind of crisis. Kathy is captured by her calling; Steve is blocked from her. Both are increasingly alone. "I was so stressed out. I was in the hospital. The kids were at home. I felt guilty. I'd get home at midnight, up at six. They were asleep," she says. "I can now put words to it."

Fight or flight?

Steve is the one who fights. One Saturday afternoon, he puts her in the red Dodge Colt and drives her to the parking lot of a shopping mall. *"We're going to sit here until we get this thing settled,"* he said. *"I'm not going to lose you."*

"I think I want a divorce," she said. *"If this doesn't change, I'm going to divorce you."*

The mention of the word "divorce" makes him feel sick. She is so far away in another world. "My support came from my class," she explains. "I could communicate so much more easily with them."

"You don't talk to me," she said. *"You have to talk to me."*

"I don't know how to do this. I'm busting my butt for you. What else. . . ?"

And so they talk and talk. They sit and talk for three hours in the parking lot. "That's what turned everything around," she says. "The afternoon in the parking lot brought home who my husband was. He has such integrity. He was going to deal with things no matter how painful. That is the kind of guy he is."

Steve knows on some level what she is going through. After all, he'd flown secret missions in unmarked planes to hot spots around the world. He knows about the magnetic pull of a cause, the thrill of an adrenalin surge, the strain of fatigue. And he wants her to go for the prize and become a doctor. He also wants to keep the marriage.

He beats back the lion.

"When times get rough in a marriage, you've got to talk," says Kathy. "Marriage is a series of negotiations." That afternoon in the parking lot leads to a new chapter in the marriage. They incorporate fighting the lion into the ideology of their relationship. Even their sex life gets better, more meaningful. "There were still rough times. I was in the middle of things. But I knew: it was going to be okay," she says. "There was still the residency to complete. We knew we were going to get through that.

"Now, no matter what comes, I know we are going to get through it."

Get through it.

At St. Mary's College, Kathy was a "staff girl," the scholarship student who waited on tables six days a week. In the dining room shaped like a chapel with dark paneling, marble floors, and Gothic windows, the other girls dressed in wool dresses and pearls; staff girls wore white uniforms, white shoes, and a hairnet. Kathy's father had suffered a major stroke when she was 10 and died some fifteen years later. Growing up, "there was not enough money," she says. "I came out of a background where you always had to work. You had to really scramble to put it all together."

So does Steve, the second of six kids growing up in Fort Wayne, making it to the Air Force Academy. "We've both been in situations where you say—this is the pits. There's no way to get through it except to get through it."

> Oncologist: *"We can treat you but we cannot cure you."*
> Steve: *"What do you mean?"*
> Oncologist: *"We can treat you and you'll do fine."*
> Steve: *"So I don't have to worry about this for fifteen years?"*
> Oncologist: *"More like seven."*

Kathy sees him take the information as a body blow. It's her turn to beat back the lion. After the first day of therapy, which lasts seven hours, she takes him home and puts him to bed. He is shaking with cold. She wraps him in blankets. The top of his head is burning—as if it's about to come off. She holds him. Steve goes through this every Friday for four weeks. And he repeats the cycle every six months for two years. Each time, he tolerates the treatment a little better. "I watch him like a hawk," says Kathy. Steve grows stronger and resumes his consultant work. Kathy continues to practice.

The agenda of their marriage is about to change again. "We both want to take more time to be with each other and do what we want to do," says Kathy. Cut back on work a little, travel together for fun, plan more visits with the grandchildren. "We're talking more about what we'll do in the future," she says. "We're on the same page."

At church, when Kathy and Steve counsel young couples who are about to get married, they always tell them about the afternoon in the parking lot when they learned how to fight the lion. As Kathy looks back on the narrative of their long married life together, she says: "The tapestry is more beautiful with all the knots and threads in it."

For couples like Kathy and Steve, earlier struggles build up the secure base of their relationship, which helps the marriage flourish in this later-life stage. Call it "marital empowerment." You've been tested. Each test awakens the relationship. The awakening prevents burnout. And the empowerment enables you to meet the next test.

✦

It's true: *Come grow old with me; the best is yet to be!* Older couples are generally happier than middle-aged couples. Just as older people are generally happier than younger people—the *positivity* factor that comes with age. You arrive at a zone of acceptance and contentment.

Among 50- to 59-year-olds, nearly 50 percent of married men and more than 46 percent of married women are with their first spouse, according to 2001 data from the U.S. Census Bureau. They have survived the high-risk divorce years. They look forward to retirement, grandchildren.

The fiftieth wedding anniversary is a glorious celebration of a long relationship. Around the table is the circle of kinship—the community of friends and family that has sustained the couple over five decades. Ushers and bridesmaids reminisce about the couple's courtship. Adult children arrange a collage of photographs of their life together. One by one, the guests stand up to say how much this couple has meant to so many people—how much they have meant to each other. Husband and wife are intimate witnesses of each other's lives. When it comes to crafting a legacy, they have the advantage of joint authorship. They remember the struggles of youth, the places of childhood. They connect to families of origin. They oversee an extended family—without the complications of divorce and remarriage.

But a long marriage has special burdens. Some couples never learn how to fight the lion as a "we-team." Or they forget. They avoid confrontation. It's comfortable, predictable. Over the years, they drift along together in velvet stagnation. There is not a lot of engagement. To stay alive, you go outside the marriage—the real you is in the office or at a book club or with the children. Or in someone else's bed.

The marriage hits the mute button. Conflicts hide underground. So does affection. Husband and wife don't talk to each other very much. You can glimpse the marital shutdown in restaurants: the couple in the corner, eating in silence; his mouth set in a permanent snarl, her eyes vacant as she cuts into a lamb chop; two people who seem paralyzed in habit and regret.

No, no, you say. It could never be as bad as that.

Marital satisfaction seems to follow a U-shaped curve: high starting out, declining over the next ten years, hitting a low when children are teenagers, climbing back up after the children leave home and couples get into the retirement years.

Yet, very little attention has been focused on marital satisfaction in older couples. Until now, who cared? The National Survey of Family Growth by the National Center of Health Statistics stops at age 44. But older couples can provide perspective to young couples, particularly those at the bottom of the U-shaped curve.

The long-term marriage study performed by West Coast psychologists Robert W. Levenson, Laura L. Carstensen, and John M. Gottman offers a rare glimpse into the marital quality of men and women who have spent most of their adult lives together.[2] "Old marriages have reduced potential for conflict and greater potential for pleasure," conclude the authors of the study. "Overall, this preliminary snapshot of the nature of marriage on the threshold of old age is a positive one."

The researchers followed 155 couples, about half between the ages of 40 and 50, the other half between 60 and 70. Most couples were white and upper middle class. "Older couples develop an ability to use positive emotions like affection more effectively. They are better able to calm themselves down and negotiate conflict," says Levenson. Over many decades, the intense volatility of youth moves into a more peaceful phase of contentment. But it's not a quiet void. "It's companionship and friendship and support. We now see that late life is not a period of wasting away. [It is a period of] self-actualization," continues Levenson. Couples reinforce that continuing process of development in each other and share

---

2. Robert W. Levenson, Laura L. Carstensen, and John M. Gottman, "Long-Term Marriage: Age, Gender, and Satisfaction," *Psychology and Aging* 8, no. 2 (June 1993) (hereafter referred to as the "long-term marriage study").

the adventure of a new chapter. The priority of chemistry and physical attraction gets superseded by trust and respect.

In long-lasting *good* marriages anyway.

What about those couples who stay in *bad* marriages decade after decade? Some relationships seem to mellow out. As people age, the rising tide of *positivity* seems to lift all marriages. But it's not clear whether those happy marriages in later life were happy to begin with, or whether there is "a process in which old wars are diminished and marital bonds are strengthened," point out the study's authors. The data offer clues that couples who were unhappy earlier in their marriage may find happiness together later on when they enter the Golden Pond stage.

Research tends to be skewed because happily married couples are more likely to participate in studies than unhappily married people. "There clearly are unhappy couples that stay together over the long term despite their difficulties; we know far less about these troubled long-term marriages than about those that are happy," explain the authors.

◆

You make accommodations. After a while, the marriage may not seem to be so troubled. You don't even try to make your ideology of love fit the reality of the relationship. You find your comfort level. One way to avoid conflict and get what you're missing is to become involved in another relationship. This is the triangle marriage.

The two of them are lying in bed, watching the movie *Die Hard* with Bruce Willis, on television. *"My hero,"* she whispers. Bruce is beaten up, bloodied, unbowed—Yipee Ki Yay! *"You guys,"* she sighs. He puts his hand up her sweater and unhooks her bra. She unbuttons his shirt and plays with the spongy white hairs on his chest. She is not his wife.

A photo of his wife and two children circa 1975 sits on the bureau. Paul and Glenda Kowalski*[3] are still married. A commuter marriage, he explains. He lives in Gloucester on the North Shore of Boston. His wife lives

---

3. Throughout the chapter, asterisks indicate that names, identifying details, and some events have been changed.

in Hingham on the South Shore. She runs a fancy plant and flower business: lilies at Easter, balsam wreaths at Christmas, impatiens in many colors for pots in summer, wedding decorations, and funeral arrangements. He's allergic to plants. He says his wife treats him like a boxwood that needs pruning. "If we lived together, we'd be divorced," he says with a grin.

"Why do you stay married? Don't you want to be happy?" asks the other woman. *"I am happy,"* he says. *"No, you're not. You're in bed with me. You haven't had sex with your wife for ten years!"* He pulls her bra free and starts rubbing her breast, flicking her nipples. *"You're too romantic,"* he says. *"You see everything in black and white."*

For ten years it's been like this. Pat Grumbach* is divorced with three married daughters. She is a case manager in Child Protective Services. She meets Paul, a computer program specialist, when his firm is hired to upgrade the department's records. Paul gets a studio apartment to be close to his work. When the job is finished after a year, he stays on in Gloucester. He likes the rocky coast. He finds another job at a home security company. His wife stays on the South Shore.

Paul and Pat see each other two nights a week and talk on the phone in between. They go kayaking, whale-watching. She takes care of him when he has a colonoscopy—and he does the same for her. They talk about their children. They enjoy their long nights together in bed.

Except on weekends. Except at Christmas and New Year's. Except on Valentine's Day. Except on birthdays. Either Paul goes to Hingham or Glenda comes to Gloucester. And next week, Glenda wants to take him on the Beacon Hill garden tour in Boston.

Paul and Pat are naked, now. He floats his hand gently across her thigh. They take turns stroking each other—an arm, the belly. She finds his penis. On the screen, Bruce Willis is covered in blood, vanquishing the enemy. She climbs on top of Paul. So good to be wrapped around another for a moment when nothing else matters. So good to be alive and work the old nerve endings, to feel the surge. *Yipee Ki Yay!*

The movie is over. The phone rings. Paul leans over and picks it up: *"Hi, honey. . . . Really? . . . When . . . That's great. . . . Sure. . . . Uhhh*

. . . *nothing much.* . . ." Pat starts getting dressed. She wants to go home to her little Cape on an acre of land in Beverly. It gnaws at her: how it's so easy for him to go from her in his arms to his wife on the phone—without moving a muscle. "It's a little uncomfortable for me," she says. "He picks up the phone—it's a specific informational call: *What time are you getting in?* He's okay about it, but not comfortable. It's not easy for him. He tries not to lie. But he clearly is by his activities."

For women like Pat, it's a timeless dilemma. One day, she's willing to settle on Paul and the limits of their love and not let his allegiance to his wife get in the way. The next day, she's outraged and wants to be Number One. The day after that, she's okay with the arrangement. "There are times when I feel very jealous. His wife has opportunities to do things with him that I don't," she explains. But shortcomings can also turn out to be advantages. "I like my independence. I've lived alone for more than fifteen years. I was married for twenty five years." The relationship gives her the freedom to be with her family, go on vacations with friends, stay late at work if she has to—and even date other men. And so, she settles for part of a loaf.

For men like Paul, it's not so much a dilemma as an exercise in compartmentalization. He has perfected the art of living simultaneously in separate spheres. The only way to keep his marriage going, he says, is to live apart. He is grateful for Pat; they are so happy together. But he doesn't want a divorce. He just wants peace. He likes spending holidays together as a family. Glenda was a good mother. She stood by him early in the marriage when he was fired and couldn't find a job for eight months. So, he settles for two half-loafs.

For wives like Glenda, such an arrangement minimizes day-to-day tension. It also gives her the freedom to pursue her own dream. This way, she can throw herself into building up her garden design business and hit the party circuit searching for more clients—without having to deal with Paul's grumpiness. Does she know about the other side of the triangle? Perhaps on some level, she knows. Paul doesn't even like to touch her, and sometimes, she feels so alone. But she's a strong woman and she focuses on the glass half full. She refuses to think about what he's doing when they are apart. She's committed to the marriage and to him; she can count on his support—the time she had a gall bladder attack and he came rushing to her side. They have a history. They enjoy grandparenting together. She settles.

The next morning Paul calls Pat. They talk about the fishing boat that exploded in Gloucester harbor. They talk about Pat's daughter, who is about to give birth—her third grandchild. They laugh and make a plan for next week. *"I love you,"* he says. Then he sits down to write a condolence letter to a widow whose husband had been principal of the high school and was like a second father to Paul. *Remember when I was courting Glenda and she stayed with you? Glenda asked you: "Do you think Paul will turn into a Male Chauvinist Pig if we get married?" You backed me up! And today Glenda has her own business. She's running the world! . . . So many good memories. . . . We both send you our love and sympathy.*

Paul is deeply rooted in his relationship with Glenda. At the same time, he is increasingly attached to Pat. All three are settling for the triangle marriage. The arrangement works as long as all three support the status quo.

Triangle marriages can last many years.[4] They have their own truth. But they are not static. The relationship between Paul and Glenda is changing. They are spending more time together now that they have grandchildren. They don't bicker as much.

The relationship between Paul and Pat is also changing. At first, it runs on high-intensity passion. "It's all been very romantic. We enjoy a lot of the same things. It's always a date," says Pat. "If his wife died tomorrow I'm not sure whether either of us would want to get married. We like it the way it is." Yet, over time, they have become more like . . . an old married couple. Pat sighs. "The more I see him, the more I see things that piss me off," she continues, like not opening the door for her, not taking out the garbage when he stays over in her house. She tells him off when he starts backseat

---

4. Charles Kuralt, the folksy television correspondent, spent twenty-nine years in a triangle marriage until his death in 1997. He supported his wife in New York City and his mistress and her family in Montana. The details of his double life came out after his death.

driving. *"You and my wife—you think exactly alike,"* he says. Last year Paul gave Pat a silk blouse for Christmas; this year he gives her an umbrella.

At the same time, Paul and Pat have become closer . . . and more committed. In the beginning, he would say: *You enrich my life.* Now they say to each other: *I love you.* Pat's daughters grow concerned. They wish their mom would get a *whole* guy. When Pat goes off with friends for a week of skiing in New Hampshire, Paul feels the bolt of jealousy. He says to her: *"I had a physical pain in my chest. In that moment I realized how much I cared for you."*

What happens if one of them gets sick? One evening Paul suffers what seems to be a stroke. He can't remember where he parked the car. Or the name of the president. Pat rushes him to the Emergency Room. She thinks to herself: Who does she call? His son? His boss? His wife? *Hello, this is . . . I'm a friend . . . we were having dinner. . . .* The symptoms go away and Paul is released from the ER.

After a certain age, you may be more accepting of parts of a loaf. You don't want to be alone in these years. There is liberation from *shoulds* and *ought nots* once children are grown. You say to yourself: no one is getting hurt. Some men and women are more comfortable in partial relationships than in all-consuming ones. There is tenderness and commitment on all sides in a triangle marriage. "I can't see us just ending it," says Pat.

✦

But "partial" in relationships is sometimes another word for "problematic." Fate intervenes to upset the status quo. Or someone looks in the mirror and says: *I can't go on like this.*

There are hidden costs to staying in problematic relationships. The toll is greater on women. Men benefit from marriage—any marriage. But women seem to benefit only from good marriages. In the long-term marriage study, a review of research over the past twenty-five years finds that, in general, husbands report higher rates of satisfaction in marriage than wives do. Compared to single men, married men are happier with their lives. This is not true for women. Single women generally report *greater* life satisfaction than married women do. And although women benefit from good marriages, those who are in unsatisfactory relationships have more physical and psychological problems than either married men or happily married women.

"The health cost exacted from staying in a dissatisfied marriage is paid primarily by wives," conclude Levenson and his co-authors in the study. "We believe that in our culture, confronting marital conflict and attempting to heal an ailing marriage have become primarily the responsibility of wives. The cost that wives incur in taking on the emotional and physical work associated with this responsibility is extracted from their mental and physical health reserves. Husbands, in contrast, buffer themselves from this process by withdrawing from conflictive interactions. This withdrawal may function to protect husbands' health, but it adds significantly to the burden placed on wives."

How much satisfaction are you getting in a relationship? How much is the relationship taking out of you? Your health and well-being depend on how you make the calculus.

✦

A counterpoint to compartmentalization at this stage of life is the drive toward *authenticity* and *integrity*. That requires integrating the separate and sometimes conflicting spheres of your life and your psyche. Marriages that draw closer in this period have usually attained a level of transparency. Not that this is a time to confess all your buried secrets. "In some instances compassion trumps honesty," says a good friend in her 90s who knows much about love. At the same time, it seems, a certain amount of candor is necessary for attachment.

Some long-married couples lose their candor and have to go through a painful meltdown to get it back. Over many decades, they have each moved into different compartments that require secrecy. When the compartments collide, they face a moment of truth in the wreckage.

"I asked him: Are you having an affair? I pressed him. He said, yes. I was totally cool about it. I knew I had had an affair. I was as guilty as he was. I wasn't going to tell him, ever. It didn't bother me for about thirty-six hours. And then I started going crazy," says Julie Rostow,* 51. "I couldn't *not* tell him about my affair."

The marriage explodes. The affairs are different. Her husband, Frank, has flipped over a woman at work. They are both smokers, and they meet on the sidewalk outside the building. *Do you want to have lunch?* The affair is electric . . . and shallow. The wife's affair with a married man has been going on for ten years. The two are film buffs; they spend hours talking about *Rashomon* and *The Seventh Seal*. About *Love Story*. (Love *is* having to say you're sorry.)

When you have an affair, you create a watertight compartment for it. "You think you can keep it a secret. You say to yourself: this has nothing to do with my spouse. I still love my spouse. This unacknowledged part of me was enacting a separate life," she explains. "But when the walls break down, the two parts of yourself are forced to confront each other. . . . It is catastrophic. It's like a tsunami. The truth was explosive. I've never suffered like that."

The gap between what you think you are and what you have actually done exacerbates a mutual sense of betrayal. It's like finding out a person you thought you knew is a green-fanged monster. He didn't see her as someone who could sleep with another man. She didn't see him as someone who could sleep with another woman. They didn't see themselves as betraying the marriage.

Their three sons are at college. For a year, they suffer and fight. His nightmares from Vietnam come back. He stays in their split-level house in Oak Park, Illinois. She travels to the rooming house in Oaxaca, where she spent the summer before they married. *Get out!* He writes her huge block-printed letters. *I hate you; I love you!* She comes back to their house, gets a bulldog, and cuts her hair. He takes up hunting with his younger brother. She cannot live with a man who kills animals and birds. She plants corn in their backyard, her mind turning to the Kansas farm where she grew up. He is suspicious—where is she going? He follows her in his car. She watches him—what is he up to at the gym? Time brings some solace. They spend hours together, plowing the past over and over, talking for the first time in years, struggling to understand, slamming the door shut—opening it again. "We both tried to break away because it was so painful," says Julie. But they'd always come back because, after so many years, their attachment is strong. "We didn't know it was there," she says. In a long marriage, you take attachment for granted, she says. "When something disrupts it, you see it."

Some couples are so disassociated from each other that any attachment has been drained away. But chances are, if you've been together for many decades, you've built up reserves of bonding. You may not realize how enmeshed you are. In the crisis of betrayal, you may be just as hurt and angry as younger couples. But unlike individuals whose relationships are just starting out, you are able to draw on this reserve of attachment.

After the wounds heal, you may look back at the meltdown as a necessary awakening. "We could never be this close if we hadn't told each other," she says.

◆

"How do you achieve forgiveness? If you don't, you can't move on. You can't go on," says Berkeley psychologist Philip Cowan. Forgiveness is a major task in this period of truth and reconciliation: forgiving those who hurt you, disappointed you, enraged you—not just spouses, but children, friends, colleagues, former partners, and parents. Making amends to those you have hurt and then forgiving yourself for what you have done and left undone. Forgiveness does not mean erasing the reality of the injuries or missed opportunities. As is often said: forgiveness means giving up hope for a better past.

In the process, you may become grateful for all those you have loved and who have loved you. This is the payoff of sticking together.

The Cowans have been married for fifty years and have fought the lion several times through attacks of illness and periods of estrangement. They have explored the dimensions of marriage as researchers, while cementing their bond as spouses.

"I'm just feeling so blessed and so good about where things are between us," says Carolyn Cowan. "What most stands out for me is that when Phil and I met, we were very young and now we've been together very many years. In the early part of our married life with children we had some rough times—which were a total surprise to us. What I now know is that we were very lucky because we were able, ultimately, to use those rough times to learn some things, not only about ourselves but about marriage."

Wisdom in relationships is based on knowledge. To be known—and to know another person—and still to cherish each other: that is the measure of a rich, enduring relationship, whether with a spouse, a child, a friend—or a lover. Longevity makes sure you have a last chance to know a person . . . and be known. In this deep knowing is the heart of love.

10

Boomerang Couples

Variation on the Vietnam refrain: you have to destroy the marriage to save it. The conflict is too raw, the betrayals too searing, the disappointments too many. You go your separate ways. And then, perhaps years later, you come back together again and build a new relationship—as in the arc of a boomerang.

In rare cases, you get divorced and then remarry each other. Statistically speaking, you have been married twice and are serial spouses. But your two marriages are to the same person. Isn't that one long relationship? Yet the two marriages are very different.

The larger population of boomerang couples involves those who go through rough periods and are apart for a while, then come back together to form a new relationship—all within the marriage. You take a break from the marriage without getting a divorce. You may live in separate places. In this phase, you are mainly on your own.

The boomerang model highlights the important role of singlehood in the New Normal of "marriage." A single period, rather than being stuffed into a secret compartment, is an open chapter and has legitimacy. It's part of your relational narrative.

Whether you get a divorce or have a temporary separation, the time apart rewrites the ground rules of any future relationship. Couples who get divorced do not expect to get back together—it's a temporary surprise when the time apart leads to remarriage. Couples who take a sabbatical do not usually expect to split up—but it's a risk that the time apart may lead to a permanent separation or divorce.

You don't know how it will turn out when you make the break—or your partner does. More immediate is the challenge of being single.

Cecilia Rivero*[1] has always been a "good girl"—one of five children, the first in the family to go to college, the pretty bride with black hair and a crucifix around her neck who marries Tommy Rivero before he ships out to Vietnam in the Army; now she's the mother of three grown children and a guidance counselor in the San Antonio school system.

One Saturday morning at breakfast she tells Tommy: "I'm leaving you. I want a divorce." He blows up at her—*Crazy bitch!* "That's why I'm leaving you," she says. For thirty years of marriage, he's been a bully, she tells him; a whole lifetime, she's lived in a house of chronic verbal abuse. She is 56 and she wants out. Her two married daughters understand. She earns a steady salary—more than Tommy does working on construction jobs in a depressed economy. She has her network of girlfriends. She's thought about this for years.

Tommy can't believe it. Cecilia who goes to mass and never raises her voice as long as he has known her. She gets a lawyer and files for divorce. Tommy watches the end of his marriage as though he were on the shore watching the crashing of a wave. Cecilia leaves him in the house and rents an apartment in another part of town. She has her own money; she has a support team. She starts a new life. By the time he comes to—the marriage is over.

Cecilia relishes her freedom, the quiet of the morning. It's not long before she falls in love with a co-worker—a man in the process of a divorce, who teaches biology in the high school. He's very different from Tommy: a decade younger and a bit of a lost boy; he does yoga and subscribes to

---

1. Throughout the chapter, asterisks indicate that names, identifying details, and some events have been changed.

Men's Health magazine. They immediately connect. She awakens sexually and emotionally. Slowly the walls around her body and her psyche come down—the walls she had built up to ward off her husband, to protect herself from his permanent rage. She learns how to give of herself: with her degree in psychology and newfound independence, she helps her lover work through the pain of his divorce, his anguish over leaving children at home, his anger at his wife—at the whole female gender. *What do women want?* Cecilia tells him. She tells him things that she was never able to tell Tommy. There are some bumps—the way he flirts with younger women when they go to a party together. The way he complains. About everything—his wife is late bringing the kids to him on the weekend, the school principal doesn't care about science. The romance runs its course; the breakup stings. But by that time, Cecilia has become a wiser woman. She starts thinking about the man she left.

Four years after the divorce, Cecilia and Tommy are sitting down at TGI Friday's. From time to time they meet and talk about the kids. He asks her about her work—what's this he hears about oral sex in middle school? She rolls her eyes and then she tells him. . . . She asks about his work—he's found a regular job as a maintenance supervisor at a Holiday Inn. They order steaks, and Cecilia says in an offhand way: "What would you think about getting back together?"

Tommy puts his head down on the table and starts to sob. He's missed her so much. His sister got him to a therapist after the breakup. He goes into a men's group. He spends more time with their daughters; he emails their son in the Army, who has had two tours in Iraq. Before the divorce, he would let Cecilia handle everything to do with the kids, everything to do with the house, everything to do with their marriage. He didn't know what a burden he was then, didn't know how much he was hurting her, he says.

After a few months, Cecilia and Tommy get remarried in their daughter's living room. In this case, it takes a divorce to break the dynamic of the angry bully–stoic victim that characterizes the first marriage. It also takes the time apart for Cecilia and Tommy to change—not their personalities, but their behavior and their attitudes about what a marriage *should* be. Psychologists point out that a relationship is shaped both by behavior and by ideology, your set of expectations for your partner, your idea of "marriage." How you behave often reflects your ideology. If you have a negative idea from past experiences with parents and previous relationships, you are primed for trouble. "Relationships are two things: One, behavior. Two, idea," says Berkeley psychologist Philip Cowan. "They are both powerful. The idea may be more powerful. The idea can color things—negative and positive."

With the intervention of therapy, Tommy is able to understand his negative ideology of generalized anger—and he sees how much it has cost him, including the loss of his wife. That leads to a change in behavior toward Cecilia: he is nicer, more appreciative. Cecilia comes to understand the rigidity of her ideology: how a husband should be either a perfect prince or a dragon to avoid, outsmart, or slay. Through her affair, she experiences the nuance and complexity inherent in love. That leads her to change her expectations of "marriage" and her behavior toward Tommy: she is more open, more giving.

Liberated from the past, they are able to form a new relationship. After a while, they become like other older couples—facing retirement, coping with health problems, taking care of grandchildren . . . figuring out what they want to do over the next decades.

Many couples, like Tommy and Cecilia, have to have an ending in order to have a beginning. Otherwise you can't break free of the old dynamic that has snuffed out the earlier relationship. You keep trying to rework the past. There's always a danger that once you're in the marital routine again, you'll slip back into the old relationship.

It's important how you regard the time apart once you are back together. If you try to delete that chapter from the narrative—erase it as an unfortunate interlude best to be forgotten—you are likely to start nurturing the Big Grudge: *How could you have left me like that—humiliated me in public?* Or you beat yourself up: *How could I have done that to you? How could I have been such a jerk, such a sicko? . . . How could I? How could you?*

If you keep saying to yourself *How could you/how could I*, you're stuck in the old marriage. You aren't free to start over. Liberation from a destructive relationship depends on mutual acceptance of the past. You accept your partner and you accept yourself. You respect each other's separateness. You acknowledge the arc of the boomerang in your story.

✦

Some boomerang couples break up early in their lives and don't get back together until they're much older. Maybe you are just too young when you first meet—too immature emotionally to sustain an enduring relationship. You leave the marriage as an unfinished couple. You get divorced and move on to several more chapters on your own. Along the way you become more mature. You reframe the past. A spark from old love remains. The challenge when you rediscover each other is to start over as though you were both somebody new.

Susan Corey and Jules Eisenberg live in Redondo Beach, California, in a sprawling mission-style house with stark white walls, arched doors, and a plant-laden patio. Susan has just celebrated her 60th birthday. Jules is fifteen years older. This is their second marriage to each other. The first time they were a couple, she was 30 and he was 45. After a six-year marriage, they got divorced. They don't see or speak to each other for more than a decade.

When they reconnect, it's a different relationship. Susan makes the point: she doesn't cook anymore. "Forget it," she says. "I don't even wash lettuce. I get it in a bag, ready to eat." Jules smiles and puts the steaks on the grill.

They first meet in 1975 at JG Melon's in New York City. They are both hanging out at the bar. Jules is a divorced father of two children with dark sexy eyes and a warm smile. Susan is nymph-like with long blond hair, a free spirit of the '70s. "Jules and I just locked eyes, and it was absolutely love at first sight," she says. They talk that night until there is no one else left in the bar. He says he'll see her next week at a party. As the days go by, she wonders if she's dreamed all this—too many glasses of wine;

maybe the guy is a mass murderer. At the party, he taps her on the shoulder and she turns around: "I was totally like: *Oh! He's really cute!*"

> He: *"I want you to make a phone call. Just dial this number."*
> She: *"Okay."*
> He: *"When they answer, give them your name and ask if you have a reservation."*
> She: *"All right."* She makes the call and gets an airline. *"Do I have a reservation?" "Yes,"* replies the voice on the phone, *"you're going to Dallas."*

A weekend in Dallas! Jules whisks her away. The dynamic is set: he is the leader; she is the follower. "I was just totally overwhelmed," she says. "I just thought this was the neatest thing that anyone had ever done. And so I started traveling with him . . . and everything else."

They live together and buy a weekend house, complete with peach orchard, in upstate New York. They get married in the garden beside the pool there. On the outside, it's a *House Beautiful* scene. On the inside, the rumble has begun. Susan is so thin, so insecure. "I was always worrying about what I should wear, what I should say. I was a different person with different people," she says. Jules looks after her, he gives her direction. Look at the peaches, they're almost ripe. He buys her a freezer and a Seal-a-Meal food storage system so she can make peach pies and freeze them. "And I did it. And I hated it. I hated it!" she says. "I made like nine pies in one day."

The marriage is going down. "I'm just not happy. I'm losing my identity," she says. "He was always right, I was always wrong. . . ." And so Susan does what many men and women do in a May Day marriage situation: she has a pole-vaulting affair. What better way to even the score with Mr. Dominant than to go outside the marriage and have the last word? The night before Thanksgiving, she blurts it out: *"I'm having an affair!"* Jules doesn't understand—how could she be unhappy? *"You know, this guy is not the problem,"* she says. *"The problem is that I'm feeling like*

you're the teacher, I'm the student. You're the father, I'm the child. I'm losing
myself. I've become like this chameleon."

Jules knows the man, a high-flying advertising executive in the publishing corporation where Susan works. Jules has sensed it—the way she
knows how to get to his place for a company party without looking up the
address. How could she? All the times she'd call up to say she'll be late
coming home from work. Very quickly the immensity of the betrayal overwhelms him. "I was destroyed," says Jules. He created a world for her—
and this is what he gets in return? Shock turns to rage. He wants nothing
to do with her. He changes the locks on the apartment. "I was pissed," he
says.

The reasons for a divorce are specific and unique to each couple. But
the underlying problem may be the structure of the relationship. With
such a skewed balance on the marital seesaw—Jules the parent, Susan
the child—the relationship gets stuck. Instead of changing the dynamic,
they break up the marriage.

After the divorce, they build separate lives. Jules moves to Los Angeles, not too far from where Susan's family lives in Pasadena. Susan stays
in New York City—where Jules grew up. They get involved with others.
They each have a chance to review the script of how they behave in intimate relationships—and why.

In Jules's first marriage, the dominant-submissive dynamic with his
wife is reversed and he is the one who has a pole-vaulting affair. He feels
that he has no control over his life. He isn't making much money. He
feels beholden to his in-laws. "I was bored at being corrected all the
time," says Jules. He is also overcome when his sister dies of breast cancer and her husband commits suicide. The dual tragedy weighs him down
with responsibilities for the extended family. It's as though there is no oxy-
gen in the air around him to breathe. In his marriage, he is feeling pushed
down and around. In his job, he is trapped. His one escape is business
travel. Every month or so, he would travel to Texas for the company. In
hindsight, it seems inevitable that he would have an affair. "She relieved
all my anxieties and pressures from things that were going on back east,"

he says. "She didn't really end up being anybody in my life," but the affair gives him "the opportunity to think about what the heck I was doing . . . how I wasn't succeeding in what I was doing . . . how I was trying to get out of the marriage."

The affair explodes the marriage; Jules and his first wife get divorced. Then, like many serial spouses, when he gets involved in the next relationship he reverses the script. With Susan, he makes sure he is the one in control. He's more secure financially. He's enjoyed being a bachelor on the town. He's more confident with women. When he meets Susan, she is so young and unformed. The exhilaration he feels when he sweeps her off her feet—rescuing her, molding her Cinderella style. Even though the dynamic would eventually doom the relationship, he is stuck on the high of sweeping her away.

In Los Angeles, he follows the same script when he has a live-in relationship with another woman. "She was young and exciting," he says. She is also needy. He replays the tape: rescuing prince in charge. But ultimately, the woman is too needy, he discovers. She gets caught up in the drug scene of the 1980s. Jules cannot rescue her. He cannot take care of her. When he ends that relationship, he finally gives up his role of Rescuer in Control.

It's a painful but necessary education. "I'm more understanding and more mature," says Jules. "You learn a lot; some good and some bad, but what it does is it changes your outlook on who you are and what you're doing."

Susan, too, gets an education in her single period. She is a glamorous independent woman before television's *Sex in the City* popularizes the genre. She has multiple relationships. She gains weight; she loses weight. Who is she? The question takes her back to her childhood and the divorce of her parents. She remembers the day in the garden when she and her four siblings learn that Mother is leaving them to follow the love of her life, as she would later explain. But back then the five children don't understand; they are stunned and bereft. Their father is in the airline industry, and the children are largely brought up by housekeepers and a disapproving grandmother. When their father dies, Susan is 20. She grows up with a yellow caution light blinking inside: don't get in too deep because marriage can be hazardous. Meanwhile, she is popular with boys; they fall in love with her, she falls in love with them; if it doesn't work out, that's okay, no hard feelings: the way to avoid heartbreak is to avoid the chains of caring too much. Yet she is searching for Great Love.

In this period of singlehood, she visits her mother, who has started a second family in rural Mexico. Susan reconnects to the heartbreak of childhood—to the love she lost and now regains. She and her mother make up for the time apart and become close again. Her mother talks about the decisions she made and why. Susan goes deeper—into who she is, into what love is.

"If you aren't sure of yourself, if you don't know who you are and what you want, you can kind of get swept away in the other person's idea of what you should be," she explains. Who are you supposed to be? "Or it could be your job that shoots you in a direction you don't want to go. It's only time that allows you to figure out what it is that you want."

She gets the time she needs to figure out how she can put the "I" in "marriage." She changes her script in relationships. In an eight-year liaison with a younger man, she becomes the pursuer, the initiator. When he wants to have children, she tells him no. She learns how to speak for herself in close quarters. Her decision leads to the end of their romance. They remain friends. Meanwhile, she reviews the past with a different idea of herself and relationships. She thinks about Jules, how she's sorry she hurt him. Her sister-in-law, who is living in Pasadena, remarks that she hasn't had closure with Jules.

Eleven years go by. It is midnight, Eastern Time, when the call comes through. *Do you know who this is?* Susan knows. Jules explains that he has just run into her sister-in-law, who urges him to call. *How are you?* They talk for three hours. And by the way, on his way to Europe next month, he will be stopping at Kennedy Airport.

Susan goes to meet him; as in the movies, she goes to the wrong terminal, she races to another terminal, her heart in her throat—what if she misses him? And then she finds him at the American Airlines counter. "When I saw him—you know—it was kind of like the way I first saw him at JG Melon's: he is just absolutely the love of my life," she says. They just stand there and hold each other. "We had the sparks. Those kinds of things don't go away," says Jules.

Like burn victims whose wounds have healed over with time, they are finally able to touch each other again. They remember the good parts of the past. "We were in love when we met, we loved each other, we enjoyed each other's company. Suzy was very young and I was much older," says Jules. "She has been through a lot, and so have I."

They are cautious. They conduct a bicoastal romance for a while. "The first thing I was able to convey was how heartily sorry I was," she says, "to hurt someone like that and to do something like that when he didn't deserve it. I didn't know what else to do. I was just immature. And the rest, he just knew." How the affair could have occurred, how she could still love him. Who they really are now.

As they go forward, Susan keeps her "I" in the relationship and holds on to a realistic idea of the other "I." Jules has to rebuild his trust in her and let her be who she is. Being older is an asset. "You live with her. You live with the person who you think is being honest and mature in more ways than she was before," says Jules. "That's where we are now."

They change the old dynamic. "When I came back I remember saying: *the woman who left is not the one who's coming back. I'm a completely different woman,*" says Susan. Then she smiles. "I don't make peach pies."

Sometimes she'd swing too far the other way on the leader-follower scale: in a restaurant, she'd order his drink, and he'd say: *"What are you doing?"* It took a while for them to settle in, to feel secure, to establish a fair partnership.

After nine years of living together as a couple, Jules suggests they get married.

She: *"Whatever for?"*
He: *"It would be prudent."*

She: *"Oh, bowl me away with your romance!"*

He: *"Well, I've just been thinking that if something happened to me, you wouldn't even get my Social Security."*

She: *"If there's money in it, I'm your gal!"* (laughter)

It's a different kind of dialogue and a different kind of relationship than the first time around. They have another wedding in another garden with the same bride and groom and the same cast of family. And a different marriage.

A few years later, they quit their jobs and start a real-estate business together. Jules has the business savvy; Susan, the eye for houses and design. They both have people skills. Like many older couples starting a new chapter, they become partners in business as well as in marriage. "We're going to work together. We're going to create another life," says Jules. "Susan is working hard at it. We do it together, we enjoy it. It's a lot of fun."

"We're such a team—that's a great thing," says Susan.

One question nags at boomerang couples: Did you have to go through all that pain and upheaval to save the relationship? Susan looks back on her narrative. "I needed to go away to grow up," says Susan. "I wish—my only regret—I wish I'd had the hindsight to have stayed and grown up with him. But we'll never know whether that would have been possible," she says.

They don't dwell on what might have been. What's the point? Besides, weaving their time apart into the narrative of their relationship together has strengthened their survival skills. They've been tested, alone and together. That makes them less afraid of the future.

Sometimes when Susan wakes up in the morning and Jules is sleeping so soundly, she thinks that he's not breathing. Because he's older, she lives in the shadow of his mortality. "I just can't imagine—if he goes before me, I'm going to be tremendously sad. But I also know that it's not the end of the world; it will just be the end of my world with him. It's a real fear— he's the love of my life. If I lose him, it's going to be a tremendous loss. But I also know that I've gone through so much that I'm a survivor." And so is Jules, if fate were to go the other way. They are both survivors.

Jules and Susan have been together now for sixteen years. Or a quarter of a century, if you count both marriages. Or more than thirty-five years, if you count the time that they've known each other.

There are situations—as with Susan and Jules—where you have to be on your own to make the necessary changes in your intimate script. The oppressive crowding in a stuck marriage doesn't allow for mutual growth or personal insight. You have to put a lot of distance between past and future to make sure you don't repeat the early draft of the relationship.

Some boomerang couples don't make it. The reasons for the first breakup also cause the second breakup. Chronic problems with immaturity, infidelity, or drug and alcohol abuse can reemerge with fatal consequences. People are who they are. Personalities are set. What *can* be modified are attitudes and behavior. But these changes come slowly through experience and honest self-evaluation. A successful boomerang marriage like Jules and Susan's requires two essentials: growth during the time apart and a different dynamic in the return relationship.

✦

Maybe you just need a break. You don't want a divorce, but you'd like a vacation from being married, especially if you've been together for many years. A time-out is a chance to pursue a personal dream—you move to another city to go to school or take a new job. Or you need a retreat, a time alone, respite from a frantic life, a period of solitude to reflect and renew. Perhaps you are in a flat-lined marriage and don't know how to get the heartbeat of the relationship going again. The only way you can blast out of an atrophied marriage and catch up on deferred growth is to have a period of separation.

Writer Joan Anderson chronicles her sabbatical from a long marriage in *A Year by the Sea*[2] when she lived alone in a cottage on Cape Cod. "I'm beginning to think that real growing only begins after we've done the

---

2. Joan Anderson, *A Year by the Sea* (Broadway Books/Random House, 1999), pp. 145, 154–155.

adult things we're supposed to do," she writes. At that time, her sons are grown. Her marriage has stagnated. She needs private space to renew. Her husband gets a new job in another city. She refuses to go with him. She needs time to be alone. After a year, they get back together.

"Perhaps we were simply tired souls who hadn't the energy for anything but inertia, both shutting down and keeping our feelings to ourselves," she writes, as she builds her own life, watching the seals and coping with frozen pipes. Perhaps a time-out is important especially for women in a generation where couples married young, had children quickly, and wives deferred to the needs of children and the work life of their husbands as they shouldered the main burden of maintaining the family and the marriage. "Maybe separating was the sanest thing for two confused people to do, coming coincidentally as it did at menopause—hmmm, men-o-pause, a pause from men. Perhaps all women in long-term relationships should consider it," continues Anderson.

Not only is the time apart a complete break from the old marriage—but getting back together is conditional on building a new kind of relationship that is more engaged and egalitarian. The decision to stay in the marriage "is intentional, not a mere matter of convenience," writes Anderson. "If we are to have a future, it must be a collaboration, where each has a hand in the plot and contributes to the stage directions."

This sets a high standard for relationships in this season of life. The New Normal is a voluntary and collaborative relationship. If not, what's the point? There have to be positive reasons to stay together. A separation can be a dramatic attempt to invigorate a marriage. There is no etiquette on how to take a good sabbatical from your spouse. Whatever your pathway, the goal of a time-out is regeneration—of yourself, your partner, and the marriage.

◆

Donna and Adam Williams* have all the props of success: Academic posts at the University of Oregon. A grown son and daughter. A lovely house with a view of the mountains. He is an engineer who helped start a small company in wireless technology. She has a degree in public policy with a specialty in water resources. They are 62 and 63 and have been married thirty-nine years.

And they have been living apart for five years. She's loved it; he hates it.

Donna is an optimist. She grows up in Gary, Indiana, and never lets the dumb-Pollack jokes bother her. She knows she will never stay in Gary, where her father works in the steel mills. She wins a scholarship to Smith College, graduates summa cum laude, and goes on to earn a degree from Columbia University's School of International and Public Affairs.

Adam has a forlorn look in his dark brown eyes. His father, stern and Calvinist, who could trace his ancestry back to eighteenth-century farmers in New Jersey, is a housing inspector in Trenton. His mother flees Berlin just before the War; she reads the poetry of Heinrich Heine to put herself to sleep at night. Every afternoon, she greets Adam when he comes home from school with the same refrain: *being good is not good enough—do better!*

Adam and Donna meet in the library at Columbia University and quickly become a couple. "He was smart, sexy. He introduced me to another world," Donna recalls. "While we came from different heritages, at the important level we had the same values, the same drive for academic achievement."

They travel together in South America. They take hiking trips in the mountains and go river rafting. When Adam turns 30, he tells her he wants to start a family. She says, *not yet.* She's in graduate school, studying for exams: *Hey, it's got to be good for me, too!* It's a disagreement on timing—not on the desire to have a family. They go on to have two children. But the disagreement is a foretaste of the struggle that erupts thirty years later.

Adam never wants to leave Portland, where he has surged ahead in his career. His company is successful and he's known as Mr. Wi-Fi. He's done—*better!* He's found the way to achieve the highest level of achievement, of happiness. Mostly Donna has gone along with his grand plan. Once the children are in school, she gets an appointment at the university in environmental sciences. She keeps up her ties with the Center for Energy, Marine Transportation, and Public Policy at Columbia's public policy school. But after twenty years, the leadership in her department changes, their grown children are working in different cities; she's ready to do something else.

In 2002, her big chance comes through: a fellowship sponsored by the American Association for the Advancement of Science (AAAS) to work in Congress on environmental issues. A two-year assignment. She's excited to go to Washington and work on policy issues from the inside. She brings the news to her husband: Couldn't he get some telecommunications work from the government and come to Washington, too? Adam says No! Why would he want to change anything in their lives?

Donna takes the fellowship. "This is the first thing I've done that required not being able to accommodate him," she says.

A whole world opens up for Donna. She revels at being in the hot center of politics. She makes new friends. She finds a condo overlooking Rock Creek Park.

A whole world shuts down for Adam. How could she? They both want something from each other that they are not getting—but that something is illusory. Donna wants to stay married. So does Adam. But they are both angry and disappointed with each other. Adam feels injured; Donna tries to make it up to him. They play "hurt-me, hurt-you-back" games: when she suggests that she fly back to Portland for the weekend, he says don't bother. When she invites him to Washington to see the cherry blossoms, he's too busy to make the trip. Sometimes weeks go by without a phone call or an email message.

One year stretches to three years, then to five. Donna shifts from Congress to the Environmental Protection Agency. Throughout, Donna and Adam hang on to each other, hang on to the marriage. They keep up a family tradition: the summer vacation in wild country. They share a history of trips into nature—hiking, canoeing, mountain climbing. Before children, with the children, and after the children have left home. Back to just the two of them. This summer they take a canoe trip in Montana to follow the route of Meriwether Lewis and William Clark in their historic expedition across the Northwest to the Pacific and back. Adam and Donna leave the two coasts behind and go to Big Sky country—away from the frenzy of the city, away from the torment of their split-apart marriage. They sleep in a tent. They go to a Pow Wow on the Blackfeet reservation. They stay in a teepee for a couple of nights. He stops worrying that she's not there. She stops worrying about her hair (what he thinks of her, whether she's measuring up). They loosen up. He calls her Wild Running Hare (Hair); she calls him Buffalo Bull (Headed). They are strong paddlers in their canoe.

When they come to the White Cliffs along the Missouri River, Donna looks up at the sandstone cliffs and thinks about her marriage. In the quiet except for the dip and pull of the paddle, she wonders whether this is the way of a long marriage: a passage by the white pillars of calcite, sculptured by eons into grand cliffs, shooting up 200 to 300 feet, and then a stretch of the darker stone, the rust-colored hematite. She paddles along through light and dark. When the white cliffs stop and she comes into a stretch of brown, she holds her breath, a few more strokes, and suddenly the white cliffs appear again. She is reassured. Can she trust that the white stone will always reappear after the dark? She stares at the cliffs, hoping that the wild splendor of alternating sandstone reflects a similar pattern in relationships. She rests her paddle and turns around to look at Adam in the stern: he is concentrating on guiding the canoe. Will the white cliffs reappear in their marriage?

After five years of living apart, they turn to a novel solution: they draw up a postnuptial agreement. Like a prenuptial agreement, the postnup addresses the financial obligations in a marriage and divides separate and community property. For Donna and Adam, negotiating the postnup is a way to break the impasse of their separation and lay out a blueprint for staying together.

They agree to maintain separate households. They also agree to spend more time together. The postnup stipulates that they will not be apart for more than ten days at a stretch. The goal, they say, is to recommit the marriage.

Donna is in a different place when they sign the agreement. The sabbatical has served its purpose. She fulfills her dream to be in the heady world of Washington politics. She's had "her turn." She is ready to "go back" but under different conditions. She has some flexibility in her work. After retiring from her full-time job in Washington, she gets a contract with the federal government, which allows her to work on policy projects out of the office. It is important for her to maintain her Washington life. She keeps her apartment in DC—but she spends at least two and a half weeks of every month in Portland with Adam.

The sabbatical has also served a purpose for Adam. He realizes how much he misses Donna. His mistress is his work, and so he doesn't have a large circle of friends outside of the office. He's lonely. In the years of the separation, he translates a lot of his rage into concern about money: how outrageous that the wealth he has created should go to support his wife going off like that. Why should he pay for her new life in a new apartment? The postnup gives him reassurance that his financial resources are not at risk. Donna is able to support herself in Washington—she is able to carry the condo. Adam doesn't feel so ripped off. In this way, the agreement dampens his rage so he can focus on the emotional assets of the marriage. They started out so much in love. They go back to the moment in the library, the shared history of children, the memories of travel.

The tenor of the marriage shifts. They build up the positive elements in the relationship. Donna becomes more available to Adam. Adam softens toward her Washington life and spends weekends with her in the condo. (That counts as together time.) Instead of fighting about what they don't like in their marriage, they focus on what they've always liked about each other. Donna admires what Adam has achieved in his work. He's impressed with what she's done in Washington.

Donna becomes more sympathetic to his issues: when to retire; should he retire? Perhaps when he's 70, he says. The jolts of getting older depress him. He wears a hearing aid and takes cholesterol-lowering medication. On the canoe trip in Montana, he suffered pain in his arm and worried about his heart. Donna looks after him, gets him checked at a clinic. No longer is he the husband who is blocking her; he's a man who needs her.

They bring their opposite views of life to each other. Adam sees the glass as half empty. He tells her *"I love you. I'm so sad we're in this situation at this time of life."* But Donna sees the glass as full. For her, this stage of life "is a liberation," she says. "I want him to be part of it. It makes me so sad [that he resisted her Washington chapter]."

His sadness, her sadness. Slowly, cautiously, they find ways to relieve their sadness and bridge the gulf between them. They hold each other in bed and snuggle like two spoons. The newness of the relationship is stimulating. There are no flat lines in this marriage. They are starting over.

Separate lives *can* lead to more interesting lives. In a successful sabbatical, the separation fosters personal development and makes possible deferred dreams; you acquire an edge of mystery that forces your mate to take another look at you. As a man married more than forty-five years says of his wife: "I'm always discovering something about her."

✦

The postnuptial agreement is a relatively new legal contract for married couples, and it is not recognized in all states. Unheard of twenty-five years ago, this mid-marriage document is gaining a foothold in American matrimonial culture. Like its better-known cousin, the prenuptial agreement, the postnup is responding to two demographic trends: the overall aging of the population and the increasingly common pattern of marriage, divorce, and remarriage with its complicated legacy of children from different relationships. The postnup defines the financial relationship of spouses during marriage, in the event of divorce, and at death. It requires a full disclosure of debts and assets. It can include drawing up a family budget and deciding who will pay the heating bill.

Older couples may want to draw up a postnup if one of them inherits a large amount of money—or a cabin by the lake that has been in the family for generations. A postnup could ensure that the cabin goes to the children and is not part of the marital estate in a divorce or at death. Serial spouses often sign a prenup before they get remarried. If not, they may turn to a postnup to take care of children from previous marriages and to sort out separate assets and obligations. There are other legal avenues to accomplish this. But with a postnup, both spouses are involved in the resolution of potential disputes; difficult issues about money are brought to the surface.

In negotiating your financial stake in the marriage, you air your fears and search for what is fair. It's a way to avoid fighting over money in the future. For couples like Donna and Adam, the postnup can remove money as a source of tension in the marriage so they can repair their relationship.

But using a postnup to heal a troubled marriage is controversial. "There are cases where that's advisable," says Gregg Herman, a family law attorney in Milwaukee. "But I only recommend it where there is an equal desire to stay married and work on the marriage." These are committed couples with "soft" problems of incompatibility from struggling with retirement issues to coping with boredom. These couples also benefit from counseling and joint therapy, he says.

The postnup is not recommended for couples who are confronting the "hard" problems: physical or mental abuse, infidelity, substance abuse. Nor for people who are really planning to break up and want to use the postnup as a Trojan-horse settlement in any future divorce battle.

Couples are rarely in the same place when they go through a break point. One may be more dissatisfied than the other—or more eager to make changes. It is the same with a sabbatical. Taking time apart may help couples with "soft" problems, who have an equal desire to stay in the marriage. But just living apart is not likely to fix a marriage with "hard" problems.

As many men as women take a recess from each other. Separations are often part of the natural rhythm of a work history. He takes a job overseas; she stays put—she's working and is excited about a new assignment. Sometimes a time apart leads to the end of the marriage. He falls in love with a co-worker . . . or she does. It's not long before they part ways permanently.

What are your motives for a time apart? To pursue a goal—to put some excitement in your life? Or to escape a destructive or empty situation at home? You take a break *because* the marriage is in trouble. Perhaps you are too exhausted from a "bad" marriage to have enough energy to end it. Or to change it. You need your own space for a while. Living apart gives you time to prepare for another chapter; it gives your adult children a chance to see you as two separate people. If you go on and get divorced, maybe it won't be such a shock. And maybe, you think, there is always a chance to get back together.

A separation is a gamble: heads, the couple is renewed; tails, the couple breaks up.

And for some couples, living apart becomes a permanent condition of marriage. You get into the rhythm of seeing each other only now and then. You keep your commitment to marriage and your commitment to freedom. This is the living apart, loving together arrangement for the long-married set—another variation on the New Normal.

11

Throwback Romance

You fall in love with the girl who got away, the boy next door, an old crush, or just someone from an earlier stage of life. There's something magical about finding new love in a familiar face. A throwback relationship is a kind of homecoming. It fits into the overall agenda of going back and reviewing your life—of connecting the dots of experience from the beginning.

The poster child of throwback romance is Donna Hanover, the ex-wife of former New York City mayor Rudolph Giuliani, who edited *My Boyfriend's Back: Fifty True Stories of Reconnecting with a Long-Lost Love*. After her divorce from Rudy, Hanover reunited with her high school boyfriend and they married a year later.

Throwback relationships also have some of the benefits of long-term marriages: here is someone who knows your origins before you became who you are. They bear witness to where you were and how far you've come. You don't have to spend a lot of time gathering data to know a person's résumé. It seems like . . . destiny.

"My philosophy is, this was always meant to be," General Douglas John O'Connor, 76, told the *New York Times* when he finally married his teenage sweetheart, Jeanne O'Brien Conway, in 2007. They dated in youth and parted: both married others. They kept in touch as couples. After they both were widowed, they began another courtship. "This was the girl of my dreams, the girl I had on a pedestal when I was a young man," said the groom. Getting married almost sixty years later is "as if the greatest dream you ever had finally came true."

There is nothing like a dream come true to awaken the regenerative powers of love. Life is worth living again. But throwback couples, so steeped in the spell of the past, have to grapple with the realities of the present. People can change significantly since seventh-grade science class or that football weekend in college, or even since that business conference a decade ago. The danger is that in the infatuation phase of falling in love, couples project an overidealized image onto each other, perhaps burnished over the years with fantasy. It becomes all the harder to sustain such an image in the daily rhythms of a relationship. You may pick up where you left off, but you've each had separate lives. There's a lot of catching up to do and new urgency to accommodate reality.

◆

Bill and Susanna Dinant*[1] have been together for eight years—or forty-one years, if they count back from their college romance. They fall in love at the University of Wisconsin in 1966. Susanna, a freshman, meets Bill, a senior, in the lobby of the women's dorm. He has come with the boyfriend of her roommate. The three of them go off for the evening and she goes back to her room and studies. The next day, as she is coming downstairs to the lobby of the dorm, Bill is walking in. With characteristic feistiness, she says to him: *"Oh, hello. Did you come to take me out for coffee?"* He smiles and replies: *"Yes."*

"We went out for coffee and that was that," she says. They have an intense one-year relationship. An English major with a laid-back laugh, Bill helps organize the protest against Dow Chemical Company and the use of napalm in Vietnam. Susanna follows him. She wants to be a public defender. After Bill graduates, they go their separate ways. They get married to others and start separate families. Bill ends up teaching American

---

1. Throughout the chapter, asterisks indicate that names, identifying details, and some events have been changed.

studies at a small Midwestern college. After law school, Susanna works for the Justice Department and then moves to Chicago where she starts her own firm specializing in gender discrimination in employment cases.

On the thirtieth anniversary of the Dow protests, the university alumni magazine publishes a feature on student activism. Susanna, now divorced with two teenage daughters, sees Bill's name in the article and wonders what happened to her old boyfriend. Susanna's name is cited in another article because of a 1970 piece she wrote on feminism. At this point Bill is also divorced, his three children are grown, he's retired early from teaching; he, too, wonders what happened to that feisty freshman. They track each other down. After emails and phone calls, they decide to meet in Madison at the scene of their romance. Susanna, who has arrived the day before on business with the university, waits for him at the Rathskeller, a German pub at the student union. It's snowing and Bill is late. He has a two-hour drive. Susanna is nervous. Bill comes through the door, covered in snow. They order "Rathskeller Ale" and dinner. "We connected as if thirty years hadn't passed," says Susanna. Four hours fly by. When they finally walk outside, the snow has stopped, the night sky is clear with sparks of stars. "Bill grabbed me," she says. He kisses her. Long and slow, so long and so completely, he kisses her. "The Big Kiss," she says.

A hasty midlife courtship begins. Bill soon moves to Chicago and six months later, they get married.

Behind the wonder of the Big Kiss is a more troubling reality. Bill, the soft-spoken, brilliant teacher who could recite *The Leaves of Grass*, has suffered a closed-head injury from a bicycle accident ten years earlier. The signs are scarcely noticeable. He has all the charm and warmth of his undergraduate self. But he knows his brain is not working right. That's why he retires early—the classes have become so tiring, the students so frustrating. Susanna insists he come and live with her: she is making a good living in her law practice; her house is big enough, especially now that the girls are in college. Bill pulls up stakes to be with her. But he gets distressed with the suddenness of being part of someone else's family— of moving into *her* house in *her* city. He feels like an outsider in the place he is supposed to call home.

Both have changed substantially since their year together at the University of Wisconsin. Bill is still that dashing soul mate whose kiss in front of Memorial Union changes Susanna's life. But a different side of him emerges. First the colorful language: swearing a blue streak from a man so gentle and poetic. Then: a combination of edginess and aimlessness so alien to the energetic student protester and inspiring English teacher of the past. A whole day lost in front of the TV. An angry outburst over Susanna's mother—whom he never knew because she had died a decade earlier but whose photograph hangs in the hall. A morning spent looking for an old plastic yogurt container—Bill won't throw anything away, and so boxes of empty bottles and used food containers stack up in the basement.

Susanna, too, has changed. She is no longer the freshman looking up to the senior, but an experienced lawyer and an independent woman. She has raised her children and managed her life for almost a decade before re-falling in love with Bill.

The challenge for men and women who come together in their 50s and beyond is to integrate the previous chapters of their partners with their own. Stepchildren are usually involved. Adult children may be thrilled that Mom or Dad is getting remarried—but they aren't always too happy about the new person in the house. Blending families is more complicated than blending books and dishes acquired in earlier decades. Susanna's daughters worry about Bill's weirdness and their mother getting stuck; Bill's children worry about their father and his increasing need for care.

At the same time, there are gaps for Bill and Susanna to fill in—to understand who each of them has become and how that is different from long-ago remembrances. "You have the idealized romantic picture of each other. After a while, you have to encounter the person as he is—and as you are to him. It does not always meet expectations," says Susanna. "Then you decide: Can you accept him? Can you work with that? Can you build something from a realistic perspective—or not? Am I better off with him or without him? Is this what I bargained for? Do I take what time is left and look elsewhere? Every marriage has that line in the sand. The decision is made consciously or unconsciously."

Bill and Susanna leave her house and move into a townhouse in downtown Chicago—a fresh start. But Bill's symptoms continue. The low point comes when Susanna is unpacking the boxes, the packages of her former life, and thinking: "Oh, no, what have I done! . . . Is my marriage a disaster? Do I put my tail between my legs and run? Oh Lord. Oh Lord, what am I going to do?"

Susanna and Bill make the decision—unspoken—to stay together. They learn how to accommodate their new reality by accepting who they are *now*. To begin with, their roles in the relationship are reversed. In the flush of young love, Bill was the leader. In their marriage, Susanna takes charge. She has to. She consults medical experts about head injuries. She goes to a therapist to help her deal with her feeling of disappointment and to understand Bill's situation. At the same time, she knows how much Bill loves her. In her first marriage, she did not feel valued or cherished. Bill gives that to her. He also gives her something else: the feeling of being needed—of being essential to him. "I decided I was going to stay with him," she says. "He needed me."

Now they exchange a different set of vows. Her wedding gift to him is acceptance plus caring. She accepts the colorful language. She accepts that he is going to spend his time watching television. He has his routine. He likes to browse in the bookstore and find new restaurants for lunch. They have a nice time together. "I accept him as who he is," says Susanna. She also cares for him, providing a social structure and safe environment for him. He has her unconditional support.

His gift to her is acceptance plus freedom. He accepts that she is a vibrant doer in the community, a leader in the law and in women's rights, a frequent-flyer mom whose two daughters are now married, one in Providence, one in San Diego. "He has never, never said I shouldn't do something. He's never put his foot down and said: *you're doing too much.* I am free to pursue my interests, visit the children. He's pleased when I do something well." She has Bill's unconditional support.

As they get older, they find increasing contentment in their marriage. They enjoy what they share—taking a drive in the country and discovering a new town, sitting down to dinner together—and are able to fulfill their individual potential in separate spheres.

One advantage in making their separate-but-together relationship work is that they each know how to be single. Both spent more than five years alone after being divorced. Bill is comfortable being by himself. Susanna's need for independence goes back to childhood. Her parents were horrified that she wanted to go to law school and become "a ball-breaking feminist," in her father's words. Susanna grows up wanting the approval of her parents, but not their restrictions. She remembers the summer of escape when she is sent away to camp to be a "little Indian," according to the camp brochure. They live in teepees. They eat meals in the Pow Wow Lodge where the dining room is painted bright yellow, the chairs are bright red, and on the walls are images of white antelopes and boys and girls fishing in a stream. To Susanna, the camp is a symbol of freedom. She remembers running barefoot and hollering on the warpath. "I could wear a loincloth. I could run around. I could chase baby deer. I could be Huck Finn. I could go swimming in my underwear. I could be a wild thing," she says.

In her marriage to Bill, Susanna can be a wild thing, running free, sustained by Bill's support. She can be who she really is—and so can Bill. "Even when, superficially, there may be a temper tantrum," she says. "That's not the real thing between us. I know what the real thing is."

To know the real thing, like Bill and Susanna, is to combine the Big Kiss with mutual acceptance and support. That is the formula for turning throwback romance into an enduring relationship. You carry the bolt of love from the past—but you have to learn how to cherish each other through accommodation and hard experience. It's another variation on settling.

✦

For the thousands of men and women who become single in this period, there are many opportunities to rediscover friends from previous chapters and perhaps find a partner among old acquaintances. You go back to your class reunion—a premier mixer for dating and re-mating in this stage. You adjust for balding heads and thicker waistlines and see the kid with long hair in a face with fine lines. You listen to the Rolling Stones . . . the Jefferson Airplane. *Whatever happened to* _____? It's quickly apparent who is married, who is divorced or widowed—who is available, who is not.

You find each other at funerals that bring you back to a hometown you left years ago. A death prompts a letter of sympathy that leads to dinner. You connect at grief groups. That's how my 80-year-old cousin found his third great love: he was answering the help line of the widowed persons organization in Washington when the woman at the other end of the phone said: "Are you the same John that used to drive a red MG?" Turned out they knew each other decades ago when they were both working for the federal government.

You meet at weddings of the young. That's how another cousin met his second wife—they were part of the parental wedding party of older friends and family members. The parents of the bride had known them both separately for decades; their instant romance was a throwback by proxy.

You go online and search. Not necessarily for a relationship, you say to yourself, but to retrieve a piece of your past. A friend tells me about reconnecting with his old girlfriend. There were good reasons for breaking up more than forty years ago. He's content in his marriage, but he wonders what happened to her. He finds her. She is married, too. They exchange messages, reminisce about their glorious bike trip around Holland one spring. He feels good about reconnecting.

At the same time, hooking up with an old flame can spell trouble.[2] You can get sucked back into a difficult relationship. Many romances of youth are better left in memory.

---

2. An extreme example of a throwback romance gone wrong is in *The Visit* by Freidrich Durrenmatt. In this dark comedy, an older woman returns to her hometown and reconnects with her former lover in order to seek revenge on him for having jilted her when they were young. The woman, now rich, offers to subsidize the town with her millions in return for his murder.

The problems with a throwback relationship can be subtle. Without re-alizing it, you may be using the romance to rewrite an earlier chapter in an attempt to resolve "unfinished business" from the past. You shine light on the dark places of childhood by loving someone from that period—a strategy where a new love literally kisses the hurt and makes it feel better, as a mother would heal a child. This is unconscious, of course. You meet someone from high school days and Cupid shoots an arrow through your heart. It's a double challenge: to create a real relationship while working through your private agenda.

George Dickinson* is a screenwriter in Hollywood. That is, when he's employed on a television series or a movie. He falls in love with movies as a kid growing up in Lexington, Kentucky. Every Saturday afternoon, he'd go to the matinee movie and hang out with Western cowboy heroes. That love never dies. Not like his two marriages, which end in divorce. Women like him; they tell him he looks like Clint Eastwood. He knows where that conversation is going to lead; he's been around the track a few times.

When the doctor in Lexington calls to say that his mother has pancre-atic cancer, he goes home for the first time since he left for California at age 18. Except for flyby drop-ins on the way to New York, George has stayed away from Kentucky. Every year he'd bring his mother out to the West Coast for a long vacation—to get to know his two daughters, to watch the movie stars on Rodeo Drive, to marvel at the Pacific.

He lets himself into the house where his mother moved right after the War. Everything about Lexington is smaller than what he remembers. The hill he mastered as a 6-year-old on his bike doesn't exist anymore—it's a mere gentle rise on the road. The big kitchen where the sun pours through the window in the afternoon, where he would sit and talk to his mother after school—it has room for only two chairs. His father died in the War, after the armistice in Europe is signed, in a truck accident near Munich; George is born two days later. His older brother is 4; but there is something wrong with him, he doesn't talk. Fifteen years later, he drowns at a summer camp for the mentally retarded.

A photograph of his father in uniform sits on a table in the living room, along with a photo of his brother on a horse. His father: pure Eastern Kentucky who went east to college and spent most of his time acting in plays. The Hasty Pudding show, his mother would boast. She is the granddaughter of a coal baron. After the War, the family has a silver tea set but no money. His mother goes to work in the administration office of the University of Kentucky and is home by three every afternoon.

Saturday: movie time. Westerns with his best friend, who has two parents and lives in a large house down the street. *The Man from Laramie, Bad Day at Black Rock, Gunfight at the O.K. Corral.* George vows then to get as far away as he could from Kentucky.

The doctor tells him three months.

When he walks into the Markey Cancer Center at the University of Kentucky hospital, he sees a familiar face, reminiscent of Grace Kelly in *High Noon*, the perfect unattainable blond of his teenage years, the daughter of a mogul in the thoroughbred industry, a fixture at the Keeneland Race Course. Her mother and his mother had been classmates in school; but growing up, they all lived in worlds apart.

"George, George," says the voice. *"I can't believe it. Hollywood. Omigod, you look like Clint Eastwood!"*

Jenny McIntyre* has the charm and confidence of having always been a beautiful, seductive woman. Too seductive, perhaps, with three marriages, multiple affairs, and a live-in relationship with one of the trainers in her father's horse farm. People talk, but she doesn't care. She has a mission, she tells him: to provide support to families with cancer. Her daughter is a cancer survivor, treated for Hodgkin's disease four years ago and is doing well, she says. How do families that don't have resources deal with major illness? She's started an organization to help families cope—with doctors who don't talk to each other, with bewildering insurance forms and the emotional fallout on all members of the family. She puts her arms around him and hugs him. *"Whatever you need,"* says Jenny.

George falls deeply in love with her.

He looks after his mother, who enters a hospice facility and lives four months. "Jenny saved me," he says. Mostly he stays with Jenny in her house. He meets her two sons; the younger one is starting college, the older one is working for her father. Her daughter is finishing up at Vanderbilt University.

Jenny takes him to the country club, where he sees more familiar faces in a room of blue blazers. *"Hey, George! Loved Hawaii 5-0!"* No, he wasn't involved with that show. *"Ever run into Nicole Kidman?"* He smiles. It's January and cold and he misses California weather. *"Do come next Saturday, we're having a party,"* says a matron who once had pigtails. Jenny squeezes his arm, gives him a sultry smile, and walks him around the room. *"George—great to see you,"* says another classmate. Jenny breaks off to greet a gentleman from Virginia who has just bought a horse from her father.

Over the months of his mother dying, he also sees his childhood movie buddy, who married a girl next door and just took early retirement from the Jif peanut butter plant. They've kept up over the years. *"You and Jenny,"* says his old friend. George smiles: Maybe this is it. Maybe she's the one. *"Be careful,"* says his friend. *"She's like her father—always checking out the next racehorse."*

After his mother dies, George sells the house and sends the family stuff to his daughters. He keeps his clothes and books at Jenny's. He returns to LA and starts up a long-distance relationship. He enjoys the visits with Jenny—going back to the rolling hills, so beautiful and serene to him now. He connects with old friends and cousins. He begins a new screenplay, the story of a family out of the Kentucky mines. *"Sounds dark,"* says Jenny. Her favorite movie is *Seabiscuit*. She's excited about a 2-year-old in her father's stable. *"A winner,"* she says.

George remembers the horses at his grandparents'—two stubby ponies, mellow with age—a simpler barnyard scene with chickens and pigs. It's been a long time since he was around that musky smell of horse and leather. Jenny's smell: the combination of sweat, flesh, muck . . . and the grease of money. He is standing in front of her father's stable in early spring. The air is heavy, not like California. He watches the thorough-breds out in the new grass. Two chestnuts, and a bay: each weighing 1,200 pounds—high-priced, high-strung, high-maintenance. A trainer comes around the corner, leading another potential winner of the Kentucky Derby. George steps aside . . . and says to himself: *What am I doing here?*

He doesn't want to let go of Jenny, her soft skin, her enthusiasm for everything, her ability to make the party go. She hooks into a deep place. Jenny is the princess who has chosen him to be her knight—something that never would have happened when they were young. But the commute is draining—he organizes assignments in New York so he can stop off in Lexington. They see each other less frequently. Out of sight, out of mind? He is the one who initiates visits now. Once he calls her and a man answers. One of the trainers who'd come in to feed the house cats while she is at a horse show in Virginia.

George takes on a grim determination not to lose her, to push ahead as a couple. "I really loved her," he says. In previous relationships, he has been the bolter; this time he wants to see it through. He's as sure as he'll ever be. Couldn't he write as well in Kentucky as in California? His daughters grow concerned—Appalachia over Orange County?

One evening in late September he arrives at the Lexington airport and they go to a new restaurant, a little fancy, and Jenny is bubbling over about the horses and her trip to Virginia, and then she tells him her big news: the gentleman from Virginia, the one who bought a horse from her father, he's a big deal with the Virginia Horse Show Association in Lexington, Virginia—he's asked her to marry him and she's so excited: this is it; she's finally going to settle down. They plan to split their time between the two Lexingtons. . . .

He stares at her. . . . BITCH! He doesn't say anything. Three weeks earlier they were in bed together. *"Now, I didn't lead you on,"* she says. *"We were both free."* George mumbles: *"Yes . . . free . . . we certainly are free."* She tells him how special the Virginia gentleman is, how they are going to be partners and raise horses together, how he is endowing her little cancer organization. George breaks in: *"I thought we had a future."* She flutters; how could they—he'd never leave LA . . . really! *"But we must stay in touch,"* she says. *"Now, your clothes and books—shall I send them to LA? . . . And you have to let me know about your play. . . . You'll always be on my Christmas list."*

George is glad he ordered bourbon on the rocks. He finishes his glass and takes one last long look at her. She's pointing out the specials on the menu. He gets up from the table. *"Take me off your Christmas list,"* he says. And then the cowboy walks out of the saloon.

It takes a while for George to recover. He holes up in his daughter's house in Newport Beach and starts working on his screenplay about the tangled lives of coal barons and miners. He hangs out with his two grandsons and walks the beach. He begins to feel lighter. Always takes two to ruin a relationship. He put so much pressure on Jenny to take away the darkness of his childhood. Maybe that kind of infatuation can morph into love. But he was so steeped in his own agenda with the death of his mother. The throwback romance was too much in his head, too little about the person behind the princess mask.

He ends up with good memories: those delirious months together. Jenny made him *want* to be back in Lexington, the first step in confronting his past. The rest he does himself: he keeps up with his old friends and newfound cousins. He gives a lecture on movies at the university in honor of his mother. He promises to bring his daughters to see the Kentucky Derby. He's hoping his screenplay will be made into an HBO movie. He's 60 years old and feeling good.

A throwback romance can light a fire in you. As with George, it can also camouflage a deeper process in your own personal development. A loved one may help you experience the past in a new way—that's often the role of friends and family and partners. But you alone are the one to revise the script and settle the past.

It helps to step back after the first rush of throwback infatuation and figure out: how much of this passion is driven by a desire to rewrite the past—and how much is fueled by the quality of the relationship? Is there a mix of common interests and values that lay the groundwork for companionship? As George learned, without a real knowledge of each other and a shared template of what's important, a romance withers. Just because the person is a throwback doesn't mean there's an automatic foundation for love.

◆

Some people never let go. You're stuck on the First Great Love. You hang on to its fever, its fantasy. You don't let others get close because you are already "taken." That's when a throwback romance becomes a fatal engagement.

Linda Koenig* gets out her grandmother's cracked Old Willow teapot to make tea—a new ritual now that she's retired from Wall Street. The teapot is the one family piece that she's kept. Not like her mother in Kansas City who hordes everything from Linda's report cards to boxy red-vinyl pocketbooks from the 1950s. Linda is a minimalist. She wears Manhattan standard black—foldable, washable, wrinkle-proof pantsuits—and she never checks a bag when she flies. Her motto: travel light. But now she wonders if that explains why she is single after two marriages and numerous flirtations. Perhaps hoarding is a sign of attachment: people who keep things and live in the clutter of knickknacks and broken furniture have the same psychological "drivers" as people who make commitments in marriage—they are able to live in the clutter of a daily relationship. Not Linda. Sometimes she thinks she shed two husbands the way she gave her two (slightly worn) winter coats to the clothing drive at church.

She pours a cup of tea and admires the gilded teapot with its famous Chinese blue design. She is 66, glamorous with silky gray hair, hazel eyes, and a slightly mischievous smile. After all, she has a lifelong lover. *He* called and left a message yesterday: *"I love you. . . . We should have married."*

They meet their senior year in high school. Jim Hills,* a newcomer to Kansas City from New Jersey, handsome, athletic, the quick Irish grin. He asks her to dance at the class gala in the gym. "There was a wonderful feeling of comfort and warmness. We danced all night. I went home wild with excitement and did not sleep a wink," Linda recalls. They date and neck in the car. "Intense longing on my part," she says. But after she comes back from spring break, she hears that Jim is taking other girls out to parties. She is heartbroken. She is 17. She heads east to college and ultimately to a fast-paced career in banking.

But the pattern is set: intense connection followed by heartbreak. He reappears and disappears throughout her life. At Barnard College, he would suddenly arrive at her dorm. "I would immediately fall into his arms," she says—afterward, no word for months. Then a letter: *"I miss you. . . ."* She'd write back. Nothing. Every time she goes home to Kansas City, she sees him. "It always felt the same—but it always ended the same," she says. On one visit—she has her first big job at the Chase Manhattan Bank—she ends up spending the night with Jim in his new apartment. This is it, she thinks. They will be together forever. A few days later, she learns from a friend that Jim is planning to get married . . . to someone else. She picks herself up and goes back to New York. A few years later, Jim reappears. He's about to go to Vietnam and calls her. "He wanted to know—*did I love him?* He said he loved me. He missed me," says Linda, adding: "He had a wife and a child on the way."

His reappearances disrupt her two marriages. Her first husband is an antipoverty lawyer; they have a 2-year-old son when the phone rings at her desk. Meet me in a hotel. He tells her (again) that he misses her—that he loves her, that she is the only one. "It excited the old feelings," she says. "He made me feel fully alive." She sees what is missing in her marriage, propelling her to break up with her husband.

After her first marriage breaks up, she and Jim see each other every month or so for the next several years. One weekend they meet in Las Vegas and have wild sex at the Flamingo Hilton. But after that, not much. "He'd come here. I'd go there, but nothing is happening," she says. Linda goes into therapy and eventually remarries. "The marriage was not very happy, but it was not bad," she says. As with many blended families, there are strains between the stepparents and children—her son and his two daughters. Her husband has taken over a nonprofit agency to provide job training and assistance to people with disabilities. He is rarely home before dinner. Jim calls her. *"I think about you all the time,"* he says. A few months later, Linda goes to their thirtieth high school reunion; her husband is too busy to go with her.

Linda and Jim dance in the old high school gym. *"I should have married you,"* he tells her. They start up all over again. "I was intoxicated," she says. They meet in Atlanta and Pittsburgh under the cover of business meetings. They spend two perfect days in Atlantic City. "He said he was leaving his wife and we would live together," she recalls. Finally! She decides to leave her husband and make the commitment to Jim. "It is at this point that I felt the relationship was fully realized. I made an adult choice to be with him and give it everything I had. I was determined to be positive."

She separates from her second husband—breaking his heart. He is a nice man, she says. She doesn't want to hurt him. But this other is so powerful, she says. Then Jim withdraws again. He returns to his wife. At this point, Linda is hurt, but how could she be surprised? She reinvents her life. She focuses more attention on her son. She moves to a different section in the bank and becomes a mentor to younger women in business. She gathers around her a network of friends. She starts dating again.

Jim doesn't change. Every couple of years, he contacts her. "I no longer had any belief that we would live together, but I still wanted to see him. The intoxication was never the same, but it was a lot of fun and very comfortable," she says. "We had conversations that I never had with anyone else, and he made me feel very beautiful."

Fifteen years after the high school reunion, Linda, 62, returns to Kansas City for several weeks to take care of her 86-year-old mother, who has broken her hip. At a party with old friends, she runs into a high school classmate—an attractive woman who lived for many years in Washington and worked for the FBI. "I asked her why she had moved back," begins Linda, "and she said: *'Well, I've never mentioned this, but at our high school reunion, Jim Hills asked me to move back and live with him. But he didn't leave his wife.'"*

Linda is speechless. "I simply had no capacity to understand this. The happiest period in my life had apparently been duplicated with someone else. Who knows how many others are out there?" Linda leaves Jim an angry voice mail message: *you'll not be hearing from me again.* The final break, she says.

But the pattern has become a ritual. He starts calling her again.

> He: *"How are you? Did you love me?"*
> She: *"What's wrong?"*
> He: *"The doctors say I have Alzheimer's disease. . . . I love you. I*
> *wish we were living together."*

Now they talk three times a week. Jim hangs on to early memories, the high school dance, the first kiss. "He wants as much love and support as he can get," she says. "I'm happy to give it to him. I'm not angry at him anymore." He calls on his cell phone so his wife won't know. But this is the end game. In a while he won't be able to dial the numbers and his wife will take the phone away.

A big part of Linda is relieved. There's an edge of triumph over a man who promised so much and delivered so little, who hurt her and abused her. But he is also "the love of my life," she says; the wild, wicked, sexual adventurer against whom her husbands and other suitors seemed so pale. "The unavailable fantasy is more powerful than the available reality," she explains. "It was always easy to slip back into this fantasy life." Jim is the rail of lifelong passion, undiluted by sharing a bathroom year after year.

Besides, this shadow relationship has given her the space to grow. "Deep down, I don't share well," she says. No baggage. No burdens. No things. She needs a lot of room to be her true self. "I now realize just how well he has served me: he comes, he goes. I cry, I long, I languish, and then I reinvent myself." In a life of continual reinvention, she's created a family that includes three grandchildren; she's built a distinguished career; she is surrounded by her chosen circle of loved ones. She is comfortable with herself.

Meanwhile, Jim and Linda are true to each other in their fashion. She is gladdened by his phone calls, his mushy words of love. A very long engagement! The tension of an on again, off again affair is gone. No more agonizing—*will he, won't he; should I, could we?* They've settled in for how much longer they have. They are fixed on the basics: *I love you.*

Linda pours another cup from the Old Willow teapot.

Intermittent gratification has a powerful impact on behavior. The sometimes yes, sometimes no relationship can be more compelling than one that is all yes, or one that is all no. It also traps people in doomed situations like a gambler hooked on a slot machine. How much is this passion taking out of you? Those moments of ecstasy can exact a high price. They leave out the committed engagement part. You don't learn how to negotiate what you need and desire in the close quarters of intimacy. You are so attached to fantasy that you become immune to others who could perhaps bond with you in the more complicated zone of reality. No earthling can compete with the fantasy lover.

How much does a person miss by hanging on to an impossible love object? At this stage of life, the resilient don't go to the graveyard of regret. They find the positive in the past—and the future. For Linda, this strange finale with Jim is a peaceful reconciliation between the longing for great passion and the need for emotional safety—which for Linda, like many people, involves a lot of private space. Her intimate narrative is made up of moments of high-risk romance and long stretches of self-made security. Mixed in are loving relationships with children, grandchildren, friends, and neighbors. Linda is content.

✦

The modern throwback romance has enduring appeal because it adds a new twist to the old Romeo and Juliet tale. The plot is familiar: Boy and girl fall desperately in love. Girl's parents block the marriage. At this point, nobody dies. It's the 1950s. Brokenhearted, the two go their separate ways—for the next thirty years. In 1900, when life expectancy was less than 50, that would probably be the end of the story. But not today.

With longer life spans, the couple can ultimately triumph with a happy ending. The challenge is to rewrite Shakespeare's ending so that it remains true to the fairy-tale beginning. Or you turn it around: you use the original romance to sustain the new sequel.

Jenifer and Stephen McDermott live in Greenville, South Carolina. They have been married about twenty years. But their romance begins fifty years ago in Steamboat Springs, Colorado, at a summer camp for theater and dance. Jenifer, 20, is a junior at Vassar College, an aspiring actress; Steve, five years older, is a musician—a conductor and composer. For him, the moment of falling in love comes when he watches her audition for the starring role in the play *Ondine* by Jean Giraudoux, with her husky voice, her Audrey Hepburn looks (Hepburn starred in the Broadway performance), her seductive elegance. For her, the moment comes one night when they are running down a mountainside and they hold hands under the stars. "We had our different areas. His was music. Mine was theater and dance," Jenifer recalls. Their love unfolds in "that whole artistic, creative context"—the aphrodisiac of sharing youth, work, and dreams. He asks her to marry him.

Her parents intervene. Jenifer is the only child of older parents, a proper girl sent to private schools, dressed in organdy dresses and black patent-leather pumps, raised with a governess. Her father, career army, would not allow defiance in his troops or in his daughter. Jenifer obeys. She knows the cold look of rage in her father's eyes. She also knows her parents' love. She could not—would not—defy their wishes. They want her to marry someone suitable—a lawyer or a diplomat, not an artist. They expect this theater phase to pass—an interesting experience for a debutante, but not a life.

And so, Jenifer breaks off the relationship with Steve and destroys his letters. *For never was a story of more woe/Than this of Jenifer and her Romeo.* They disappear from each other's lives.

In the next chapter of her narrative, Jenifer goes on to marry Mr. Right and have three children, another kind of love story. They live in Houston. But the relationship starts to unravel. It's a raw, difficult time for Jenifer with the death of her parents and the breakdown of her marriage. In 1980, she and her husband divorce after twenty years of married life. Throughout, Jenifer keeps up her love of theater. After the divorce she goes to work full-time in theater development.

The years go by. She thinks about Steve and wonders what has happened to him. In 1985, on a visit to Chicago to see her grown daughter, she recalls that Steve went to college in Chicago. Well, why not. Through the college's records, she tracks him down in Little Rock, Arkansas. "I wrote a careful letter thinking he might have a fat wife and five children," says Jenifer. A month later, Steve replies: "You have totally turned my world upside down. I never dreamed I would hear from you again."

And so begins a furious exchange of letters written, as before, in longhand on yellow legal paper. Steve tells her that he has had other relationships but never married. She writes him about her marriage, her children. Steve explains how he pursued a career in music, becoming the music director at a college in Missouri, teaching the history of dance and music. She describes her continuing work in the theater. Finally her daughter says: *"Mom—is writing all you're going to do?"*

They arrange a meeting in Houston. When they reconnect, "it was like we were 20," she says. The magnet of attraction to a person in your past is so potent, explains Jenifer. When you are young, "you are your truest self." Then social pressures and the passage of time take hold and "you lose yourself for a while." Finally, in these later decades, "you discover who you really are," she says. Instead of sorrow and Shakespeare's "glooming peace," there is gratitude and another chance to love.

This time when he asks her to marry him, she says yes.

On Thanksgiving Day, Steve, 57, sits down with Jenifer, 52, and her three children and reads aloud his love letter of thanksgiving:

> *I am thankful that you and I found each other on that mountain in Colorado . . . thankful you sought me out . . . thankful you and I found, gently but intensely, swiftly and firmly, that our love for each other does exist as truly and deeply and strongly as it did*

thirty-two years ago. I am thankful for love's goodness, purity,
beauty, radiance, strength and endurance. And now in marriage,
we lead each other into new and vast dimensions, spaces,
terrains. I thank you, Jenifer, just for being. You are a miracle in
my life.

On the wall of their house hangs the framed Thanksgiving letter. The romantic glow has settled down. They survive that gasping, *oh-dear-what-have-I-done* period. Steve, 78, enjoys music recitals. Jenifer, 73, is on the board of the local theater and is active in an interfaith project. She looks up at the framed letter. To be called a miracle! "That's pretty outstanding. You could live on that for a long time. It's my intention to be that miracle for as long as I can. I have a reputation to keep," she says with a smile.

"It's the most profound kind of affirmation," she continues. "There is nothing I wouldn't do to hang on to it now," she says.

12

Serial Spouses

The grandchildren issue the wedding invitation. The grown sons are the ushers. The bride and groom are grandparents. Susan Leonard, 60, and Ed Thornton, 68, walk down a makeshift aisle at the Politics & Prose bookstore in Washington, D.C., to exchange their marriage vows—turning the generations upside down. Yet the ceremony is traditional, with flowers and music, a reading from *The Little Prince*, champagne, and cheers.

Newlyweds of a certain age belong to an experimental group in the laboratory of marriage. You're not looking to the institution as a framework for raising children or establishing a work life. You seek intimacy, comfort, and companionship in the final decades of life—which could be thirty or more years. You may not even get legally married, but you become a couple and make the shared commitment to love and cherish. All this puts you in the vanguard of the New Normal, which places a high value on mutual fulfillment.

You differ from younger couples in important ways. The Leonard-Thornton merger illustrates the elements of a late-stage union: rich *relational history*—Susan is divorced and Ed is a widower, *life empowerment* rooted in experience and personal development (they know who they are), *complementarity* of interests and ethics (what attracted them to each other), and a sense of urgency (how much time is left?).

Ed and Susan are shaped by their pasts. Susan's first marriage lasts thirty years. She and her husband marry young but, over time, the relationship burns out. "We didn't know each other anymore," she says. After a divorce ten years ago, she turns to a career in the federal government and creates a circle of women friends. She goes out on dates. A period of singlehood "was extremely important. My identity changed from being wife and mother to being a professional woman," says Susan. Without this time on her own, she wouldn't have been ready for another marriage, she says. "I had to have some bad experiences—and some mediocre ones—to find out what I wanted and to be clear about it."

It is the same with Ed. He changes in a different way. All through his career in running nonprofit organizations, he is a hard-charging alpha male. But when his first wife develops cancer, he makes a dramatic shift. He stays home for six months to take care of her. After her death, he goes back to work but he has no heart for it. He decides to leave the zoom zone of work. For a while, he manages a bookstore. Then he starts a nonprofit company to provide transportation to older men and women to go to the doctor, or to the symphony. If Susan had met him during his aggressive career days, she might not have liked him very much. But after his wife's death, Ed redefines himself. By the time Ed and Susan meet, they are different from the way they were.

Both are ready to mate. They each decide that they want to share their life with someone—before they meet—and are proactive in their search. Susan enlists friends and colleagues to help her find a partner. She cleans out her closet so that she would wear only clothes that were suitable for a date. She makes up a list of forty-three characteristics that she is looking for in a mate—likes to have fun, willing to challenge me, does not smoke, loves sex. She is about to search online when a mutual acquaintance puts Susan and Ed together. On the first date, she is so nervous that afterward she forgets what he looks like. But she remembers that he told her he had gone to see the movie *A Beautiful Mind* and enjoyed it. That was a movie she had liked, too. On her list of desired qualities, Ed scores 83 percent. If there were deal-breakers, they want to know early so "we could finish before it got started," she says. Both share this sense of urgency. "When you're young, you think you've got all the time in the world. When you're older, you know things could change."

Both are looking for a Long-Term Person with similar tastes and values. In the New Normal, there is more bonding between "like" and "like." Gender roles tend to blur as people get older. Men are not so rooted in work; women become "a little feisty," says historian Stephanie Coontz of The Evergreen State College in Olympia, who is also director of research and public education for the Council on Contemporary Families. "You find greater blending. Male and female stereotypes are softened. That augurs well."

Ed and Susan discover much in common. Both love to read, so the bookstore is a perfect setting for their wedding. Friends and family gather around the stacks of books. More champagne. More giggles from the grandchildren. The traditional family expands—incorporating previous ties into their new bond. Susan's former husband and his second wife attend the wedding. At subsequent family reunions with the grandchildren, Ed and her "wasband" are thrown together. And Susan likes to hear stories about Ed's first wife. They have dinner with Ed's former father-in-law.

The newlyweds go through a greening period—after all, they're used to having their own space. But age has taught them to be more tolerant and generous in love. "I think we're both more conscious of the preciousness of life. The power of forgiveness is important to us. Living with anyone is an opportunity for blame and criticism," says Susan. Ed continues his transportation service. Sometimes they both drive a client to a far-off destination. Susan has started a new career in fabric art. "We try to be present to one another. We don't take things for granted," she says. No chance of drift, this time. They avoid angry blowups by "going to the positive end of the scale and being grateful for what we have," says Susan. "I'm very happy."

✦

Re-coupling in this stage is a phenomenon of healthy longevity. Most newlyweds over age 50 have been married before. Many have been divorced;

as age rises, an increasing proportion has been widowed. As more people live longer and are able to re-couple more often, the serial spouse is likely to represent the dominant pathway in the New Normal of marriage.

For couples like Ed and Susan, marriage is the ultimate symbol of an enduring relationship. They want the wedding ceremony with its public declaration of commitment and call to the community for support. As Susan says: "We didn't want any back door. We wanted to commit to the relationship and give it 100 percent. We're in this or we're not—nothing in between."

But many other couples form committed relationships without the legal tie. The problem arises when one wants to tie the knot and the other does not. Can you settle and stay together?

The two of them meet on match.com. They both have been widowed and are in their 70s. "He kept on sending emails and it just worked out. He has the best sense of humor," she says. They become a couple. They plan to get married. The invitations are sent out. Her goddaughter, a harpist with the symphony, is going to play at the wedding.

A month before the wedding, he says: *"I want to talk to you."* They sit down at the table.

> He: *"I want to tell you that I cannot get married. I don't know why but I just can't."*
> She: *"No! You won't do that to me!"*
> He: *"Yes. I have to. I cannot marry you. I love you and I want to be with you, but marriage—I never want to get married. I don't want to marry anybody."*

She is in turmoil. How could he? She breaks off the relationship. But he won't go.

> He: *"I know I hurt you and I'm really sorry. Please try to understand. . . . It took courage for me to do that."*
> She: *[Expletive!]*

Indeed, it takes courage to be honest—even at the risk of losing the one you love. He explains why he cannot embrace the legal strictures of a marriage. Both have complications from the past. He is responsible for a granddaughter who was disabled from an injury in a car crash. She is responsible for a son with mental retardation. These entanglements require boundaries, he says.

He loves her; he wants her. Can she accept him as a lifelong companion—without a wedding band?

"I gave in because I missed him and I decided that I didn't want to break up with him just because I wasn't getting *all* of what I wanted," she says. Their sex life is good. He's an engineer who likes to fix things around the house. "It's the best relationship I've ever had," she says.

A year after the nonwedding, they have a commitment ceremony. Out go the invitations: Same guest list—adult children and grandchildren. Same location—a garden with blooming flowers. Same pledge to love and to cherish. In front of their community of family and friends, he plights his troth: *"I want to tell you how much I love you. I am committed to you for the rest of my life."*

In the New Normal, committed coupledom is a form of "marriage." Many older men and women want to keep their names and their family obligations separate. They may choose cohabitation and live together like a married couple. They can own property together. They accompany each other on doctors' appointments. They take on the grandparenting role with each other's offspring. Late-stage cohabitation is like a bonus marriage.

Another variation is to live in separate households. Or in different cities. These are the living apart, loving together (LALT) couples. Sometimes, the issues are practical: you live in different places because that's where you work. Or you just like having your own address. Instead of a room of your own, you want a place of your own. "My girlfriend lives two miles away," an old friend and former colleague tells me. "She's lived in her house for twenty-five years. She doesn't want to move. And I love my house. I look out on the river. I don't want to move. But we're as close as a married couple could be." They see each other every day. They sleep together—sometimes at her place, sometimes at his place. They spend the holidays together. They travel together. He helps her tend to her mother, who is suffering from Alzheimer's disease. She stood by him when his mother died a few years ago. They both have grown children. She is a widow. He is divorced, a veteran of one marriage and another long-term relationship. The way these serial spouses ensure a balance of closeness and private space is to have separate addresses.

The issue in all variations of the New Normal is commitment. Some people want to get married with all the trimmings. Others find the construct of a legal marriage too limiting. Yet you love another and want to make a 100 percent commitment to a relationship. There are no hard rules for coupling in this stage of life. You have more flexibility in the structure of the relationship. Whatever works best for two people is the right pathway. Married and unmarried—living together or living apart— you face the same challenges that confront all serial spouses: to build an enduring bond out of the legacy of previous relationships.

✦

Serial spouses can seem similar in tastes and background, but their intimate narratives may be different. You both like Chicken Cacciatore, foreign movies such as *The Counterfeiters* and *Grand Illusion*, and hiking. You share the same religion and have the same level of education. But your history in previous relationships is divergent. New partners have to create a common intimate zone out of sometimes contrasting experiences.

Brooke Swenson is stunningly beautiful with shoulder-length white hair; Charles ("Chuck") Morosini has warm sexy eyes, a gentle manner. They've known each other for forty years. Brooke and her former husband and Chuck and his former wife were good friends. After their spouses died, they found each other in a new way. Brooke lives in a farmhouse in Connecticut; Chuck lives in a small town in New Hampshire. They are a LALT couple.

They have much in common: same age (both in their early 70s); same sense of humor; shared history—all those times together as separate couples, the knowing of each other's children. But for all their similarities, their intimate narratives are different. Chuck has had one marriage that lasted forty-seven years. Brooke has followed the serial pathway of marriage, divorce, and remarriage. When they become a couple, the single track of a long marriage is joined with the multiple track of sequential relationships.

Brooke's story is rich and varied. Both of her marriages start with a *coup de foudre*. Chapter One with her first husband: "He knocked my socks off," says Brooke. It is a quick romance. After four months, they decide to get married. A perfect fit on paper—Main Line Philadelphia and Proper Boston. They have two sons. But the relationship is overwhelmed by her husband's alcoholism. After five years, they get divorced.

Chapter Two: She is a divorced woman in the early 1960s before the divorce revolution takes hold a decade later. To break up her marriage is to go against family and social convention. The following two years are a test of survival. She takes the boys and lives in New York City. But her single period is short. Within two years, she re-couples with a man eighteen years older.

Chapter Three with Eric Swenson: a charismatic, mentoring husband—a father figure. "I was madly in love with him, too," she says. "Eric and I could talk about anything and everything." Eric proposes on the beach. He brings her into his world of publishing, expands her horizon on national affairs; she becomes a Democrat and develops a passion for politics. They have a daughter. It is a long marriage of nearly forty years.

In the halls of a university, students learn as much as they can from the professor, and then they break away and become stars in their own right. In the rooms of a marriage, the same evolution may take place: the wife[1] blossoms under the tutelage of a knowledgeable husband and then at a certain point she evolves into her own person. That's what happens with Eric and Brooke. Eric has the leverage of age—and with it comes the Entitlement Syndrome: entitled to be the one who is always right. "I was

---

1. This process can also occur when a husband blossoms under the guidance of a supportive wife. As he becomes more his own person, he may want to break away from what he now sees as an oppressive mother figure.

deferential to him. It took me years to think and say: maybe I have a point to make. We did things his way for the longest while," Brooke recalls.

When she becomes more assertive, the relationship has to change. In Chapter Four with Eric, they negotiate for a fairer balance. After Eric retires and is at home, they have to figure out how to be co-partners and exist in the same space. Eric is thinking—how can this whippersnapper, nearly twenty years younger, have a better idea? "I didn't want to be right. I just wanted to be heard," says Brooke. Eric softens. He is struggling with jolts of loss—he no longer goes into work; his golf game is off; sailboat racing becomes too risky. He doesn't want to lose his place in the marriage. He appreciates Brooke's talents, especially her feats as a chef. One time, with the garden overflowing with zucchini, she makes a whole meal of different gourmet versions of the vegetable. *"You are very clever,"* he tells her. The meal prompts her to do a cookbook of zucchini recipes.

Chapter Five: The dynamic completely changes again when Eric develops congestive heart failure. Brooke, who had looked after her parents in their later years, becomes the caretaker. "I returned to my accommodating self. . . . He appreciated that," she says. The role balance is reversed. Eric is now the receiver, the dependent one. Brooke helps him get around. "We were devoted."

The marriage has evolved from student and teacher to negotiating co-partners to care-giver and receiver. After his death, Brooke begins another chapter. She is on her own for about two years, content to garden, to be with her grandchildren, to write about her political opinions, her feelings about life.

Her next chapter is with Chuck.

If Brooke's story is a landscape of peaks and hills and valleys, Chuck's topography is more like the plains. His narrative is simpler. There is less overt turmoil. He marries young, at age 23, when he's a medical student. It's an old-fashioned, shotgun wedding: his wife, Helen, is pregnant. "I obviously liked her. I grew to love her. It was a good marriage," he says. They have three daughters. Their relationship deepens. "No separations, no big fights. It was a nice marriage." He'd had many girlfriends in his youth, but after marriage he's a faithful husband. He becomes a successful cardiologist. He retires from practice at age 66. "I couldn't stand the paperwork." Meanwhile, he develops a hobby—woodworking.

Chuck and his first wife were a popular couple. Both are raconteurs. Their life runs smoothly until she develops thrombophlebitis. She has few symptoms, and the doctors don't find cancer of the ovary until her final surgery. She never knew the diagnosis and died four days later. "I felt sad," says Chuck, but he's a doctor and he's familiar with death. "I'm a pragmatist. Something I can't do anything about—I get over it. I was saddened. We had a good life. One of us has to die first. I thought it was going to be me." After her death, "I figured I'd play out the string," he says. "I was perfectly content. I'll do my woodworking."

And then he falls in love with Brooke. Very quickly, he is caught up in the thrall of the *coup de foudre*. "Look at her—she's gorgeous!" he says. "Sometimes I feel like a teenager." He spends more and more time thinking about her, calling her. "It's entirely different. I didn't knock her up. I didn't have to get involved with her. This is something I entered fully, without hesitation. I really love her. I'm a little surprised."

For Chuck, the *coup* is a new experience. But not for Brooke. That is the major difference between them. Brooke worries that her slightly lower-voltage feelings are unfair to Chuck. But he recognizes what he calls their asymmetric balance and accepts it. Their challenge is to bring the more passionate rail (his) and the more companionate rail (hers) into one track of growing attachment.

Like young lovers, they are tentative at first. How to know what the other wants? How to please each other? They go through an early O. Henry phase.[2] At the restaurant: Do you drink still water or sparkling? The first time, he orders the bubbly water, but she notices he doesn't drink very much. Maybe he prefers regular. The next time they go out, she says:

---

2. O. Henry, "The Gift of the Magi," the short story in which two lovers sacrifice what they hold dear to give each other what the other would most prize.

"Let's order regular tap water." He doesn't drink very much of that either. The next time, he automatically orders regular water because that's what she suggested at the previous meal. Finally, after half a dozen dinners—and with some amusement—they figure out that they both prefer seltzer.

The romance is ignited by Chuck's daughter, Dana Reeve, the widow of Christopher Reeve, chair of the Christopher Reeve Foundation. Dana suggests her dad bring Brooke to a gala fund-raising event with a cast of stars from Robin Williams and Meryl Streep to Brooke's neighbors, Joanne Woodward and Paul Newman. Chuck and Brooke make a glamorous couple—she with her sparkling white hair and trim figure, he with the sexy smile. *"I'm his escort,"* jokes Brooke. Meryl Streep with a twinkling eye inquires: *"Are you from the service?"* That sends Robin Williams into an imagined dialogue between Chuck and the head of the escort service: *"Do you want the white hair or the midget?"* Laughter all around. More champagne, more toasts to the beauty and heroism of Dana Reeve.

After the gala, Chuck's daughter emails Brooke: *"Soooo great that you came. You looked beautiful. I hope my Dad was a gracious and fun escort."*

But the high of romance is mixed with sorrow. After the gala, Dana is diagnosed with lung cancer; she dies four months later at age 44. It is a terrible loss for Chuck. In a cruel irony, Eric's daughter from a previous marriage—also named Dana—dies the following summer. Chuck and Brooke draw closer.

Over the next few years, they establish their rhythm as a couple. They support each other in sickness; when she has a shoulder operation, Chuck takes care of her. When Chuck falls and hurts his hand, Brooke gets out the first-aid kit. They develop a pattern of teasing and appreciating each other. He kids her for having decade-old Band-Aids. With his hand all bandaged, he can't cut his toenails. Brooke gets out his nail clip. *"Best clip job I ever had,"* he jokes. There's a sensuous excitement between them. She calls him Love-Dove. He calls her Boo-Chick. "Her sense of humor is way better than I thought it was," says Chuck. "It's imaginative. I have a sense of humor. We laugh a lot."

Brooke and Chuck are finding ways to bridge their intensity gap. Chuck has to make sure that passion doesn't drive him crazy. For someone who has led a very stable relationship existence, this burst of feeling can be overwhelming. To be *in love* is to be made vulnerable to fatal questions of doubt and torment, such as: *Am I as good as . . . ? Who loves you more?* His answer: nobody.

Chuck's advantage is his pragmatism. What he can't change, he accommodates. For Brooke, learning to accept Chuck's love is a matter of learning to accept herself and her own self-worth. "It's an interesting reality to find that there is someone who likes you—just for who you are," she says.

Living apart gives them space to work out their dynamic. Brooke needs "alone time." After a lifetime of focusing on others (husbands and children), she relishes her independence. Finally, it's her "my time." With separate addresses, she doesn't feel smothered and is not prevented from spending time with her grandchildren who live nearby. Chuck also gains: he is not dependent on her for daily emotional attention; he has his own life in New Hampshire. He's taken up golf again. He's made more than forty-five big pieces of furniture—cupboards and tables and beds—and is working on a chest for Brooke.

Brooke grows in her appreciation of Chuck; he even drives like a man at peace with himself. Chuck, meanwhile, is playing out the string of passion. He always feels a jolt of excitement when he pulls into her driveway after the three-hour drive from his house. He delights in the way Brooke starts the day with a fistful of almonds, the way she gets down in the dirt in her garden, the way she makes light of the ordinary tribulations of life.

Brooke and Chuck are settling in.

Relationships often start out with different intensities of passion. Once you get beyond the starter romance, you find out whether unequal emotions and expectations at the beginning of a relationship can morph into mutual love and a real bond.

Initial love is notoriously mercurial. The intensity of feeling does not predict the long-term quality of the relationship. In a study of younger men and women who were followed over a thirteen-year period, researchers Shanna E. Smith and Ted L. Huston of the University of Texas,

Austin, found that "newlyweds who would later divorce had the levels of affection and feeling of love that matched or exceeded those of newlywed couples who would stay married."[3]

Some people need the hit of falling in love to jump-start a new relationship in this stage of life. Or maybe, as with Chuck, it's a long-awaited first. The problem with infatuation is that adoration puts the love object on a pedestal. "Even though your partner may believe you're perfect, you know you're not. That makes you feel vulnerable," says psychologist Laura Carstensen, director of the Stanford Center on Longevity. To be known and accepted is what love is, Carstensen points out. You want to be in a relationship—and part of a circle of intimates—where you don't have to be perfect. "To be accepted is the key to long-lasting love," says Carstensen. "In old age, you really want to be known."

✦

Sometimes, a subtle competition begins between present and past relationships. You think, New chapter: No interference from lingering ghosts. No photographs on display of the former or the ex. You even put away the family photographs of the kids on a camping trip from long ago. The collection of Robert Parker novels that a previous husband loved? Into the basement or to a used-book store. The wing chair that came from a former mother-in-law? Unload it with an adult child. No bringing up: *"Well, when Judy and I went to Disney world in 1985. . . . "* No cutthroat comparisons: *"Well, Dennis used to make sure the gas tank in the car was always filled. I thought you'd get the gas. That's why I ran out on the freeway and had to get towed."* Unsaid in the unflattering comparison: *you sonofabitch!*

But you can't erase the past. Perhaps in the first wave of divorce—as part of a couple in your 30s, for example—you can re-couple in hopes of

---

3. Shanna E. Smith and Ted L. Huston, "How and Why Marriages Change Over Time: Shifting Patterns of Companionship and Partnership," in *Continuity and Change in Family Relations: Theory, Methods, and Empirical Findings*," edited by Rand D. Conger, Frederick O. Lorenz, and K.A.S Wickrama (Lawrence Erlbaum Associates, 2004).

making up for earlier "mistakes." You are young enough to re-roll the tape of traditional adulthood and create another family unit with stepparents and blended children, homework and soccer games. But not if you are over 60. Sure, you have regrets; but you can't write off most of your life as a "mistake." You can put the photographs away, but not the complex legacy of relationships. Whether you are divorced or widowed, you bring the imprinting of the exes into your new relationship.

Making peace with the past involves integrating sometimes conflicting chapters into one comprehensive narrative. This is what John Updike does in the novel *Villages*. The hero, who abides in the silky comfort of a well-financed retirement, uses creative memory to bring together his multiple, disparate, secretive chapters into one cohesive love story. He thinks of his first wife every day even as he lives with his second wife. In his dreams, all the many women he has known and made love to morph into a "generic oneiric wife-figure," writes Updike. When the hero wakes up, he's not sure whether the image is of his first wife, or his second wife, or yet another female. Or even what house he is living in. The past blurs in the blender of his imagination.

You don't want to glamorize earlier love so that no new partner can measure up. At the same time, you don't want to diminish a previous partner in order to justify your current situation. You make an accounting to shore up your narrative. As psychologist and author Pamela Regan describes the accounting process by people who divorce: "Accounts are not always accurate, and individuals involved may create vastly different accounts of the same situation. Nonetheless, accounts allow their creators to satisfy a need for control and simple understanding."[4]

In a new relationship, you have to develop a comfort zone for past relationships. It may become natural to bring up previous spouses in the normal course of conversation: *"When Joe and I were living in New York"* begins a woman referring to her first husband, who had abandoned her with two small children. The conversation is about traffic jams in Manhattan.

---

4. Pamela Regan, *The Mating Game: A Primer on Love, Sex, and Marriage* (Sage Publications, 2003), p. 174.

Now, happily remarried, the woman recalls how she almost didn't make it to the hospital to give birth to her second child. *"Sally and I used to go to the Poconos every summer,"* says a man recently re-coupled after a long first marriage. The conversation is about family vacations. And what about the recent news report on the radical Weathermen of the late 1960s? *"Sounds like your first husband, dear,"* jokes a woman's third husband. *"At least he didn't vote for Bush,"* she sighs. *"No, that was my first wife. That's why Bush won,"* he replies. Everybody laughs.

The more confident you are in yourself and in the new relationship, the easier it is to absorb your different legacies. This is important because a major task in this stage is to steward the extended family of adult children and grandchildren, not to mention friends and colleagues who are in your intimate circle.

Remarriage in this stage can upset the links between generations—especially in the wake of late divorce. "Older children are in a stronger position to question decisions that parents make," says developmental psychologist Adam Davey, one of three researchers in a Temple University study on intergenerational relationships.[5] "Adult children can place stronger judgments on the decisions that their parents are making." When Mom or Dad shows up with a new mate, adult children quickly size up the new person. Not just in terms of their parent's happiness, but they gauge the impact of the new relationship on their welfare. There are practical consequences. Men and women who re-couple later in life spend less time and money on their adult children and their families. "Marital transitions that occur when children are adults tend to reduce support from parents to children," concludes Davey. The new partner may try to drive away what are seen as hangers-on from a former life. Wicked StepMonster stories abound in which a last-gasp spouse snatches the inheritance away from adult children and grandchildren.

---

5. Adam Davey, David J. Eggebeen, and Jyoti Savla, "Parental Marital Transitions and Instrumental Assistance Between Generations: A Within-Family Longitudinal Analysis," in *Interpersonal Relations Across the Life Course*, vol. 12, edited by Timothy J. Owens and J. Jill Suitor (Elsevier, 2007).

The disruption of support goes the other way, too. Divorce and remarriage when children are adults tend to reduce support from offspring to older parents if they become frail and dependent. This is especially true of older men who remarry, according to Davey and his colleagues at Temple University. Women who remain single after a divorce, however, are likely to retain the support of adult children.

In a new relationship, much depends on how open you are to the children and grandchildren of your mate. How careful you are in cementing the bonds in your own family so that people don't feel left out. When you're young, you worry about your mother- and father-in-law. When you're older, you think about adult children and grandchildren-in-law. In traditional adulthood, you focus on raising young children. In these later years, you focus on stewarding a large, sometimes fragmented, extended family.

✦

Sometimes it takes many relationships to get the real thing. You keep getting involved but things don't work out. And then you finally settle down. The difference between earlier relationships and the current one? "I grew up," says Priscilla Schumann,* 64. She's been married to her "last" husband for fifteen years. "He's the first of three husbands and intermittent affairs to get it right. This is the first totally real relationship I've had that wasn't informed by the movies."

A first marriage at 19 to a Marlon Brando type: "We were wet and hot," she says. "It was a case of mistaken identity. We weren't who we thought we were. We were what our masks were." Second marriage to a Marlboro Man: "I spot the guy literally across a crowded room," she says. "Most interesting man I've ever seen." But it's another mismatch of needs and desires. "I was demanding milk but I was in the hardware store. He couldn't give me what I needed." An affair with a much older man: "Utterly brilliant. Bald. . . . An old guy," she says.

This exciting, sensuous, chaotic, and ultimately unsatisfying pattern continues for twenty years. When she reaches 45, she figures she has to get her act together. She is struggling on many fronts: the death of her father, the meltdown with her second husband, frustration in her job, and concerns about her children living in an unstable marriage. At this point she meets Husband Number Three: "I can relax with him. I don't have to stage-manage the climate. I trust him entirely. It's been a wonderful marriage," says Priscilla.

Finally she gets a real person. And so does he. "Each of us knows very accurately who each of us really is. We respect each other. We trust each other. We're much more confident," she says. They need a lot of separate space. She doesn't like feeling trapped; he gives her a wide berth, especially in recent years. "In a funny way, the closest I have come to having my singlehood is now," she explains. Her husband walks with a cane and wears two hearing aids. He no longer enjoys going out or listening to music, so she goes off to concerts and the theater with other people. She's about to take an Elder Hostel tour in Mexico with two women friends. She keeps up her circle of friends. "We manage our intimacy when we're together but we're not together all the time."

Mainly, she says, you have to be ready for a real relationship. "Ripeness is all! Readiness is all. If you're not ready, it might come along and you wouldn't know it," she says. It took until she was nearly 50 to be ready for the real thing. "It's awfully good to be with someone now—even if it's not lights, camera, action."

✦

Maybe you are a creature of habit. You keep repeating the same relationship with a different face. Or it's a different relationship but it has the same ending: divorce. You get tired of having relationships not work out. Poor choices? Bad luck? Something you don't understand about love? About the opposite sex? The dark side of being a serial spouse is that you never get it right, even as you try and try again.

Some people don't ever get it right. They grab the high of a new romance and when the relationship doesn't work out, they move on, older but not wiser enough.

Other people try to change the pattern.

Ron Browne, 65, of Cleveland, has a deep radio voice, silver curls, and penetrating hazel eyes. He knows his pattern: He changes fields every ten or twelve years—he starts out in education, switches to the broadcast industry, changes again and gets into the retail running-shoe business. Now he works in aging and wellness programs. And he changes partners in the same rhythm. His three marriages each last about the same amount of time as his work focus. But it's going to be different now. He's in his final career, he says. And he's in his final marriage to Jacquelyn, a psychotherapist who is also a specialist on aging.

"We look at it differently. We're wiser. We are more life-experienced. We're looking to build a life together in the second half of life which looks a little different. We're not constrained or distracted by having kids at home. We're both settled into careers," he says. "We're still sexually driven but not to the same extent. We have the experience of life decisions that we regret and we have learned from these experiences. We are more careful."

Ron's first marriage "just wore out," he explains. He marries while in college. They have two daughters. They are both teachers and struggling financially. His first wife "is a wonderful woman," he says. "It was a very committed relationship." They divorce after twelve years.

The second marriage blows up: "I was single. I had this fantasy about a woman, a local TV anchor. I was enamored of her," he says. One night they happen to meet in a restaurant. It is a fast-lane glamorous relationship that becomes his second marriage. But there are logistical problems. She works nights and he works days so they don't have much cross-over time. "I believe I screwed up. That one had real potential," he says.

The third marriage implodes: "We had this instant connection," he says. But his third wife also has teenage children. The family goes into therapy. "Stepfamilies are really tough," he says. "We finally threw in the towel. At that point I said to myself: I've tried this three times. Either I've had bad luck or I'm not good at this. I'm going to try to change the way I go about this."

He is 51 and the way he changes is to stay single. He moves into a 600-square-foot efficiency apartment in downtown Cleveland. He gets rid of his car. He goes through a low dark period. "Depression is a double liability for men because men aren't good at talking about it. You get stuck in a bottle of booze or go to a baseball game." He picks up books instead of women. He reads about depression and male psychology. Relationships with his children improve. He stops drinking, except for a glass of wine now and then. He pays attention to his body and runs in marathons. He starts writing about "male menopause" for a fitness website.

His single period lasts twelve years. "I grew up. I became more self-confident. I think I had a clearer vision of what my life was—and where it was going," he says. "I learned to be alone. I learned to be comfortable with myself. It wasn't fulfilling or pleasurable just to have someone in bed at night. That's a huge lesson—a big turning point in my life. I came to the point where I could say: if I'm like this for the rest of my life, that's okay."

When he starts work on an aging project for a foundation, a new world opens to him. He's especially interested in how men deal with aging and he facilitates men's groups. He meets Jacki at a conference. Her story is very different. She is ending a thirty-year marriage. He worries that she hasn't had a period of time to be on her own. She explains that she was alone for years in her marriage. They discover they both like classical music. They both like to run. They work in the same field. But she lives in Florida. "We like to say we fell in love on the phone," he says. They commute and get to know each other. After a year or so, they decide to marry.

Ron moves to Florida where he and Jacki become another couple in their 60s enjoying a new chapter in the sunshine. But their marriage is a relationship totally different from what they each have known in the past. For Jacki, it is an awakening. "With Ron, it's really like a dream come true—but different when you're 60 than when I was daydreaming at 16 for love," says Jacki. For Ron, it is a stable attachment. "I feel more settled. I'm confident that this will be my final relationship," says Ron. "And this is my final career—unless at 92, I open a lemonade stand on the beach."

✦

Some couples experience meaningful intimacy for the first time in this stage of life. Don Gold, 62, is coming out of a long unhappy marriage and sinking into depression when he finds Cynthia, 67, on eHarmony.com. Their late-blooming love is "more beautiful and effortless than I have ever experienced, and far more wonderful than I had ever chanced to dream," he says. Cynthia, single for decades, also had a long unhappy marriage. "Don is the perfect one," she says. "I was looking for something I didn't have in the first marriage—deep understanding and communication and spirituality."

Now they are married and living in Temple, Texas. Every morning they sit at the kitchen table and look out the window and talk about the world and its meaning. "I had never met a man who could express his emotions to me as clearly as Don," she says. Don remembers the first time they made love and then slept wrapped in each other. "It's been some years since that first night together," he says. "We still look forward to coffee each morning and the same bed each night."

Other couples find each other after long happy marriages. Newlyweds Ruth Johnson-Mullis, 85, and Leonard Mullis, 87, of Littleton, Colorado, are veterans of the one-track pathway. Ruth's first marriage lasts sixty years; Leonard's, almost fifty-nine years. Ruth's first husband was a union plumber in Miami; she was a draftsman and worked on building bridges. Married out of high school in World War II, they retire in their 50s to the mountains in Colorado. After her husband suffers a stroke, he is paralyzed on one side of his body. Seven years later, Ruth is a widow. Loneliness eventually overwhelms her. "I can't stand this. I am so lonesome I cried," she says.

Leonard, who becomes a librarian after retiring from the Air Force, is also widowed. "I began to realize—I'm pretty lonesome in the house," he says. They each go on match.com. Ruth is worried—who wants an 84-year-old woman? "I did," says Leonard. To meet in person, he drives forty-five miles to her cabin in the mountains. There are no restaurants so she serves him lunch. "From that point on, I was a dead duck," he says. "We just clicked. I can't explain it," says Ruth. They connect their pasts: both grew up in Florida; both went through World War II. "We were raised in the same manner. We were raised in the same era. We have so much to talk about," she says.

They look fondly on each other's previous marriage. "If a man stays with a woman for fifty-nine years, he's not going to run away from me if I'm not perfect," says Ruth. "The fact that she stayed married for a long time, that was a plus," says Leonard. They marry after a few months. "At my age, I don't believe in long engagements. No use fooling around," he says.

✦

The many pathways to love merge into one framework for "marriage" in an age of longevity. The New Normal is inclusive of all those who love— whether you're married or unmarried, in a new relationship or an old one, whether you've been single for one year or twenty. You know something about love now. This intimate wisdom spreads into all your relationships.

You have the advantages of age over youth: a greater tendency to see the positive, more readiness to forgive, and in the shadow of mortality, more gratitude and urgency to make the most of what you have.

It is fall; I come back to the town where I grew up and go through the woods to the brick house on a hill to visit a family friend. I open the front door: the familiar raspy voice, shining smile, and firm hug. He is 97 years old. He had been an usher at my parents' wedding nearly seventy years ago. Now he is the patriarch of a large clan and an even larger network of children of his friends and friends of his children. He has had two marriages. His first wife—whom I remember from nursery school days—died after struggling with Parkinson's disease for twenty-five years. After a while, he married again in his 70s. His second wife was a childhood friend of my mother's. She died several years ago and he is a widower again.

We sit by the fire in the library. Outside, the maple leaves are red and gold. On the table is a bank of photographs: a black-and-white snapshot of young men on skis—he and my father and their friends on Mt. Washington in the 1930s. The formal graduation portrait from the late 1950s of his daughter—my friend and classmate. Photographs of his sons. Several color scenes of grandchildren and great-grandchildren. In the corner, a painting of his second wife as a young woman—they had known each other when they were teenagers.

He has time to look back. What, I ask him, is the key to relationships in these later decades?

He thinks for a moment and says: *"Consideration. . . . Consideration for the other."* This is the age advantage, he continues. Your identity is secure. You know something about life—its unfairness and its promise. You've lived through the inevitable disappointments and unexpected twists. You've overcome the loss of loved ones and reveled in the joy of finding love. When, with maturity, the "I" is more securely established, it is easier to think of the other "I" in the relationship. It is also essential. The glue of attachment is empathy. *Consideration for the other.* All the others—the ones no longer present, the ones just born, the ones you are holding in your arms.

This is the gift of great love, as time goes by.

Epilogue: The Circle

"Granny—what happens to you when you die?"

The question comes from Brooks, my grandson, age 7. We are all sitting at the kitchen table: Brooks and his cousins Sophia, 6, and Lila, 4. Their mothers—my daughters—are upstairs, sleeping in, and Granny is in charge. What happens when you die? Too early for this! I get the coffeemaker going, find the Cheerios, pour the milk.

"Yeah, Granny, what happens?" asks Sophia.

I dissemble. "Well, I'm pretty young," I begin. "I'm probably not going to die for a while." Finally the coffee is ready and I pour myself a cup. Maybe we can now talk about something else. Silence. Three pairs of brown eyes stare at me. The children wait for an answer.

"Well, I won't be here anymore," I mumble and take another sip of coffee. The children look confused. Not here? Not in the house? Brooks points to the kitchen cabinets. "But what happens to all your stuff?" he asks. That's easier to answer: "Your parents will take care of the stuff," I say brightly. The children, only slightly reassured, keep staring at me. I have to focus on the question.

How to explain the roll of generations, the natural cycle of birth, life, and death? The notion of peace everlasting? Sophia and Lila and Brooks are so young. Life lies ahead of them.

"When I die, my body will be gone . . . but one part of me never dies. My love for you never dies. When I die, all my love jumps inside of you," and I turn to Brooks and tickle his chest. He smiles. Then I tickle Sophia and Lila. All my love jumping inside you. More giggles.

"You know, let's say you have a big test one day and you're nervous. Just before the test, you can take a deep breath and say to yourself: My granny loves me!"

"That's great, Granny," says Brooks.

"I have an idea," says Sophia. "What if we put a picture of you on the wall and then when we get up we can say: Good morning, Granny!"

"That would be wonderful," I say. "We'll always be in touch."

"Good morning, Granny," they all shout and burst out laughing.

Lila waves her hand at me. She hasn't touched her Cheerios: "Hi, Granny!" I blow her a kiss. "Can I have a waffle?" she asks.

✦

Love never dies. That is the message in all the stories in this book. Longevity's gift of time is also a gift of love. From the first kiss to the final good-bye, we grow in love from others and in giving love to others. As time goes by, the love within us spreads out to many more—a human chain of connection that transcends generations.

My love for my grandchildren begins with the love my grandparents gave me. Their photographs hang on my wall. In between is a rich roster of loved ones: husbands, friends, companions, cousins, parents, and children. We may focus on a partner in a long relational life, but we thrive in a circle of intimates—the ones we love and who bear witness to our lives.

With each interview I conducted for this book, I was inspired by the power of love. The interview itself is an intimate act: anytime there is a revelation of truth and a sharing of experience, there is bonding. Breaking down superficial barriers and getting to the bedrock of a person's life is like breaking bread in a ritual of friendship. The men and women in these pages have become another kind of circle of kinship.

They also reveal important features of loving in an era of living longer, healthier lives:

- *Resilience.* The twin of love is loss. In every story, I found jolts of pain and sorrow. The blows come in many guises, from the deaths of loved ones to the deaths of dreams, from the breakup of a relationship to the slower pace of estrangement and disappointment. And yet, perhaps because loss tears open the heart, the capacity to love can grow stronger with age. I think of my friend Becky Lescaze, who went through a divorce and lost her son in a traffic accident. Or psychiatrist Bob Butler, who lost his wife to cancer. Most people in these pages were able to recover from loss and find renewal in loving relationships—all kinds of relationships, across multiple generations. A mark of resilience was the ability to nurture a circle, finding invigoration in multiple connections and common purpose.

- *Focus.* Relationships are hard work. It takes time and effort to build and maintain close bonds with loved ones. Virtually everyone in the book made relationships a priority. It helps to start creating a circle early in life—reaching out and caring for others. In later years, you reap the rewards for the bonds built up over decades. These circles of chosen kin are the bulwark against tragedy, the stage for joy.

- *Happiness.* Older people are happier than younger people. Study after study confirms that, in general, older men and women are more content and satisfied with life than younger ones. This positive sense of well-being does not reflect an absence of problems. Quite the opposite. Many people in these pages have dealt with major crises in the past and are confronting new problems in their health and financial status—and in their relationships. But they have more perspective on outrageous fortune and more appreciation for what goes well. The emotional ability to control negative feelings and enhance positive ones improves with age. As a result, older men and women rate themselves as happier than those who are younger. And happier people tend to have happier partnerships—whether it's a long marriage like Philip and Carolyn Cowan's of Berkeley or a new partnership like Jacki and Ron Browne's in Miami. They also have stronger circles.

✦

My intimate circle is precious. Its active members are relatives and close friends—male and female. We share secrets and laughter and the daily fare of life. The circle includes friends from childhood and college. Friends from more recent passages—from work and travel. Nine-year-old children and 90-year-old confidants. The circle is home. As one male friend said to me after the breakup of my second marriage: "You can always come here for Christmas." Just recently we were reminiscing about our long friendship. "You were there for me when my mother died," he said. So much shared memory . . . so much solidarity.

As someone who followed the serial pathway and had two husbands, I make special places in my heart for them, too. That both relationships ended in divorce is not the final word. The first marriage brought two wonderful daughters, joyous moments, awakening into adulthood; the second marriage was an adventure of two soul mates, a great love, mutually reinforcing and creative. I can hear his voice inside me whenever I lose my nerve . . . or embark on a new path: Go for it! And then his trademark laugh!

Now a single woman, I know the joys of love and romance. I bring new friends into the circle. I also draw on memory. Place and time are mixed up with different jolts of passion and partnership. From the exotic of the Taj Mahal in India to the everyday movie theater and neighborhood restaurant, place is connected to intimacy. I remember: the "High Place" in the mountains of Jordan; the Ghan in Australia, the train from Adelaide to Alice Springs; the Lincoln Memorial in Washington, D.C.; the harbors of Tangier and Hong Kong. Then there are beaches and woods and rocks and hills and highways and airports. Each moment in my life of relationships endures like a geographic spot on a map.

As time goes by, the vault of love fills up inside me. By now I am a philanthropist with riches to give away.

✦

It is late afternoon and I am hurrying to set up for the party: my younger daughter's tenth wedding anniversary. Both daughters were married here on this island in Maine. They are always close to my heart. The circle gathers—my intimate circle and the larger circle of extended family and friends. The guests arrive: toddlers and teenagers, parents and grandparents; the formerly married, the never married, the currently married, and the newly married.

One by one, they stand up to give a toast, sing a song, tell a story.

I look out at the mass of youngsters screaming across the field—they weren't here ten years ago. A whole new generation has been born. I find my cousin, my playmate from when we were their age so long ago. You must remember this. We hug. A soft breeze comes in from the southwest. The ferry goes by. The children take turns on the swing. More hugs, more laughter. But also a note of sorrow: another cousin, who is in his 80s, is in hospice care now. Bittersweet are these milestone celebrations.

An eagle flies in and sits on a nearby tree. We all stop and look. Majestic, proud, defiant—the eagle turns its profile to the crowd. Silence . . . awe. Look! Look! Catch a glimpse before it goes. And then the eagle spreads its wings and flies away.

I survey the gathering and see interlocking circles of couples and individuals, bound together by shared experience and the ties of love, loss, and friendship. These circles embrace us, sustain us. On the front lines of longevity, we have a mission: to keep loving and caring for others, to steward future generations, to craft a legacy by weaving our past into the present.

And then we fly away.

The children are ready for cake and ice cream.

"Hi, Granny!" *Good morning, Granny.*

Selected Bibliography

Quotations throughout the book that are neither footnoted nor included in the list below resulted from personal interviews.

Bair, Deirdre. *Calling It Quits: Late-Life Divorce and Starting Over.* Random House, 2007.

Bratter, Bernice, and Helen Dennis. *Project Renewment: The First Retirement Model for Career Women.* Scribner, 2008.

Butler, Robert N. *The Longevity Revolution: The Benefits and Challenges of Living a Long Life.* PublicAffairs, 2008.

Butler, Robert N., and Myrna I. Lewis. *The New Love and Sex After 60.* Ballantine Books, 2002.

Cherlin, Andrew. *Marriage, Divorce, Remarriage,* rev. ed. Harvard University Press, 1992.

Cohen, Gene D. *The Creative Age: Awakening Human Potential in the Second Half of Life.* Avon Books, 2000.

Coontz, Stephanie. *Marriage, a History: From Obedience to Intimacy, or How Love Conquered Marriage.* Viking Adult, 2005.

Delillo, Don. *Underworld.* Scribner, 2007.

Durrenmatt, Friedrich. *The Visit: A Tragi-Comedy,* translated by Patrick Bowles. Grove Press, 1994.

Fromm, Erich. *The Art of Loving,* Harper & Row, 1956.

Ford, Richard. *The Lay of the Land.* Knopf, 2006.

Freedman, Marc. *Encore: Finding Work That Matters in the Second Half of Life.* PublicAffairs, 2007.

Gottman, John M., and Nan Silver. *The Seven Principles for Making Marriage Work.* Crown Publishers, 2004.

Gruman, Jessie. *AfterShock: What to Do When the Doctor Gives You—or Someone You Love—a Devastating Diagnosis.* Walker & Company, 2007.

Laken, Virginia and Keith. *Making Love Again: Hope for Couples Facing Loss of Sexual Intimacy.* Ant Hill Press, 2002.

Levine, Suzanne Braun. *Inventing the Rest of Our Lives: Women in Second Adulthood.* Viking, 2004.

Lipsyte, Robert. *In the Country of Illness: Comfort and Advice for the Journey.* Knopf, 1998.

Lynn, Dorree, and Florence Isaacs. *When the Man You Love Is Ill: Doing the Best for Your Partner Without Losing Yourself.* Avalon, 2007.

Miller, Sue. *The Senator's Wife.* Knopf, 2008.

Minot, Susan. *Evening.* Knopf, 1998.

Moen, Phyllis, ed. *It's About Time: Couples and Careers.* Cornell University Press, 2003.

Person, Ethel S. *Dreams of Love and Fateful Encounters: The Power of Romantic Passion.* American Psychiatric Publishing, Inc., 2006.

Roth, Philip. *Exit Ghost.* Houghton Mifflin, 2007.

Rowe, John W., and Robert L. Kahn. *Successful Aging.* Pantheon, 1998.

Sedlar, Jeri, and Rick Miners. *Don't Retire, REWIRE.* Alpha, 2007.

The Transition Network and Gail Rentsch. *Smart Women Don't Retire— They Break Free: From Working Full-Time to Living Full-Time.* Springboard Press, 2008.

Updike, John. *Villages.* Knopf, 2004.

Resources

Many organizations provide services and information about aging. Most focus on health and financial issues. But a recurrent theme in making the most of the bonus decades after 50 is the importance of relationships and social engagement. The agencies listed here are committed to expanding opportunities for older men and women and enhancing their well-being—as well as their status in American culture.

AARP: A nonprofit, nonpartisan member organization for people over 50. The family section on the AARP website focuses on love and relationships, life after loss, grandparenting, and care-giving.
601 E Street NW
Washington, DC 20049
1-888-OUR-AARP (1-888-687-2277)
www.aarp.org

Civic Ventures: A nonprofit organization aimed at tapping the talents of baby boomers in retirement. The Next Chapter project provides information and connections for people who "want to make a difference in the second half of life."
114 Sansome Street, Suite 850
San Francisco, CA 94104
415-430-0141
info@civicventures.org
www.civicventures.org

Experience Corps: A nonprofit national program for 55-plus men and women who wish to serve in community schools.
  2120 L Street NW, Suite 610
  Washington, DC 20037
  202-478-6190
  info@experiencecorps.org
  www.experiencecorps.org

International Longevity Center (ILC): A nonprofit international research and policy organization "formed to educate individuals on how to live longer and better, and advise society on how to maximize the benefits of today's age boom."
  60 East 86th Street
  New York, NY 10029
  212-288-1468
  info@ilcusa.org
  www.ilcusa.org

National Council on Aging: A nonprofit organization with a national network of more than 14,000 organizations and individuals who serve older adults. Members range from representatives of senior centers, employment services, and consumer groups to leaders from academia, business, and labor.
  1901 L Street NW, 4th Floor
  Washington, DC 20036
  202-479-1200
  www.ncoa.org

National Institute on Aging (NIA): One of the institutes of the National Institutes of Health. The NIA provides leadership in aging research, professional training, and consumer health information to "understand the nature of aging and to extend the healthy, active years of life." It is the primary federal agency on Alzheimer's disease research.
  Building 31, Room 5C27
  31 Center Drive, MSC 2292
  Bethesda, MD 20892
  301-396-1752 / 1-800-222-2225 / TTY: 1-800-222-4225
  www.nia.nih.gov

Project Renewment: A retirement model for career women. Based in California, Project Renewment provides tools to form small informal groups to help women who are leaving the workplace.

   Helen@projectrenewment.com

   Bernice@projectrenewment.com

   www.projectrenewment.com

Stanford Center on Longevity: An interdisciplinary center at Stanford University studying human development over the entire life span, with expertise in mental health and emotional well-being as well as in global health, physical mobility, and financial security.

   P.O. Box 20506

   Stanford, CA 94305-0506

   650-736-8643

   Info-longevity@stanford.edu

   www.longevity.stanford.edu

The Transition Network (TTN): A membership organization of midlife women in transition from career to new opportunities in the workplace and the community. It provides information, mentoring, and regular meetings on specific subjects, from retirement planning to renegotiating relationships. Formed in New York City, TTN has chapters in San Francisco, Houston, Denver, Chicago, and Washington, D.C.

   Ansonia Station, P.O. Box 231240

   New York, NY 10023-0021

   212-714-8040

   www.thetransititionnetwork.org

WomanSage: A national, nonprofit, membership organization of midlife women based in California that focuses on financial literacy, health, beauty, careers, care-giving, and relationships. It offers a news-based website, annual conferences, and monthly "salon" meetings.

   949-222-4210

   info@womansage.org

   www.womansage.org

Index

Asterisk denotes fictional name; text in parentheses after a name describes the experience, issue, or type of relationship illuminated in the discussion of this person.